Teachers, Pupils and Primary Schooling

Continuity and Change

Edited by
Paul Croll

CASSELL

Cassell
Wellington House
125 Strand
London WC2R 0BB

127 West 24th Street
New York
NY 10011

British Library Cataloguing-in-Publication Data
A catalogue record for this book is available from the British Library.

ISBN   0-304-33660-2 (hardback)
        0-304-33659-9 (paperback)

Typeset by Action Typesetting Ltd, Gloucester
Printed and bound in Great Britain by Redwood Books, Trowbridge, Wiltshire

Contents

Preface

This is the second book to emerge from the work of the PACE (Primary Assessment, Curriculum and Experience) research study of the implementation of the National Curriculum and associated changes in primary schools in England. In the first volume we documented the impact of the National Curriculum at Key Stage 1. In the present volume we report on the continuation of the study as the first cohort of children to experience the National Curriculum moves into Key Stage 2. The period from the late 1980s to the mid-1990s, which is covered by the research so far, has been one of very considerable change in many aspects of the curriculum, management and organization of primary schools. This change was largely centrally imposed in an explicit attempt to raise educational standards through a common curriculum and rigorous assessment arrangements and to make schools both more accountable and better managed. A number of issues relevant to these aims will be discussed in the chapters of this book. It is important to note, however, that these changes were introduced without any systematic study of the aspects of education to be 'reformed' and with no mechanism put in place to monitor the impact of the changes. The belated recognition of some of the problems with the National Curriculum and the widely welcomed Dearing Review came about following the action of the teacher unions rather than from any systematic enquiry into the operation of the changes in school. It is quite extraordinary that wide-ranging changes affecting the education of millions of children and the working lives of hundreds of thousands of teachers could be introduced without either a research base or an ongoing evaluation. Of all public services, education is the area with the least governmental commitment to research into its operation and effects, and yet it is a service which absorbs a very considerable level of publically funded resources and which is widely acknowledged to be of fundamental importance to the lives of individuals and the public good more generally. The PACE project has been generously funded by the Economic and Social Research Council and, together with a few other individual projects, has contributed to our understanding of contemporary educational change and to Sir Ron Dearing's review of the National Curriculum. But *ad hoc* projects of this kind cannot be a substitute for a governmental commitment to rational and research-based decision-making.

A particularly unfortunate feature of the neglect of research in educational decision-making is that it makes it impossible to bring to bear the experience of the teaching professional on such decisions. The evidence presented in this and our previous book shows how the systematic study of teacher experience and teacher opinion is essential to an understanding of the possibilities of change and the impact of reform. Without such a mechanism for involving teacher experience in educational policy we are left with the clumsy mechanism of industrial action, the process by which teachers collectively brought about the Dearing Review of the National Curriculum. The evidence presented here shows the commitment of teachers to the principle of a National Curriculum and the thought and effort they have put into making the changes work for children. As we enter the promised period of stability the PACE study will continue to document and analyse the issues faced by schools, teachers and pupils.

This book differs from the previous report on the PACE project in that it consists of separate attributed chapters and a single editor rather than being the product of joint authorship. However, both the writing of the individual chapters and the overall editorial direction of the book have benefited immensely from the collaborative work of the members of the PACE team for which I am grateful to my colleagues.

Paul Croll
Reading, 1995

Acknowledgements

All the chapters in this book are based on research carried out as part of two linked projects funded by the Economic and Social Research Council, R000231931 and R000233891. The third phase of the study has also received ESRC funding. The contributors to the book wish to express their thanks to the ESRC for the continued support of research into a major educational reform and for the helpful comments of ESRC officers and panel members. The project has involved working with the same schools for a period of six years and the PACE team members are extremely grateful for the continued cooperation of headteachers, teachers and pupils. Their openness to our enquiries, at a time of considerable pressure and strain, is a tribute to the education service and made data collection a rewarding experience.

A great many people have helped with the research, and particular thanks should go to Jenny Noble, who worked with the research team in conducting interviews and classroom studies, and Mike Taysum, who has managed the organization and analysis of a large and complex data set. Alyson Kington helped in processing the data used in Chapter 9. Thanks are also due to Pat Abbott, Jim Campbell, Tony Edwards, Ann Filer, Caroline Gipps, David Halpin, Ann Lewis, Ian Menter, Yolande Muschamp, Jennifer Nias, Oz Osborn, Claire Planel, Ros Pollard, Sally Power, Colin Richards, Christine Stone, Mike Wallace and Pearl Wilson for their continued interest in and support of the study. The PACE team has been fortunate in their secretarial colleagues, who have so efficiently supported the conduct of the research and the writing of this book. They thank Jacquie Harrison, Viki Davies, Sarah Butler, Elspeth Gray, Sheila Taylor and Lynn Cook for their contribution to the research. An earlier version of Chapter 2 appeared in the *British Journal of Educational Studies* and is reproduced by permission of the editors.

Notes on Contributors

Dorothy Abbott is a Research Associate at the University of the West of England

Edie Black is a Research Associate at the University of Bristol

Patricia Broadfoot is Professor of Education and Head of the School of Education at the University of Bristol

Paul Croll is Professor of Education at the University of Reading

Marilyn Osborn is a Research Fellow at the University of Bristol

Andrew Pollard is Professor of Education at the University of Bristol

Chapter 1

Introduction

Paul Croll

1.1 A context: policy and project
1.2 Continuity and change
1.3 Research on primary education
1.4 The PACE project and the present book

1.1 A CONTEXT: POLICY AND PROJECT

This book arises from a large-scale Economic and Social Research Council funded project studying the impact of the National Curriculum on primary school education in England. It is an interim report on that project: neither the policy implementation nor the research project have fully run their course at the time of writing in mid-1995. The study was designed to follow the first cohort of children to experience the National Curriculum from the beginning of their schooling throughout their primary school careers. It was funded by the ESRC in three stages: the first, covering Key Stage 1 (ages 5–7), was completed in 1992; the second, covering the first two years of Key Stage 2 (ages 7–9), was completed in 1994; and the third stage is due for completion in 1997. An outline of the project design and data collection procedures is presented in the Appendix.

The work on Key Stage 1 of the National Curriculum was reported in *Changing English Primary Schools?* (Pollard *et al.*, 1994) and at the end of the project further volumes will provide an overview of the experience of the National Curriculum across the full primary age-range. The papers presented in this book focus on the experience of pupils, teachers and schools as the first group of pupils to experience the National Curriculum moved from Key Stage 1 to the first two years of Key Stage 2.

As originally conceived, the stage of the project reported here was intended to put particular emphasis on the study of continuity and progression in children's educational experience and on the extent to which the National Curriculum became 'routinized' or 'normalized' for teachers and schools as, following the original impact of 'newness', it became an ordinary part of primary school experience. These issues have remained an important focus of the study. However, other changes meant that the implementation of the National Curriculum did not proceed as planned. This stage of the study coincided with the action of teacher unions against the additional workload associated with testing and recognition of the overloaded and unmanageable nature of the National Curriculum.

It is this recognition which led to the modification of the National Curriculum following a review by Sir Ron Dearing (1994). This shift in the nature of what was being studied inevitably affected the character of the research. In the earlier book we drew on Wallace's notion of 'multiple innovation', the overlapping complex of education policy developments in the late 1980s of which the National Curriculum was only a part, as a context for understanding the processes we were studying. In this book we have used the notion of 'turbulence', a less orderly version of the multiple planned innovations, and a context of uncertainty, critique and constant policy change, to characterize the educational environment under study.

Although neither the research nor the educational changes it was designed to study are complete, much of interest has already emerged both in the earlier book and in the papers which make up this volume. We devised an approach to analysis which attempts to consider the particularity of the educational changes of the late 1980s and first half of the 1990s and which is also conscious of the enduring issues of education and schooling which underlie these changes. The discussion of contemporary education policy addresses an agenda which is, at least in part, an externally imposed one, set by the claims made for the National Curriculum and criticisms directed at it. However, at the same time we have tried to develop an analysis based on theoretical concerns over primary education and the questions to emerge from a tradition of empirical enquiry into primary schooling.

1.2 CONTINUITY AND CHANGE

The subtitle of this book indicates a major theme which informed the original design and the later analysis. The study was designed as a study of educational change, but it has, at least as much, been a study of educational continuity. This was partly because of the contrast we identified above, between the particular policy context of a major and deliberately formulated change in educational prescription following the 1988 Education Reform Act, and the longer term underlying features of educational structures and educational relationships. We embarked on the study knowing that there were certain to be echoes of other research into primary schooling and that the fundamental 'dilemmas' of education would continue to be of major importance. And the importance of continuity has also emerged in the analysis of data from the project.

The title of the first PACE book, *Changing English Primary Schools?*, was deliberately ambiguous. The title can refer to the substantive changes which were taking place in primary schools and also to the process of effecting change in primary schools. Both of these areas are also addressed in the present book. The title also contained a question mark which recognized the complexity and uncertainty of the processes being described and the impossibility of coming to a definitive judgement on them at that level of closeness to events. However, the book, while recognizing continuity, did also demonstrate the reality of change. The emphasis on the extent of the changes which had taken place was perhaps greater than that contained in other studies of primary education over this period, such as those of Campbell and Neill (1994) and Evans *et al.* (1994), although the overall picture to emerge from these and the PACE studies is generally coherent.

As is the case with some of these other studies, the PACE project found a considerable degree of continuity in the domination of the curriculum by the basic skills of mathematics and English. These areas have always taken up the major part of the primary curriculum, and despite a commitment in the National Curriculum to a broader curriculum, the introduction of a Core (the basics plus science) as the first element of the National Curriculum and as the focus for standardized assessment was almost inevitably going to lead to a continued emphasis on these areas. The PACE project showed that, while there was not a major shift in curriculum balance, the other Foundation subjects were, to some extent, squeezed further.

A second area of continuity was with regard to the maintenance of teachers' values and conceptions of teacher professionalism. Although teachers took on additional responsibilities, their core values and professional commitment remained essentially unchanged. Related to this consistency in teacher professionalism was the third area of continuity, that of pupil experience. Pupil perceptions of schooling and the demands it made on them were largely unchanged. This came about mainly because teachers' continuing professional commitment ensured that the things they most valued with regard to children's experiences of primary schooling remained unchanged. This led to a process of mediation whereby a relatively stable pupil experience of primary education was maintained despite a confused and unstable educational environment externally.

But despite these important elements of continuity, the period under study was one of real change within primary schools, and we cannot accept the claims of some researchers that teachers have mistaken turbulence for real change (e.g. Evans *et al.*, 1994). The assessment regime within primary classrooms changed markedly, both with regard to the introduction of externally imposed assessments and in the way that teachers planned their own ongoing assessment in response to external requirements. Curriculum planning and the influence of subjects on the curriculum also increased. There were marked changes in pedagogic practice, with increased teacher direction and an increase in whole-class teaching. The organizational culture of schools also changed, both because of the requirements to implement National Curriculum reforms and because of other changes resulting from the Education Reform Act. Schools shifted in the direction of being more heavily managed organizations, as heads, with varying degrees of enthusiasm, took on more directive roles. However, the collegial aspects of primary school culture also became more important as teachers cooperated with one another in planning and, to a lesser extent, implementing the National Curriculum.

1.3 RESEARCH ON PRIMARY EDUCATION

The research conducted for the PACE project was inevitably influenced by a tradition of research into primary education, in particular, a number of research projects conducted over the past twenty years. Both the research methods used and the substantive areas of enquiry relate to those of previous projects. In the discussion below we attempt to identify aspects of a number of studies where themes emerged or methods were employed which have been influential with regard to the study of primary schooling.

The first set of studies to be considered are the large-scale, quantitatively oriented, projects looking at primary schools and primary classrooms which attempted to consider the relationship between school and classroom processes and various educational outcomes. The studies conducted by Bennett (1976), Galton *et al.* (1980) and Mortimore and his colleagues (1988) are interesting for what they say about the relationships between educational processes and educational products, but also for the way in which they conceptualized the processes of, and identified the key elements in, primary education.

The earliest of these studies (Bennett, 1976) was a groundbreaking attempt to conduct process–product research in British primary schools. It was heavily oriented towards the debate over 'traditional' and 'progressive' (or 'formal' and 'informal') approaches to primary education and attempted to characterize teachers in these terms and to compare the performance of children taught by different methods. Although a variety of research methods was used, the central procedure by which teachers were categorized into different teaching styles was by their self-report of various aspects of their practice, using a questionnaire.

The various questionnaire items in the Bennett study can be grouped into those dealing with curriculum, those dealing with pedagogy and those dealing with assessment, although they were not explicitly characterized in this way. With regard to curriculum, the key element which distinguished different sorts of teacher was the degree of emphasis on an integrated curriculum compared with the use of separate-subject teaching. With regard to *pedagogy,* the main differentiating element was that of control: the extent to which teachers controlled aspects of classroom management such as where pupils sat and whether they were allowed to talk to one another and move around the classroom. (Although we have called this pedagogy, it is, of course, more concerned with the management of the class than the method of teaching.) The third aspect which differentiated teachers was the use of *assessment,* in particular the extent of formal or semi-formal testing.

Bennett's was the first of a number of studies to show that the extent of 'progressive' ideologies and approaches based on the recommendations of the Plowden Report had been much exaggerated. (See Pollard *et al.,* 1994, Ch. 1 for an extended discussion of the Plowden Report and its influence.) Teachers using different approaches varied to some extent in the expression of their educational values, but there was a commonality of view both around the central importance of the 'basic skills' and on a commitment to the personal and social development of children. Although the study was initially seen as demonstrating the superiority of formal methods with regard to academic achievement, later analysis considerably modified this conclusion (Aitken *et al.,* 1981) and, despite its original orientation, the study can be seen as showing that teaching practices and values are too complex to be categorized by a formal–informal scale.

The second of these large-scale process–product studies to be considered is the ORACLE (Observational Research and Classroom Learning Evaluation) study (Galton *et al.,* 1980; Galton and Simon, 1980). Like the Bennett study, this project was concerned to describe classroom processes in the primary school, to identify groupings of teachers using similar methods and to relate these methods to outcomes for pupils. However, unlike the Bennett study, the main basis for the description of teaching approaches was direct observation in classrooms by trained observers, rather than the self-report of teachers.

The ORACLE project was the first attempt to provide a representative picture of the classroom experiences of teachers and pupils in English primary schools based on observation. Although other data on pupil and teacher perceptions were collected by means of interviews and questionnaires, the main thrust of the project was determined by the use of systematic observation data to describe teachers, pupils and classrooms. Extensive data were gathered on teacher and pupil behaviour in the classroom. For pupils this included such variables as time on task, time distracted from work, levels of interactions with other pupils and levels and types of interactions with the teacher. For teachers it included such variables as questions and statements of various kinds, time spent giving feedback and the balance of whole-class, group and individual interactions. Data were also collected on patterns of classroom organization, seating patterns and grouping arrangements.

The ORACLE project placed great emphasis on patterns of classroom behaviour and interaction and on those aspects of *pedagogy* which could be characterized in terms of patterns of pupil–teacher interaction. Pedagogy was, therefore, mainly seen here in terms of the balance of class, group and individual teaching, the use of questions and the giving of feedback. Other pedagogically related features of classroom to emerge from the study were to do with how pupils spent their time in the classroom, typically working alone on individual tasks, and the low levels both of cooperative work between pupils and group teaching, despite the almost universal practice of seating children in groups.

Curriculum figured much less strongly in the ORACLE study than did pedagogy and interaction patterns. However, data were gathered on broad categories of curriculum content. The main result to emerge was the heavy concentration of time on the basic subjects of mathematics and language. *Assessment* was not a substantial feature of the ORACLE project.

The ORACLE project showed that certain sorts of teaching approaches were associated with higher gains in the basic skills than others and that approaches associated with whole-class teaching and increased amounts of 'higher cognitive level' interactions were particularly effective. Careful observational study in classrooms demonstrated that any attempt to locate teachers on a formal–informal (or traditional–progressive) scale did not accord with the realities of classroom practice.

Both the Bennett study and the ORACLE study were focused on classrooms. Schools as whole institutions did not really figure in the data collection or analysis (although, of course, school-level factors may have influenced some of the classroom-level variables being considered). A later large-scale process–product study, conducted in the Inner London Education Authority (ILEA) by Mortimore and his colleagues (Mortimore *et al.*, 1988) incorporated both school-level and classroom-level variables in the analysis.

The measures of classroom *pedagogy* used in the ILEA study were very similar to those of the ORACLE project (and were based, in part, on the same research instruments). Consequently the descriptions of classroom practice tend to focus on kinds of classroom groupings, the use of whole-class, group and individual patterns of teacher–pupil interaction and the extent of teacher–pupil communication. As in the ORACLE study there was less focus on *curriculum* than on these aspects of interaction and class management, but the distinction between integrated and separate-subject teaching was found to be an important differentiating feature between different sorts of classrooms.

Unlike the earlier studies, the ILEA research gave considerable attention to whole-school factors and gathered information on such variables as school policies, relationships with parents and the role of the headteacher and deputy headteacher.

There was also considerable attention given to background variables, in particular, the socio-economic characteristics of families whose children attended the schools. This had not been a feature of the Bennett study nor a major element of the ORACLE research.

This concern with the wider social context of schooling, and, in particular, the influence on school experience of factors such as social class, gender and ethnicity, has also been a feature of a different tradition of research on the primary school which utilizes qualitative and ethnographic methods and draws explicitly on sociological theory. Studies such as those of King (1978), Pollard (1985), Pollard with Filer (1995), Hartley (1985) and Woods (1990) have sought partly to address macro-sociological issues of the relationships between school and the external society, but mainly to understand schools as social organizations and teachers and pupils as social actors in them. In contrast to the large-scale, mainly quantitatively oriented studies discussed above, these studies provide detailed accounts of a small number of educational settings, using the ethnographic methods of observation, involvement and open-ended interviewing.

For the purposes of the present discussion, the importance of studies of this kind is the emphasis they place on understanding the meanings that the experience of primary schooling have for pupils and teachers and understanding how these meanings are constructed and negotiated through interaction in specific social contexts. This focus on the notions of 'self' and typification of others, and the way that both teachers and pupils bring interests and purposes to the classroom, reminds us that the social situation of the classroom is one that is created by the participants.

The contrasts between these detailed qualitative studies of particular classrooms and the attempts to get representative data across a large sample can be seen by comparing the way that the notions of teaching styles (Bennett, 1976; Galton *et al.*, 1980) and pupil types (Galton *et al.*, 1980) are used and the way that classroom strategies (Pollard, 1985) are used. The notions of teaching styles and pupil types are used to group teachers or pupils who have common characteristics on particular variables which differentiate them from other teachers or pupils. For example 'progressive' teachers (Bennett, 1976) use integrated rather than separate-subject teaching, allow a lot of pupil choice of work and seating and have little formal assessment. 'Classroom Inquirers' (Galton *et al.*, 1980) use much higher than average levels of whole-class teaching and put a lot of emphasis on questioning and problem solving. 'Solitary Workers' (Galton *et al.*, 1980) are pupils categorized together on the basis of similarity in their high level of task involvement and low levels of contact with the teacher or other children.

In contrast to this notion of style or type, strategy is used by Pollard (1985) to describe and analyse patterns of classroom behaviour and interaction. Strategies here relate to the ways in which '... teachers and children juggle with their interests-at-hand in the ebb and flow of classroom life' (p. 179). Strategies include 'negotiation', 'manipulation', 'domination', 'withdrawal' and so on. They are concerned with power and control in the classroom and in this way can be related to teaching styles. However, they also involve types of understanding of the classroom situation and reflect the influence of identity and biography (Pollard, 1985; Pollard with Filer, 1995).

A third aspect of recent research related to primary schooling which has provided an important context for the PACE research is that of research focused specifically on teachers. Research by Nias and her colleagues (Nias, 1989; Nias *et al.*, 1989) and by Broadfoot and Osborn (1993) has explored various aspects of teacher identity, teacher professionalism and teachers' work situations. While these studies did not look directly at questions of curriculum and pedagogy or the effects of teaching approaches on children, they provided a rich source of evidence on the nature of teaching as an occupation and on the values and understanding of education professionals which underpin their professional activities. Such values and understandings are also likely to be of relevance to how they react to and accomplish change.

Nias's accounts of teachers' sense of self, based on extensive interviews and observation, was concerned to describe, 'what it is like to be a teacher' (Nias, 1989). It was concerned with the way in which teachers develop a self-image based on their experiences and values and the way this affects how they understand their work situations. Teachers' satisfaction with their work emerged as strongly related to the actual nature of the work they did while dissatisfaction was related to the conditions under which they work. The notion of 'feeling like a teacher' is claimed, despite its complexity and uncertainty, to be a major part of successfully maintaining the teacher role.

A related study also focused on teachers, but this time in terms of their working situations in schools, relations with other teachers, and the nature of primary schools as organizations (Nias *et al.,* 1989). Based on case studies of six primary schools, the research was concerned with the 'organizational culture' of primary schools. It described a 'collaborative culture' in many schools based on shared understandings and values and the importance of team work. Like the study of teacher identity, the research emphasized the affective aspects of teaching and school culture and the importance of feelings and relationships. The research also showed that, however much school cultures were based on collaboration and team work, the leadership role of the headteacher was absolutely central. In this way it paralleled ILEA research described above, where, in a methodologically very different project, the headteachers' leadership emerged as a crucial whole-school factor in explaining school effectiveness.

The work of Broadfoot and Osborn (1993) was also concerned with the values and understandings of primary school teachers and focused this specifically around the notion of teacher professionalism. Uniquely, this research contrasted the concept of professionalism of English primary school teachers with that of teachers in France. The use of the comparative method enabled these authors to consider the differing understandings of the professional role of the teacher in different cultures and also the potential for contrasts between professional beliefs and classroom practice. British teachers' conception of professional responsibility was shown to be a very broad one, especially in comparison with teachers in France. Considerable emphasis was placed on the personal and social aspects of the role and their responsibilities for the development of the whole child. They also showed how this broad conception of a professional role extended to their perceptions of those to whom they are responsible, with British teachers feeling a sense of responsibility to parents, colleagues and society at large as well as to their pupils. Professional autonomy was also shown to be an important aspect of teacher professionalism and workplace relationships emerged as an aspect of their sense of themselves as teachers. The Broadfoot and Osborn research showed that perceptions of professional responsibilities were strong and had a distinct character among teachers in Britain and are likely to be an important feature of their responses to educational change.

The studies discussed so far have looked at many aspects of primary education but, unlike the PACE project, were not concerned with looking at programmes of educational reform. One project which was directed towards the evaluation of a directed programme of educational change was the research directed by Alexander (1992) which studied the Primary Needs Programme implemented by Leeds LEA in the late 1980s to strengthen primary education provision in the authority. This was an ambitious study, looking at classrooms, schools and LEA procedures and was also concerned with the educational thinking underlying practice. One of the concerns of the research was to '... demystify that ultimate article of professional faith "good primary practice"' (Alexander, 1992, p. xiii). By this the researchers meant that particular ideas of appropriate curriculum and pedagogy were used as a reference point to justify practice without being subject to critical scrutiny and without evidence on its effects on children's learning. There is, perhaps, some resonance with this critique in the teachers' views reported in our earlier book, where many teachers said that a positive aspect of the National Curriculum was the challenge it presented them to think through their values and practices and the relationships between them.

A further echo of the PACE findings which emerged in the Leeds study was the way in which the process of reform was hampered by an over-centralized top-down approach. The research emphasizes the importance both of common purposes among participants, if educational reform is to be successful, and of the vital elements of teacher ownership of, and commitment to, changes in educational practice.

1. 4 THE PACE PROJECT AND THE PRESENT BOOK

The discussion above is not intended as a complete account of research into primary education but as an indication of the research context, both substantive and methodological, within which the PACE study was located. The variety of research discussed and the importance of some of the results to emerge explain some of the tensions which were experienced between different purposes of the research.

One of the main tensions is that between studying particular educational settings in sufficient depth to share the participants' meanings and the necessity to study sufficient settings to provide a representative account. The large-scale representative studies have provided statistical accounts based on counts of time spent on curriculum areas and types of teaching method. In a study of a national educational reform it was clearly necessary to answer questions related to such variables and to do so on the basis of a substantial representative sample. On the other hand, in order to understand the educational impact of these changes and to answer questions about the nature of teachers' and pupils' classroom experience, it was also necessary to study the ways they made sense of these changes and the ways that understandings were actively constructed in classrooms. The resulting strategy embedded detailed classroom studies within a larger sample: inevitably there were times when we felt that we were not gathering enough detail and spending enough time in individual classrooms and also times when we felt that the overall sample should have been larger.

The research on teacher professionalism provided an important reference point for the study, and this was linked to the work on teacher identity and school cultures. These studies had focused on teachers, and even the studies of 'school culture' focused and teacher culture, and did not incorporate pupil perspectives. In the PACE study we tried to balance the accounts of teacher perspectives by gathering detailed information on pupils' perceptions of school and classrooms. Similarily, evidence which comes from participants' own accounts, whether teachers' or children's, can be compared with observations made by researchers.

This book carries on the account of the PACE project presented in our first volume, *Changing English Primary Schools?* Unlike the earlier book it is an edited collection of individually authored chapters. However, it is intended to have an overall coherence and to continue to develop the themes and arguments of *Changing English Primary Schools?* This coherence comes from an inter-relationship between the chapters, based both on their common use of material from the ongoing PACE programme of data collection and also from the use of common analytical themes.

The continuity with the earlier book is emphasized through the parallel organizational structure of the two volumes. The order of chapters in *Changing English Primary Schools?* moved from an initial discussion of headteacher perspectives and whole-school issues to a consideration of teacher perspectives and issues of teacher professionalism. These chapters were followed by chapters dealing with curriculum and pedagogy, each treated from first a teachers' and then a pupils' perspective. The discussion then moved to questions of assessment, first teacher assessment and then standardized assessment. Finally we attempted to bring the argument together with a reconsideration of the changes we had identified related to the theoretical concerns of the study. The underlying rationale for the organization of the book was to move from the policy and managerial context to the values and perceptions of education professionals and thence to the realities of classroom practice.

In this book we again begin with the wider context, focusing in Chapter 2 on the making of education policy and the relationship of this to the responses of teachers and schools, which has been one of the subjects of our research. We then move to headteacher and school management issues in Chapter 3, which considers the changing role of primary headteachers and the emerging tensions between an increased emphasis on managerial roles and a continuing commitment to an educational role. In Chapters 4 and 5 we consider the professional perspectives of teachers and, in Chapter 4, examine the vital issue of teacher mediation of change, while Chapter 5 deals with the intersection of personal and career influences on professional identity through case studies of two teachers. In Chapter 6 we turn to the question of assessment and show how teachers continue to see this as an integral part of the educational process and see little value in the mechanistic, externally driven assessment procedures they are having to operate as part of the National Curriculum. However, this chapter also shows the creative possibilities of the intersection between external demands and teacher professionalism in the way that those teachers with most experience of National Curriculum assessment are moving towards a planned incorporation of formative as well as summative assessment in their teaching. Chapters 7 and 8 are still concerned with teachers but also incorporate material on pupil perspectives. In Chapter 7 one of the most contentious areas of debate around the National Curriculum is examined: that of the danger that pupils who perform poorly on initial assessments will become locked into failure. Encouragingly, the chapter suggests that, at least insofar as teacher expectations drive this process, there is no evidence that it is occuring. Chapter 8 considers the practice of one teacher and shows how even the most skilful of practioners are constrained by the reality of classroom life in a way not allowed for in many prescriptions for practice.

In Chapter 9 we deal with the classroom experiences and perspectives on school of the pupils in the study. The detailed data gathered directly from pupils in the earliest years of schooling is a major strength of the PACE research procedures. Longitudinal data on pupils over four years in primary schools shows an accomodation to schooling and a progressive adaptation to the realities of classroom life and teacher control. In this and the previous book we have documented the professional ideology of teachers coming into play to mediate the impact of National Curriculum changes on pupils. This reflects a protective insistence that the interests of children come first. Ironically, however, a pupil perspective on classrooms is one of adapting their expectations and behaviour to the realization that they must pay prime attention to the classroom requirements of teachers.

In Chapter 10 we consider an area which was not covered in the earlier volume, that of special educational needs. This is an area where the tension between the claims of 'entitlement', which have been such an important part of National Curriculum rhetoric, and those of children's particular needs, which is such an important part of teachers' professional thinking, is particularly acute. In Chapter 11 Patricia Broadfoot and Andrew Pollard bring together the previous chapters and link the various empirical material presented here to theoretical positions arising both from other work and from the PACE project. The methodological Appendix gives a summary of the research design and data collection procedures. All names of schools, headteachers, teachers and pupils in the text are pseudonyms

As with the previous volume we end on a question mark (albeit a metaphorical one this time). While it is intended that the completion of the PACE study will answer many of the questions discussed here, we also recognize the open-ended nature of educational debates and the perennial difficulty of resolving the issues raised.

Chapter 2

Practitoners or Policy-Makers? Models of Teachers and Educational Change

Paul Croll

2.1 Introduction

2.2 Teachers as partners

2.3 Teachers as implementers of education policy

2.4 Teachers as opponents of government policy

2.5 Teachers as policy-makers in practice

2.6 Conclusion

2.1 INTRODUCTION

The PACE project was concerned with the introduction of the National Curriculum and its associated assessment regime, which were just two of the multiple processes of change following the Education Reform Act of 1988. Others included league tables, local management of schools opting out and City Technology Colleges. These changes have brought to the fore, in a particularly acute form, the question of the role of teachers with regard to the formulation of educational policy and the processes of educational change. Other chapters in this book will look at specific aspects of change in classrooms and schools associated with the National Curriculum. This chapter takes an overview of the place of teachers in educational change by exploring four models of teacher roles with regard to education policy and considering their applicability in the context of some of the political and educational changes of recent years.

The four models of teachers and education policy I shall outline each suggest a different role for teachers with regard to education policy and involve differing patterns of relationship between education policy and education practice. The first is a model of teachers as *partners* in education policy-making in which teachers, along with other actors in the policy-making process, contribute to policy-making at all levels and in a pluralist, 'give and take' fashion. The second model has teachers as *implementers* of education policy and draws a sharp distinction between policy-making and policy implementation drawing on a centralized, bureaucratic and hierarchical view of the educational system. The third model, which has teachers *resisting* or *contesting* education policy is, in some respects, a mirror image of the second in that it recognizes the gap between policy-makers and practitioners but, rather than see this as appropriate, regards it in terms of political conflict. The fourth model which I shall present sees teachers as *policy-makers in practice* and considers the ways in which the nature of professional activities such as teaching necessarily involve the mediation of policy through professional practice in ways which may amount to policy creation.

These models are not, of course, as clear-cut in reality as the brief discussion above suggests. I want to identify some features of the models and the ways they have been used and consider their applicability to some current policy developments. The chapter will also consider the different levels at which the models may operate, in particular the distinction between operation at governmental or quasi-governmental levels and operation at the level of the school and classroom.

2.2 TEACHERS AS PARTNERS

The notion of a partnership between teachers and other actors in the educational policy-making process has informed a number of discussions of policy-making, in particular those of the 1960s and 1970s. The notion of partnership derives from a pluralist conception of the policy-making process, involving a degree of decentralized and 'distributed' power (MacPherson and Raab, 1988). Partnership does not exclude conflict, but it does mean that various actors must see each other's roles as legitimate and that there must be a measure of agreement about common goals. Partnership models are typically characterized by a degree of ambiguity about the boundaries of influence of different actors and shifts of these boundaries in particular circumstances.

Until recently, analysts of educational policy-making agreed that the process was characterized by a partnership between central and local government. Teachers were generally, although not universally, seen as also being partners in education policy. Influential books such as Kogan's (1975) and articles such as Briault's (1976) identified central government, local government and teachers as the three key players in what Briault famously characterized as a 'triangle of tension' in the government of education.

But what exactly was meant by 'teachers' was not always the same in different accounts and there has always been a degree of ambiguity in the notion of teachers as partners in education policy. In Kogan's study of educational policy-making between 1960 and 1974, 'teachers' are the teacher unions; one of the interest groups operating in a classic pluralist account of political life. Teacher unions are also the third element in Pile's account of the Department of Education and Science where the central–local partnership was increasingly joined by 'teachers through their national organisations' (Pile, 1979, p. 24). However, although Briault is not entirely explicit about this, in his analysis 'teachers' seem to be not the unions but the schools. It is the curricular and pedagogic autonomy at school level (which may or may not be autonomy for individual teachers), which makes teachers a point on the triangle in this account.

The high point of teacher partnership is often held to be the period of the operation of the Schools Council from the late 1960s until the early 1980s. The Schools Council has been described by Maurice Plaskow as 'a hopeful act of reconciliation between central and local government and teachers' (Plaskow, 1985, p. 1). Plaskow documents the dominating role that teachers came to play in the Schools Council, and 'teachers' in this context were very clearly the teacher unions. But the Schools Council approach to curriculum development also involved a partnership with teachers at school level. The report of the Lockwood Committee, which led to the establishment of the Schools Council, claimed that 'schools should have the fullest possible measure of responsibility for their own work' (quoted in Jennings, 1985, p. 20) and many Schools Council projects were aimed at increasing teacher and school autonomy.

It is conventional in analyses of contemporary policy developments to see them in terms of an end to partnership, at least as it involves teachers and possibly as it involves local government. Insofar as the teacher partners are the teacher unions, this end of partnership seems undeniable. However, it is not necessarily the case that the less clearly defined notion of partnership with schools can be regarded as having disappeared. In the interviews with primary school teachers and headteachers conducted during the period of implementation of the National Curriculum, no mention was made of teacher associations or the representative role of teacher unions in policy-making. However, some teachers and headteachers responded in terms of a positive professional engagement with change. Examples include comments such as, 'there is a sense of achievement that we have influenced the way the National Curriculum works here' and 'We have tried to be true to our own philosophy. We do not want to change the basic system and have not had to change radically' (Pollard *et al.*, 1994, p. 73). Whether this amounts to partnership in the sense we have taken from Briault will be considered later. In terms of the distinction between different levels made earlier, partnership at governmental or quasi-governmental level has been much reduced, while partnership at school level may be continuing for some schools.

2.3 TEACHERS AS IMPLEMENTERS OF EDUCATION POLICY

A contrasting model to that of teachers as partners in educational policy making is a model which sees the role of teachers as being to implement decisions about education taken elsewhere. Such a model informs the thinking both of those who see it as the appropriate role for teachers and some of those most critical of current developments.

The writings of the New Right theorists which have been so influential in recent education policy-making were quite explicitly directed at reducing teacher influence and turning teachers into policy implementers. The notion of 'producer capture' and the argument that public service bureaucracies served the interests of their own members, rather than the interests of their clients or the purposes of the government, was a key factor in New Right thinking in education as elsewhere. From this perspective, teachers need to be shifted from being partners in policy to a role as implementers of policies determined elsewhere (e.g. Flew *et al.*, 1981).

From a very different starting point, the arguments put by critics of current education policies, focusing on claims that teachers are becoming 'de-skilled' and de-professionalized, also see teachers as relatively passive policy implementers.

Although commentators coming from such different approaches have very different value positions with regard to a role for teachers as unquestioning implementers of education policy, their account, of the actual position of teachers, or at least the direction in which current developments are tending to move them, are very similar. (Or it

may perhaps be argued that New Right theorists believe that teachers should be implementers of policy but currently are not, and their left wing critics believe that teachers
should not be policy implementers but currently are.)

Certainly, some of the documents produced by the Department for Education and
HMI/OFSTED in the late 1980s and early 1990s suggest a sharp distinction between the
determination of policy and its implementation. In such accounts the role of teachers is to
get on straightforwardly with the job of implementing the new curriculum and assessment
procedures. This is a managerially led implementation which is concerned that schools
and teachers should be clear about what is to be done and should be given training, where
necessary, in doing it. Reviews of this process are concerned with how well or badly
schools and teachers have succeeded in implementation. Problems with implementation
are seen as arising either from limitations in school management or teacher capabilities,
or from essentially technical hitches in the way the policy was designed or explained.

The DES booklet *National Curriculum: From Policy to Practice* (DES, 1989) follows
this model in being highly prescriptive and directive in tone and content. Schools are
told that they 'will want to be able to demonstrate' that they meet a list of requirements
(para 4.2) and that these will 'involve schools in considering the organisation of
curriculum, reviewing timetabling, introducing schemes of work' (para 4.3). A section
headed 'Who Does What' spells out the division between NCC and SEAC, who will
design the curriculum and its assessment procedures, LEAs, who have roles in supporting implementation, and headteachers and teachers, who need to prepare themselves for
implementation (para 9). The new order is spelt out in that 'Working with statutory
requirements will be a new experience for most teachers' (para 10.1).

In similar vein, the HMI booklet *The Implementation of the Curriculum Requirements
of ERA* (HMI, 1991) treats the content of the changes introduced by ERA as entirely
unproblematic and is simply concerned with how successfully schools have implemented
them. Schools and teachers are seen as having not done too badly, although limitations
of staff expertise have created difficulties and some schools have got their time alloca-
tions wrong. The document notes concerns about assessment and recording and about
the lateness and inadequacy of the guidelines, but this is very much within an implementation model: teachers have not been given the instructions they need. Similarly,
LEA in-service provision needs following-up to 'help teachers implement what they had
learned' (HMI, 1991, p. 26).

But not all official documentation is in this tone. The National Curriculum Council
mounted extensive consultation exercises, even before the Dearing consultation exercise
and review, which led to considerable changes in the National Curriculum and its
assessment. For example, the paper *Planning the Curriculum at KS2* (NCC, 1993c) is
an account of an extensive programme of meetings with primary school teachers and
provides frameworks for analyses of curriculum planning and examples of school practice reflecting responses to different needs in different situations rather than prescriptive
models. The paper is intended to 'share successful practice' (p. 2). A similar tone is
contained in the Dearing Report (Dearing, 1994), and the nature of the Dearing review
and its outcome implies a role for teachers beyond that of unquestioning implementers
of policy.

The analysis of the interviews with teachers conducted as part of the PACE research
did not support the view that teachers felt de-skilled or de-professionalized. Teachers
were tenaciously holding on to a professional model of their role and, in many cases, to

an active and creative engagement with policy developments. However, the interviews certainly also demonstrated that both teachers and heads felt a considerable increase in the external direction of their work and felt more constrained with regard to professional autonomy, especially in the areas of curriculum and assessment (Osborn *et al.*, 1992; Pollard *et al.*, 1994; Osborn, in this volume).

2.4 TEACHERS AS OPPONENTS OF GOVERNMENT POLICY

A third model of teachers and education policy casts teachers in an oppositional role with regard to current education policy developments. Teachers in this model are seen as resisting the imposition of policy changes. Resistance can be seen as the mirror image of implementation and, like the implementation model, comes in both left-wing and right-wing versions. In the left-wing version, teachers are cast in a potentially heroic mould, acting collectively through unions or other political groupings to prevent the imposition of change. Such resistance is held to be in the interests of pupils and frequently is explicitly intended to advance other political agendas such as equal opportunities and anti-racist approaches to education. However, it also addresses more conventional trade union issues of workloads and conditions of service (e.g. Chitty, 1991; Hillcole, 1993).

The New-Right thinkers also see teachers as often resisting change, although in their version of the model this resistance is illegitimate. Sheila Lawlor, for example, has argued that the original aims of the Education Reform Act and of National Curriculum reforms have been subverted. This has occurred both through the 'education establishment' hijacking the reforms at a formative stage and turning them to their own ends and also through trade union action preventing implementation at school level (Lawlor, 1993).

In the extensive interviews conducted in the first phase of the PACE study, relatively little evidence of resistance emerged. Only very occasionally did teachers or headteachers suggest that they would actively resist or subvert the National Curriculum or the assessment procedures, and nowhere did headteachers indicate that they thought their staff would resist the implementation of change.

Nevertheless, only a few months after the second round of PACE interviews was conducted, the teaching profession had successfully resisted a major aspect of government education policy. Union action in refusing to carry out the statutory assessment procedures led to the government having to abandon the 1993 round of standardized assessments. Following this defeat over assessment, the Secretary of State for Education announced a review of the National Curriculum, conducted by Sir Ron Dearing, a highly respected political fixer in a consensual politics mode. This review was clearly intended to conciliate the teaching profession and, as expected and almost certainly as intended, resulted in a reduction of the compulsory elements of the curriculum and a simplification of assessment procedures.

Obviously, the question arises for us as researchers of why there was relatively little in the interview data which would have predicted the widespread resistance to government education policy. Part of the reason is that the research was conducted within the primary sector of the school system, and the teachers interviewed at that stage of the study were all teachers of infant-aged children (5–7 years). The main impetus for the union action in opposition to the government came from the secondary sector, traditionally more militant and union-oriented than primary teachers, although many primary teachers supported the action. Another factor, however, is that the action against the national assessments was a collective action, while the interview situation is a very individualistic one, and the PACE interviews concentrated on individual and school-level responses. Teachers mediated the assessments in what they thought was a professionally appropriate manner, but there was no resistance in the sense of individual attempts to ignore or sabotage them.

However, there is also the question of in what respect the action of the teacher unions in 1993 can be seen as resisting educational policy. The action was represented both in terms of policy opposition and in terms of the more conventional trade union issue of workloads. Although the teachers interviewed in the PACE study said nothing about resisting the Education Reform Act, they said a great deal about the extreme pressure of work they were under. The pressure caused by the pace of change, and the extra work created by the changed curriculum and, in particular, by the assessment and recording procedures, were major themes of the interview survey (Pollard *et al.,* 1994). This aspect of the teachers' action, a resistance to increased workloads, was, to some extent, prefigured in the interviews, at least in terms of describing a situation of great pressure, considerable resentment and a feeling that the demands being made of them could not be met.

There was, of course, a tension between these two aspects of the union action: resistance to increased workloads and resistance to the content of the National Curriculum and, especially, its assessment procedures. The action was widely understood to be substantive with regard to policy, in the sense that the unions as well as many individual teachers were opposed as education professionals to many aspects of the ERA reforms. But the action was always represented publicly as being about workloads and conditions of service. With the exception of the NUT, the unions did not say that they were opposed to the content of policy but only to the unreasonable demands it was claimed to place on teachers. This distinction was crucial for legal reasons. Industrial action could not legally be pursued because of opposition to government policy but could be pursued for reasons of conventional trade union interests in working conditions. In 1993, the High Court upheld the right of NAS/UWT members to take industrial action, rejecting the attempt by Wandsworth Borough Council to have it declared illegal. This decision effectively ensured that the government's education policy would be modified but, paradoxically, it did so by establishing that the teachers were not challenging government policy.

For this reason, the notion that the teachers were acting in opposition to education policy changes has to be treated carefully. Undoubtedly such opposition was an important factor in the action but conventional trade-union concerns with workloads and working conditions were also an important factor in obtaining such general teacher support for the action. And it was by publicly establishing that they were not acting in opposition to the content of policy that the teachers succeeded in having the policy revised. As the General Secretary of one of the NAS/UWT wrote, '[we] successfully established the legitimacy of the dispute because we concentrated solely upon workload. The solution to the workload problem remains the only aim of industrial action' (de Gruchy, 1994, p. 4).

A slightly weaker version of the resistance model of teachers and education policy is the notion of *contestation.* In a discussion of the TVEI initiative, Bowe, Ball and Gold describe how an initiative which, *prima facie*, seemed to have a very different orientation to the educational values of many secondary school teachers was in fact utilized by them for their own ends. They write, 'one is struck by the extent to which an externally "imposed" policy was appropriated by the teaching profession for very different purposes to those intended by the policy' (Bowe *et al.*, 1992, p. 9). Other accounts such as those of Saunders (1985) and McCulloch (1986) also detail the way in which schools and teachers have made creative use of TVEI resources. However, the view that teachers 'subverted' (McCulloch, 1986) or 'transformed' (Bowe *et al.*, 1992) TVEI probably underestimates the degree of ambiguity and flexibility implicit in the original policy. Although an example of a centralizing influence within the education system, TVEI was still in the 'permissive' tradition of educational policy-making, unlike the changes introduced by the Education Reform Act, which gave very little scope for permissible variations in implementation. The potential for innovative approaches to teaching were always present within TVEI and were generally emphasized by the Manpower Services Commission, which administered the initiative. It could be argued that TVEI can be seen as an example of the continuation of a partnership model; and it is also relevant to the fourth model discussed below.

2.5 TEACHERS AS POLICY-MAKERS IN PRACTICE

A further model of the role of teachers in education policy-making is one which we have called 'teachers as policy-makers in practice'. This model does not see teachers as mechanistically implementing policy more or less successfully and does not see teachers as typically resisting or transforming policy. It is related to the notion of partnership but is more informal and individualistic and arises from the nature of teaching rather than from deliberate choices by partners.

This model draws on the way that teachers, along with people in similar service-oriented occupations such as social workers, doctors and the police, are constantly making choices and decisions about the way in which they carry out their work. These choices are not optional and are only partly derived from a tradition of professional autonomy. The practical reality of teachers' working situations is such that these choices and decisions arise inevitably, to an extent that people are probably not aware for most of the time that they are being made. The job of teaching, like many service-oriented professional occupations, potentially expands indefinitely in the sense that the level and range of activities in which they could engage and the demands they could meet are far beyond the time and resources available to them. Consequently, teachers must ration their time and prioritize their tasks. They also have to establish school and classroom routines, ways of getting the business of the day accomplished, in order to make sense of the constant demands on them.

The inevitable process of rationing and prioritizing, and the practical routines which accomplish these, means that professionals become effectively makers of policy as well as implementers of policy. In this model the policy-making role occurs not from choice but from the nature of teaching as an activity. In the weakest version of the model, teachers and other professionals act as policy-makers in a entirely individual fashion and influence policy as it directly impacts on their particular clients. If the choices and decisions that teachers make are purely idiosyncratic and specific to them, then the overall policy impact will be to dilute the effects of a policy initiative but not to re-direct them.

However, this individualized model of the professionals' role in policy-making can be extended if professionals in similar situations tend to act in similar ways. If, either because of similar structural or situational constraints, or because of similar attitudes and ideologies (or because of an interaction of these), teachers interpret and prioritize policy changes in consistent ways, then the outcomes of these individual actions will have a systematic effect on the practical outcomes of policy. In this model, teachers are not acting *collectively* to influence policy but are taking *common* actions in response to the realities of their working situations. Such common actions can have systematic effects and may effectively re-direct educational activities in a way that makes teachers policy-makers.

This notion is related to the idea of professionals as 'street-level bureaucrats' which is used by Weatherley and Lipsky (1977) to analyse the process of implementation of institutional-level policy in the United States, and by Croll and Moses (1989) to analyse the introduction of the 1981 Education Act in England and Wales. Both ideas focus on the inevitability of discretionary action by professionals and its potential impact on policy. However, the term 'bureaucrat' emphasizes the role of professionals in rationing access to resources and does not convey the policy-making aspect which we want to suggest that independent but similar choices made by teachers can have.

Establishing that teachers do respond in similar ways to particular initiatives and that these responses do modify policy in practice is, of course, an empirical question. An example of research of this kind in the area of special educational needs is the study by Croll and Moses (1989) of the implementation of the 1981 Education Act. The Act attempted to move practice towards the greater integration of children with special educational needs into mainstream classrooms but did not make such integration compulsory. The outcome in terms of integration was very different for different groups of children. Croll and Moses argue that teachers' relative preference for coping with different types of disabilities in the regular classroom, which was fairly consistent across teachers, explains the differential outcomes. Children with physical and, in particular, sensory difficulties experienced a considerable increase in integration while children with emotional and behavioural difficulties experienced a shift towards segre-gation. These differential outcomes were not in the legislation and were not the result of any collective action by teachers, but arose from similar patterns of response by schools and teachers to the operation of policy in practice. Another example of such a process may be the dramatic expansion of the category of 'learning disability' in the United States following the Education of All Handicapped Children Act (PL 94–142), although no such expansion was intended in the legislation (Martin, 1993).

The evidence from the PACE study shows examples of common responses by teach-ers, of a kind which has been effectively 'making' some parts of National Curriculum and assessment policy. With regard to curriculum coverage, the PACE research (Pollard *et al.*, 1994) in common with other studies (Campbell, 1993) showed that teachers were devoting a higher proportion of time than in the past to the basic subjects of English and mathemetics, even though the explicit aim of the National Curriculum was to broaden curriculum coverage. Faced with the pressure of covering the programmes of study for the Core subjects, teachers responded in a way that, unintentionally, reversed one part of the policy.

Another example is the way in which the practical operation of the standardized assessments effectively changes their nature. The research shows that faced with the massive demands of conducting complex assessments, teachers have concentrated on making sure that the assessment accurately matches a child's 'true' attainment. The standardized assessments, which were intended to be an objective and external account of children's achievement, have in practice been used to reify teacher judgements. Similarly, despite the strong criterion referencing of the assessments, the allocation of children to levels has been heavily normative, reflecting teacher knowledge of the child and a sense of ordering of achievement across the class. The PACE researchers emphasize that the teachers they observed were not trying to subvert the tests or to bias their outcomes. It was the way in which they interpreted the demands made on them and attempted to get the most accurate assessment in a difficult and pressured situation which has led to assessments intended to be independent being heavily influenced by teacher judgements (Pollard *et al.*, 1994; Abbott *et al.*, 1994; Croll, 1990).

Teachers operate as policy-makers in practice at school and classroom level, making personal and individual decisions. However, insofar as they tend to make similar decisions, these actions aggregate in a way that creates systematic effects. Common actions by teachers can create a policy-making process which parallels governmental-level processes.

2.6 CONCLUSION

These models have been presented partly as a framework to help understand the nature of educational policy-making and the place of teachers in it, and also to explore the possibilities and the limitations of different analyses of teachers and education policy. The fourth model, the notion of teachers as 'policy-makers in practice', is argued to be an inevitable feature of the education system arising from the effectively unbounded nature of a profession such as teaching and the nature of the choices which teachers must make. The extent to which the operation of this model exerts a systematic policy impact will depend on the degree of flexibility and choice in particular situations and on the extent to which similar situational locations and professional ideologies lead to teachers making similar decisions. The model emphasizes that it is not necessary for teachers to act collectively in order to have a systematic impact on policy, but that common action can arise from the similarity of the situations teachers act in and the ideas which inform their actions. We have argued that, even in the case of a very tightly constrained policy such as the National Curriculum reforms, the policies have been changed in practice in a number of respects. In the case of less tightly constrained policies such as the 1981 Education Act and TVEI, the impact of 'policy-makers in practice' has been considerable.

The notions of teachers as passive implementers of education policy and as active opponents of the policy have appeared in both left-wing and right-wing accounts of contemporary educational change. The descriptions coming from these different sources are essentially the same, the difference being in whether the policy itself is seen as legitimate and whether teacher opposition to it is seen as legitimate. The extent to which resistance to the National Curriculum and its assessment regime has been successful, and the influence which teachers' everyday working practices have had on the policies in practice, suggest that an approach to educational change which casts teachers as passive implementers is unlikely to be productive and that complaints that teachers have been de-skilled and de-professionalized are premature.

However, the notion of resistance to education policy is also not unproblematic. Analyses which focus on the 'struggle' of teachers against current policy often reflect an enthusiasm for such a struggle more than they reflect the reality of teachers' responses to policy. As we have seen, there is a considerable tension in the successful action of the teacher unions in effectively boycotting the 1993 assessments and in the debates which followed over whether that boycott should continue. The teacher unions were only able to carry out their action by asserting, and persuading a court, that they were not concerned to challenge the substance of government policy but were only concerned with their workloads. Despite being urged by some within the teacher unions to continue the action, teachers have, at least for the moment, collectively decided to cooperate with the Dearing reforms of the National Curriculum.

The model of teachers being in partnership with the government, and others concerned with education, is sometimes seen as a kind of golden age of education policy. But partnership can be a rhetorical as well as a descriptive term, and one recent commentator has referred to the 'myth of partnership' (Raab, 1994, p. 7). As we have seen, there has always been an ambiguity over whether partnership meant the formal or semi-formal arrangements which necessitate representative institutions such as teacher unions or whether it is a working partnership at the level of schools and individual teachers. We can distinguish three kinds of partnership: the partnership at the level of overall policy formation (the union model), partnership in terms of getting the details of a policy right (the Dearing/NCC consultation model) and partnership in creating educational activity in schools and classrooms. Although current education policy in Britain has moved away from a partnership with teachers, especially at the level of teacher unions, many aspects of partnership have continued in the consultation, field trials and other activities involving teachers associated with the introduction and modification of the National Curriculum. The inevitability of teacher involvement in the practical determination of policy and the difficulties which have arisen from the refusal to consult at a representative level or respond to teacher concerns suggest that governments may find a partnership model more effective in getting educational change to happen than a model based on teachers as implementers. Finally, the notion of policy-makers in practice emphasizes the inevitability of variation between policy intentions and education practice, and also the ways in which individual teacher actions can have system-wide impacts.

Chapter 3

Managing to Change? The Role of the Primary School Head

Edie Black

3.1 Introduction
3.2 For better or worse?
3.3 Power and leadership
3.4 Working together
3.5 Conclusion

3.1 INTRODUCTION

Changes implicit in the Educational Reform Act (ERA) of 1988 and Local Management of Schools (LMS) schemes have dramatically transformed the role of the primary school head. In describing the pre-war elementary school and the primary school of the immediate post-war years, Coulson states that:

> The head was often the best qualified and experienced teacher on the staff and in some schools he [sic] was the only qualified teacher. Apart from teaching, he performed a fairly narrow range of administrative and welfare functions; the comparatively stable and unchanging regime of school life made it possible for him to carry out all the school's non-teaching tasks himself. (Coulson, 1976, p. 92)

More recently Craig has argued that 'The term headteacher in the 1990s will become a misnomer. The task of headship is management' (Craig, 1989, p. 90).

These two quotations give a clear indication of one of the main dimensions of change recently experienced by heads in primary schools. Most heads can be said to have moved out of the classroom and into the office in that their role has changed from that of head*teacher* into a more managerial role.

A further dimension of change concerns that of the power of the head. As recently as the early 1980s, the power of the head was a taken-for-granted feature of the cultural world of the primary school. Alexander, for example, could then argue that 'The primary head in Britain has a formidable concentration of power' (Alexander, 1984, p.161).

Since then primary schools have been subjected to externally imposed changes, most of which have resulted in a considerable diffusion of the power of the head. In particular, heads and teachers have been propelled into new forms of collaborative working relationships (Burgess *et al.*, 1994; Nias *et al.*, 1989) and new structures of accountability to governors and parents have been set up.

In order to explore these two dimensions of change, I have analysed data from interviews carried out early in 1994 with heads in the 48 schools in the PACE 2 sample. In these interviews heads were invited to reflect on the various aspects of change they might have experienced over the time-span of the two phases of the PACE project. In order to add a further longitudinal aspect to the analysis, some reference is also made to data collected from the first round of interviews in 1990 with the 48 heads in the PACE 1 sample.

First, the transformation from headteacher to manager is explored. What does it mean for heads as individuals? How have they adapted to what most of them describe as a 'dramatic' role change? Then the broader aspects of power and inter-personal relationships within the school are explored. How free do heads feel to act as they think best? What are the implications of collegiality for the leadership role of heads?

3.2 FOR BETTER OR WORSE?

Alexander argues, as do other commentators that 'the pivotal point in the matter of how a school copes with change is the leadership provided by the head' (Alexander, 1984, p. 181).

While the importance of the head's leadership role is widely recognized, we know very little about how, in purely personal terms, heads themselves have responded to and coped with recent role changes. In this section we consider how heads now feel about their work. Has life as a head changed for better or for worse within the last decade? In what areas of their work do they feel free to act as they think best and in what areas do they feel constrained? Aggregate statistical data are used in order to give an overall indication of heads' responses. In addition, extracts from interviews are used to give a further insight into heads' responses to role change.

In the 1994 round of interviews we asked heads to comment on whether or not they felt their life as a head had changed over the last few years. It was clear that, for the majority of heads in the sample, their quality of life had deteriorated. Table 3.1 gives responses to this question in detail.

Table 3.1   *Perceptions of change in life as a head (percentages)*

No answer	4.2
Noticeably better	14.6
Moderately better	2.1
Slightly better	4.2
Neutral/mixed change	22.9
Slightly worse	4.2
Moderately worse	6.3
Noticeably worse	39.6
Other	2.1

Source: PACE 2 headteacher interviews
Sample: 48 headteachers
Date: spring 1994

Only 20.9 per cent of heads reported a change for the better (to various degrees) compared with 50.1 per cent who reported a change for the worse (to various degrees). It is significant that over one third of heads in the sample reported a change which was coded in analysis as 'noticeably worse'. Heads were also asked whether or not they found as much satisfaction and fulfilment in headship as they did five years ago (or since their appointment if this was more recent). Table 3.2 gives responses to this question. While some heads (20.9 per cent) reported increased levels of satisfaction in their job, by far the majority (54.2 per cent) reported reduced levels of satisfaction.

Table 3.2 *Satisfaction: change in last 5 years (percentages)*

No answer	6.3
Greatly increased	14.6
Slightly increased	6.3
Little/no change	4.2
Slightly reduced	12.5
Greatly reduced	41.7
Mixed: more and less	12.5
Other	2.1

Source: PACE 2 headteacher interviews
Sample: 48 headteachers
Date: spring 1994

Many heads, especially those nearing or in their 50s, spoke about their desire to take early retirement. One head said: 'I'm in my early 50s and, like so many others, I'm looking forward to early retirement.' Another head listed six primary school heads in the immediate area and three others slightly further afield, but still within the same LEA, who had recently taken or were about to take early retirement. He added: 'There's something wrong, there's something wrong if they're going.' This head's rather depressing account of experienced heads leaving the profession prematurely at the local level reflects a national trend. In a statement based on figures for England and Wales recently released to the press by the National Association of Headteachers, the General Secretary of the Association, David Hart, summed up the statistical evidence included in the statement by saying, 'The dramatic increase in the levels of premature retirement among headteachers and deputy headteachers should sound alarm bells ringing throughout the education system' (NAHT, 1994).

One head in the PACE 2 sample explained what was 'wrong' for him. He said that his life as a head had changed 'dramatically' and 'for the worse'. He went on to explain:

> I feel less fulfilled in terms of not being able to give my staff the support that I think I should in terms of resources and my time. Not being able to deliver to the children and their parents the education that the children deserve, once again through lack of resources and time. And for me personally, I seem to spend a lot of my time on things that have nothing to do with the education of children, like fiddling about with the drains and climbing on the roof, wondering whether I should pay the gas bill this month or next month. It's not what I was trained to do. Also there's the fact that I can't teach as much as I used to.

This particular head's perception of his new role is expressed in totally negative terms. He felt unable to do the things he thinks are important such as teaching, supporting his staff and delivering quality education throughout the school. At the same time, he felt compelled to spend too much of his time on 'things that have nothing to do with the education of children'. His perception of his changing role was that he had moved from the core activity of education to peripheral activities. As did so many heads in the study, he had begun to feel that he was not doing the job for which he was trained.

This head's negative response to the changing role of the primary school head was shared by many of the heads in the sample, but not all. It is evident from interview data that some have successfully made the transition from the old-style headteacher leadership role to the newer managerial leadership role.

The spectrum of responses to change can be explored by looking closely at four heads in the study. All four had been heads for ten or more years and had been in their present schools throughout both phases of the PACE project. Mr Stokes and Mrs Mockridge stand at the negative end of the spectrum. Most of Mr Stokes's negative responses were expressed in general terms of task overload and subsequent exhaustion: feelings shared by many teachers. Mrs Mockridge's negative responses were more specific to changes in the role of the head. In particular, she deplored the increasing pressure on her to move out of the classroom and into the office. Mr Sanders stands at the positive end of the spectrum in that he had totally accepted and was enjoying his new leadership role. Mr Bishop stands at the mid-way point of the spectrum. While he regretted the loss of his headteacher role, he had learned to find a different form of job satisfaction in his new leadership role.

Mr Stokes: 'plug another battery in'

In describing how his quality of life had changed, Mr Stokes spoke mostly in very general terms about being more 'pressurized' and more 'tired' than in the past:

> I would think that we're all...nearly every head that you talk to, the older ones anyway, and I put myself in that category, we feel more pressurized. I think a lot of the enjoyment, in some ways, is going because you're pressurized with paper work, you're pressurized by the fact that you've got to do something by a certain date.

As did many heads in the study, Mr Stokes talked about having to work long hours after school, either in school or at home. It is holiday time, not simply being at home in the evening and at weekends, which is now regarded as an essential respite from the remorseless grind of the daily pressures at work:

> It's changed. I think we're all more tired. You come to the end of the day and I think ... when it comes to holiday time, we're all ready for a holiday, very much so now. I'm getting now so that I do a lot of work after school. Then I go home and you've got to sit down for a while, for an hour or so and then you don't want to know anything more to do with school. It's because you are getting more and more tired I think.

Even when looking to the immediate future, Mr Stokes could only predict that pressures on teachers and heads would increase rather than decrease. He said: 'The pressures are greater now and I think with OFSTED they will only increase.' He was not alone in his fears about the extra burden that OFSTED inspections would place on schools.

An additional anxiety for Mr Stokes was that, as head, he could not let his feelings be made known to the teachers and pupils in the school. He explained:

> I was speaking to a friend who is a primary school head and he said the enthusiasm is going, it's being drained out of him. He's shattered. This is what you've got to be careful about, that you don't lose the enthusiasm, or the children don't see that you've lost it. And

the staff. It is hard at times, when you're tired but you just have to keep going — plug another battery in. You've got to keep smiling. You can't let anybody see how you feel.

Several heads echoed this anxiety. One head said he felt he had to 'put on a mask' when he went into the staffroom and another that, no matter how he felt, he had to 'keep smiling all day'.

The general statements made by Mr Stokes about being 'pressurized', feeling 'more and more tired' and, more particularly, having to work outside the official school day have also been made by many classroom teachers both in the PACE study (Pollard *et al.*, 1994) and in other studies (Osborn and Black, 1994; Webb, 1994). Clearly, heads and teachers share the burden of overload and its deleterious effects both on their working lives and on their private lives.

The second head who, with Mr Stokes, stands at the negative end of the spectrum is Mrs Mockridge. She too looked to the past and deplored most aspects of her role change.

Mrs Mockridge: 'losing touch with competencies'

When asked if her life as a head had changed much in the last five years, Mrs Mockridge responded with a loud laugh and said 'You must be joking!' Later in the interview she said that her life had changed so much (and in unwelcome directions) that she frequently asked herself 'Hell's teeth — what did I join for?'

Compared with Mr Stokes's very generalized response to the question about change in the role of the head, Mrs Mockridge had some specific points to make. Just as the head quoted earlier in the chapter had expressed objections to having to deal with maintenance problems such as 'fiddling about with the drains and climbing on the roof' she felt she did not have the competence to decide whether the school needed 'new washers or new taps'.

More deeply, at the heart of Mrs Mockridge's negative feelings about the changes in her life as a head was the awareness that she had lost touch with what she called her 'competencies'. Like so many heads in the study, she felt she was being asked to do a job for which she had not been trained. She said there were 'great lumps' of the job that she did not enjoy, explaining:

> I don't enjoy playing with telephone numbers-worth of money. Had I wanted to be an accountant, I would have been an accountant. I'm not and I don't particularly care for it. I think what I have lost and which I regret bitterly is not being able to go into classrooms on a daily basis. I do the 10 minute slot, the 20 minute slot and the 'Do you mind if I take a story?' all those kinds of 'jollies', which is after all what I was trained to do. You know, you lose touch with what your competencies actually are. So I really miss that. There are some days when the paperwork is over the top of my head and I don't see a child unless they come knocking on my door because they're poorly. That is sad; it's not part of the joy of the job.

Mrs Mockridge's statement here made quite clear the unwelcome transition from the classroom into the office experienced by the majority of heads in the study. The next head, Mr Bishop, is located at the mid-point of the spectrum. While he expressed regret at the loss of classroom contact with children, he said that he was learning how to find a different source of satisfaction in his new leadership role.

Mr Bishop: 'satisfaction from efficiency'

Mr Bishop looked back with some regret on the days when he had been a classroom teacher and had what he described as 'that pivotal influence in front of a class'. However, he also explained the sense of loss and gain that he now experienced in his changing role in this way:

> I don't see children any more apart from assembly, so that side of it ... I don't feel as fulfilled as I used to. But I suppose I get satisfaction now in a managerial sense ... through the way the job's changed and finding satisfaction from efficiency, I suppose. So the type of satisfaction I get from the job has changed.

This new sense of satisfaction had not come easily to Mr Bishop. He said that it 'has come not through training because there hasn't been any'. He has had to learn 'a load more people skills'. In spite of the lack of training,

> In one way that's been very satisfying and interesting and brought out a whole side of my personality which I didn't really know about.

His authority as a teacher and autonomy in the classroom were compared with some of the frustrations of his new role. Now, as he put it, he had to 'work through other people'. Although he enjoyed working with teacher colleagues 'because there's a lot of respect and empathy with each other' and found working with parents 'fascinating', he resented the influence of some other groups.

> The problem in working through other people is not so much colleagues on the staff ... it's more the people on the edges like governors, a diminishing LEA, people who can influence the school but don't really have an understanding of what it's like in schools. And politicians [*long pause*] they are people who deal in paper not people, and schools are people places. That's why I find them frustrating because they don't understand.

Mr Bishop had managed to learn the skills required to engage positively with his changed leadership role, but was still experiencing regrets and difficulties. In contrast, Mr Sanders expressed no regrets at all about his new leadership role.

Mr Sanders: 'I enjoy coming to school every day'

A large number of heads in the study almost invoked a sense of a lost golden age when speaking about pre-ERA days; Mr Sanders had no such sense of loss. He admitted that his workload had increased but found the work 'satisfying, challenging and very stimulating'. He explained:

> I think when I first became a head I thought I had got to the position where I thought I really wanted to be. I was a little bit ... almost I suppose self-satisfied, casual about things. Certainly in the last seven or eight years my job fulfilment has increased. I've found it more satisfying, challenging and very stimulating. I enjoy coming to school every day. My workload has increased considerably. I think I started off being a head by drifting through, really, and the school could have managed without me. I don't think it really needed a head in the same way that the school needs someone like me now.

Mr Sanders clearly derived a great sense of satisfaction from his new leadership role. In explaining why he felt that the school needed someone like him he said:

And that's because I feel more part of the team. I feel like one of ... I don't feel like the head, I feel like one of the staff.

He had no regrets at all about not having a regular teaching timetable. Quite significantly he said that he thought he had 'a better job' than the teaching staff because, as he said, 'I don't have to be responding to the demands of children all the time.'

Summary

Mr Sanders had successfully and happily managed the transition from the classroom into his new leadership role. Other heads also at the positive end of the spectrum spoke enthusiastically about the 'challenge' of the job, the 'sense of achievement' and the associated 'flow of adrenalin'. However, these heads were very much in a minority and tended to be new to what was their first headship. Both Mr Stokes and Mrs Mockridge were uncomfortable with the changes now being expected of them. Like most heads in the sample they felt they were being diverted from what they had been trained for, what they enjoyed and what they felt competent in doing. Other heads in the sample, like Mr Bishop, were located in the middle of the spectrum. While Mr Bishop shared some of the regrets and frustrations of Mr Stokes and Mrs Mockridge, he had found some degree of satisfaction in learning new skills and adapting to the changing role of the primary school head. Other heads in this position spoke of the 'steep learning curve' they had experienced before they could work their way through to even a partial sense of fulfilment in carrying out their new responsibilities.

3.3 POWER AND LEADERSHIP

In this section I consider how heads themselves felt about the power dimension of their changing leadership role. First heads' perceptions of freedom and constraint in three areas of their work are examined. Then I focus on changes in working relationships within the school.

In 1994 heads were asked to comment on their perceptions of changes in their freedom of action as a head in specific areas of their work. The same question was asked of heads in 1990, at the beginning of the PACE 1 project. Responses from 1990 and 1994 are summarized and can be compared in Table 3.3.

Table 3.3 *Greater/reduced freedom of action (percentages)*

	1990	1994
Completely free	4.2	2.1
Fairly free	50.0	27.1
Undecided	8.3	6.3
Fairly constrained	29.2	31.3
Very much constrained	8.3	33.3

Source: PACE 1 and PACE 2 headteacher interviews
Sample: 48 headteachers in each round
Date: summer 1990 and spring 1994

In 1990 just over half (54.2 per cent) of the heads in the PACE1 sample said that they felt free to act as they thought best. By 1994 this figure was reduced to 29.2 per cent. In 1990, the responses of 37.5 per cent of the sample indicated that they felt either 'fairly' or 'very much' constrained in their actions. By 1994 this figure had risen to 64.6 per cent. These aggregate statistics give a clear indication that between 1990 and 1994 heads felt that they had experienced a severe diminution in their power to act as they thought best in their schools.

In order to understand what these aggregate statistics mean in terms of the day-to-day experiences of individual heads we turn to a qualitative analysis of interview data. In interview, heads were asked to comment on how free or constrained they felt in three specific areas of their work: curriculum coverage; assessment arrangements; managing finances and resources. At this level of analysis, a more complex picture emerges.

Curriculum coverage

The majority of heads in the study felt constrained by the prescriptive requirements of the National Curriculum. Nevertheless, in principle, many heads (and teachers) shared the view of Mr Stokes.

> There are constraints, but in some ways that's not a bad thing. I must say that it's made people think about the breadth of the curriculum which, maybe before ... I must say the National Curriculum has its plus and negative points.

A few heads had an even more positive view of the National Curriculum. For example, Mr Sanders regarded recent initiatives, including the introduction of the National Curriculum, as 'positive initiatives' and 'necessary triggers'. He had not resisted them because, he said, 'I've not found there have been things there that I've wanted to resist.'

Assessment arrangements

The majority of heads in the study shared the view of the majority of teachers who were interviewed, in that they regarded assessment arrangements, particularly Standard Asssessment Tasks (SATs), as being not only an externally imposed constraint but also time-consuming and not necessarily helpful or illuminative. On the subject of SATs, Mr Bishop said:

> They're very prescriptive and time-consuming. They're really elaborate and don't give any extra information; they don't really give relevant information in some cases. They're too cumbersome.

A further objection to SATs raised by several heads was the cost to the school when supply staff had to be brought in to cover for classroom teachers who were involved in SATs.

Objections to Teacher Assessments (TAs) were not so numerous or vociferous. For example, Mrs Mockridge had this to say:

> I think the way we used to work was perhaps not so rigorous across every subject. I mean we didn't assess geography and history for example, science even. We just said 'OK, yes,

we've done this topic.' So, yes, maybe we are more constrained, but I don't know that that's necessarily a bad thing. And I don't think we're constrained in how we do it particularly, except over the SATs, you know. I think there's a fair amount of leeway to choose how you're going to do it or to choose what evidence to accept, so to speak.

Managing finances and resources

Most heads expressed very strong feelings on this topic. For example, one head said that LMS was 'the best thing since sliced bread'. In contrast, another head said that his financial problems under LMS were 'horrendous'. Such a polarization of views on LMS was noted in our earlier work (Pollard *et al.*, 1994).

The most frequently mentioned negative factor associated with LMS was that heads felt they had not been given the training to enable them to cope with their new financial responsibilities. One head in the study, Mr Sanders, stood out as an exception. On the subject of LMS he said, 'I don't have any problems there. I was in commerce before I came into education so it wasn't at all a daunting prospect.'

Not all heads were lucky enough to have had this prior experience. However, on the subject of training and support, one LEA in the study was given praise by all six heads interviewed. For example, Mr Stokes said:

> I'm fortunate that I've had a secretary who is very efficient and has just been appointed an LMS clerk for a few hours a week. We also have very good support from the LEA on this one too; they are excellent. You can pick up the phone and there's always somebody there who will come in and help you.

On the positive side of the new control over their budget, many heads said that they welcomed the 'flexibilty', the 'control' and the 'scope to make decisions' that LMS gave them. Mr Stokes gave a specific example of his new-found budgetary freedom.

> If you want to save towards a project ... for example we've spent quite a bit of money on the junior library, refurbishing it. We might have had to wait many, many years for it when we were under the LEA because everybody would be asking for a similar thing to be done.

However, there were limits to this new-found freedom. Many heads felt, as one head put it, that LMS did not really give them 'any more latitude than in the past'. Mrs Mockridge put it more explicitly:

> Under LMS there are no choices; I really feel there are no choices. Having made the decision that you want X number of people standing in front of Z number of children ... You know, I'm not proposing to have classes of 35 in order to do something different. Once that philosophical and common-sense decision has been made there are no choices except over small change, basically.

There were also differences between schools; some heads described themselves as 'losers' and some as 'gainers' under LMS. The head of one 'gainer' school, Mr Sanders, said:

> We've done fairly well on the budget; we were an initial 'gainer' when we went LMS. For various reasons we've had underspends for two or three years and this year I was enabled to put £14,000 back in and increase staffing. So there are a good number of areas like staffing and clerical hours and lunch-time supervision that I've been able to put more money into and these have been very beneficial areas for the school.

In contrast, the head of a 'loser' school explained the difficulties he had experienced in balancing his budget under LMS.

> The advantage that I had was that I had known that we were going to be a 'loser' under LMS from the day that LMS was first mooted as being the way forward, so I've been able to plan for that day when my budget was being chopped at an increasing percentage amount year by year. By judicious housekeeping, by unforeseen circumstances which have actually proved to be financially beneficial to us, like a member of staff seeking voluntary redundancy, like — regrettably — a teacher having MS, by one teacher leaving the profession altogether and not being replaced, by making a nursery nurse redundant, and a GA redundant (both forced redundancies) I'm able to face this coming financial year's cuts of £35,000 without any further job losses.

Many heads recognized that the most bitter aspect of LMS concerned staffing levels and their associated costs. Mr Stokes said:

> If we've got to find any of the new teachers' salary increase, that's where the problems will start. When people have to make decisions about whether your staffing can remain the same — that's where the worry is. I've never been in a position where I've had to make redundancies because our numbers are growing, but I know some heads who've had to face that two or three times and it's not very nice.

The dilemma anticipated by Mr Stokes has become sharp political reality as this book goes to press. Schools have indeed been asked to find the latest teachers' salary increase from within their own budgets. The outcome has been widespread revolt by governing bodies who have set deficit budgets in an attempt to resist having to make teachers redundant and so increase class sizes.

Summary

Aggregate statistics based on a quantitative analysis of interview data indicate quite clearly that, between 1990 and 1994, heads felt that they had experienced a sharp increase in constraints on their power to act as they thought best within their own schools. This finding indicates a distinct break with pre-ERA life as a headteacher. A qualitative analysis of the same data, as might be expected, reveals a more complex picture of gains and losses associated with the National Curriculum and its assessment procedures. Recent policy changes (Dearing, 1994) which have taken into account early objections raised by practitioners have served to diminish negative feelings. The tension between gains and losses in autonomy is perhaps most clearly evident in heads' responses to LMS. Under these new funding arrangements heads have welcomed the freedom from earlier bureaucratic constraints exercised by LEAs. However, this freedom only exists within narrow financial limits and also carries with it the burden of having to make painful decisions on such matters as staffing levels.

3.4 WORKING TOGETHER

Heads and teachers in primary schools are now thrown together in a new working relationship. While there has been much comment on what this new relationship means for teachers and teacher professionalism, little attention has been given to what it means for heads and their leadership role. As Southworth states, "collegiality" has become a popular notion but there is ... no acknowledgement in the writings of those who advocate collegiality that it will involve major change' (Southworth, 1987, p. 70).

Here we examine some of the tensions experienced by heads in the move towards collegiality. Heads in the PACE 2 sample were asked to say if there had been any changes in the running of the school in the past few years. Table 3.4 gives their responses to this question.

Table 3.4 *Changes in the running of the school (percentages)*

No answer	8.3
Considerable change	64.6
Moderate change	22.9
Not answered*	4.2

* NOT answered because in first two years of headship

Source: PACE 2 headteacher interviews
Sample: 48 headteachers
Date: spring 1994

Clearly, the majority experience was that 'considerable change' had taken place. Heads were then asked to comment more specifically on any changes with regard to planning co-operatively, working co-operatively, consultation between head and staff, central direction by the head and democratic decision-making. An increase in co-operative planning was reported by 89.6 per cent of heads, 70.8 per cent reported an increase in co-operative working, 62.5 per cent reported an increase in consultation between head and staff and 54.2 per cent reported an increase in democratic decision-making. These increases in co-operative, consultative and democratic activities have to be set beside an apparently contradictory reporting, by almost half (47.9 per cent) of the heads in the study, of an increase in central direction by the head.

Collaboration, co-operation and consultation

Many studies (Osborn and Black, 1994; Webb, 1993) demonstrate that since the introduction of the National Curriculum teachers and heads spend much more time planning and working together. They also spend more time together in staff meetings which are now more formal than they used to be. Mr Stokes illustrated the point:

> We do more co-operative planning now. As for working co-operatively, it depends on what you've got. If we have two classes in the same year group then they would plan and work together more. Units, for example the infants, work more together now. We now have more regular staff meetings with a set agenda which we didn't at one time. Staff meetings at one time tended to be more cosy, chatting over dates and things, now they tend to be more specific with an aim in view and the managerial meetings will be the same.

Collaborative activity on a whole-school basis is a stronger feature of the cultural life of primary schools than it was in the past. This was most evident in what heads said about curriculum development and its place within the School Development Plan. Mr Sanders described this in some detail:

> We are planning on a three- or a four-year cycle to review curriculum areas. That review process will analyse where the school is at the moment, what policies and schemes exist

and link them to assessment outcomes so that we know how effective they are. Then a curriculum co-ordinator would perhaps be engaged in INSET and then come back and deliver INSET within the school. Policy would be reviewed and perhaps revised, implemented and then over a two-year period it would have low-key monitoring. During that time resource implications would be examined and there would be a 'trickle' with it. That would then take us towards an evaluation and a review at the end of two or three years at the end of the cycle. We try to balance our curriculum areas so that, for example, each term a new curriculum area would come on stream. But during the course of any week-long snapshot there would be something happening in all curriculum areas even if it were just low-level monitoring with co-ordinators involved or the whole school involved in development in that way. It all takes time.

From this description, it can be seen that the role of teachers as curriculum co-ordinators is crucial to whole-school curriculum development. Mrs Mockridge gave more details of what was expected of curriculum co-ordinators. She explained:

We have a rolling review on the School Development Plan which now looks at each subject ... We expect co-ordinators to keep us up to date with anything that is actually new: new pieces of research, interesting articles, whatever. They are supposed to keep us up to date and put something in the staff room for us all to read. The School Development Plan gives you a warning about what the next term's subject is going to be. We work towards it by discussing it informally or discussing it in year groups before it comes before the whole staff. So it sort of rolls along. We expect co-ordinators to go to twilight meetings or curriculum meetings or whatever.

Teachers who are curriculum co-ordinators have had considerable powers delegated to them; they were regarded by heads as experts in their specific curricular field. From the descriptions given by Mr Sanders and Mrs Mockridge, it can be seen that the pivotal role of co-ordinators is a continuous one throughout the whole of the rolling cycle of the School Development Plan.

Collegiality and leadership

... collegiality will change the existing *role relations* in school. (Southworth, 1987, p. 70).

It is part of traditional assumptions about power and authority in the primary school that the head's 'zone' of autonomy is the school as a whole. Equally, it has been part of these assumptions that the teacher's 'zone' of autonomy is within the classroom (Lortie, 1969). As we have demonstrated, teachers as curriculum co-ordinators have a new role to play in whole school planning; this marks a break with previous practice and a move towards what has been described as 'extended professionalism' (Hoyle, 1974). What does it mean for heads and their leadership role in primary schools?

It is clear from a quantitative analysis of data from PACE 1 and PACE 2 that heads were increasingly aware of the fact that they had the ultimate responsibilty for running the school. In 1990 and in 1994 heads were asked: Would you say that you had a particular approach to your leadership role in the school? In 1990 there were 21.1 per cent of cases of heads reporting that they felt they took 'final responsibility' for decision-making in their schools. By 1994 this figure had risen to 37.5 per cent.

Mr Bishop put the dilemma very clearly. He was one of the many heads who reported an increase in the amount of cooperative planning and working in the school. However, on central direction by the head he had this to say:

That's grown as well. Yes, it's a bit like having [*long pause*] I mean a head can't just delegate and leave everyone else to do it all, there's also got to be some direction from the head in the middle. I hope I supply that within the systems that I set up. The head's got to stand for something.

His views on democratic decision making were equally illustrative of the head's dilemma:

Democratic decision-making. Yes, there's got to be a lot of that as well. Yes, you've got to give sometimes as well as insist at other times that this is what's got to happen. It's a balancing act. And I think the staff have got to see both aspects of the head. Staff respect a strong head but they also respect a head who will compromise and see their point of view.

Mr Stokes described himself as having 'a gentler approach than some heads, not a domineering approach' to his leadership style, but even he recognized the pressures on him to impose his views in the last resort. He said:

Central direction by the head? I said earlier maybe I've got to do more of this. I suppose you've got to do a little more now; I suppose it's beginning to come more and more that you've got to. I usually consult the staff first but I suppose the time is coming when in certain areas you've just got to say 'Right ... that's it'. We have staff meetings when we can discuss a subject, an area, but eventually a decision's got to be made and if it means, if the decision isn't unanimous, a decision's got to be made and that will be my decision.

Collegiality makes new demands on both heads and teachers; it is not always easy either in practical terms or in terms of the required shift in roles and relationships.

The findings of the PACE 1 project indicated a deterioration in the relationship between heads and their staff even between 1990 and 1992 (Pollard *et al.*, 1994). In 1994 we again asked the question: Have there been any changes with regard to your relations with your staff? Are they better now or not so good and in what way? Table 3.5 gives details of responses to this question.

Table 3.5   *Changes in head–staff relations (percentages)*

No answer	4.2
Greatly improving	10.4
Moderately improving	14.6
Little or no change	22.9
Neutral change	14.6
Slightly deteriorating	16.7
Considerably deteriorating	10.4
Mixed: better/worse	6.3

Source: PACE 2 headteacher interviews
Sample: 48 headteachers
Date: spring 1994
Note: This table indicates an almost equal balance between improvement to various degrees (25.0 per cent) and deterioration to various degrees (27.1 per cent). However, comparisons over time indicate a significant increase in the number of heads in the sample who reported a deterioration in their relationship with staff. In 1990 it was 12.5 per cent of the sample; in 1994 it was 27.1 per cent of the sample.

It must be stressed that not all heads in the PACE 2 sample were unhappy with their changing role, nor were they all experiencing tension and conflict in forging new working relationships with teaching staff. Mr Sanders, for example, described his leadership role in this way:

Yes, I think my leadership role is to encourage everybody to feel an important part of the team whether they be the caretaker or the cook or the secretary or an ancillary; I don't see the teachers as 'the staff'. So to encourage everybody to feel an important part, to have a contribution to make and to feel valued. To be in terms of their needs what would be described as a 'good boss': caring, willing to give them time, willing to talk and to listen. ... Staff are important and I know that by giving I'll get more back.

However, as we have seen, the majority of heads in the sample expressed varying levels of dissatisfaction with the quality of their working lives.

3.5 CONCLUSION

As the final question on the interview schedule, heads were asked to comment on whether or not they would choose to be a head if it were possible to have the opportunity to make the choice again. Teachers were also asked the same question about choosing to be a teacher. It is interesting that only 41.7 per cent of heads in the PACE 2 sample said they would still choose to be a head, whereas 60.9 per cent of Year 3/4 teachers and 77.3 per cent of Year 1/2 teachers in the sample said they would still choose to be a teacher.

These data would suggest that stress and pressures are working their way upwards through primary schools. The majority of teachers would seem to have adapted to change to such an extent that, if given the opportunity, they would still choose to be teachers. Whatever might be conjectured about the reason for these differences between teachers and heads, the data clearly indicate that many heads would prefer the teacher role to that of head. This preference for the teaching role has increased between the first and second phases of the PACE project. In 1990 16.7 per cent of the sample said they would choose to be a teacher but not a head. In 1994 this figure had risen to 22.9 per cent of the sample.

In expressing their preference for the teacher role, many heads looked back to the days when being headteacher meant just that. They were regarded as exemplars in a sphere or 'zone' (Lortie, 1969) — the classroom — for which they had been trained, in which they had been accorded a high level of autonomy and in which they felt competent. For many of the heads in the sample, being a head in 1994 meant the negation of all of these positive points.

Heads have a key part to play in the management of change in schools and yet surprisingly little is known about their working lives. In this chapter I have illustrated the dramatic transformation that has recently taken place in the role of the primary school head. Some heads have successfully managed the change in their working lives but, for many, the change is unwelcome. It has taken them away from tasks for which they were trained and in which they were competent. They have been propelled, untrained, into what is seen as a new set of tasks, roles and relationships. It is scarcely surprising, therefore, that so many heads in the study should express strong feelings of dissatisfaction.

Chapter 4

Teachers Mediating Change: Key Stage 1 Revisited

Marilyn Osborn

4.1 INTRODUCTION

The implementation of the National Curriculum and assessment began in the infant school in 1989 and, right from the outset, placed Key Stage 1 teachers in the front line with respect to educational change. The children they taught were the first to experience the National Curriculum from the beginning of their school careers and the first to undergo standardized assessment. Moreover, it could be argued that the changes imposed were more in conflict with the values and ethos of the infant school than with than any other phase of the educational system. Infant teaching is both a highly feminized occupation and one that has frequently been characterized by a 'caring' pedagogy and supportive workplace culture (Acker, 1995). Infant teachers had previously enjoyed considerable freedom in respect of both what was taught and how it was taught, since they were constrained neither by a formal curriculum nor by the requirements of an external examination system. As a result, the 1988 Education Reform Act placed infant teachers in a position of turbulence with respect to educational change.

Changing English Primary Schools? (Pollard *et al.*, 1994) documented these teachers' early response to change. This chapter revisits the experience of infant teachers and examines both qualitatively and quantitatively their longer-term perceptions of the impact of change on their roles, responsibilities and classroom practice. In the first part of the chapter I draw upon a series of interviews with two women teachers who taught in the same school and who were roughly at the same point in their teaching careers (both had been in teaching for over twenty years and had been teaching in the same school for over ten years). Their interviews suggested that the reforms impacted on them in rather different ways which cannot be explained either by a different educational context or differences in age or gender. Some tentative explanations for their different responses are suggested.

The second part of the chapter sets the study of these two teachers in a wider context by drawing upon three rounds of interviews carried out with the PACE sample of Key Stage 1 teachers in 1990, 1992 and 1994 in order to investigate changes over time in teachers' priorities, perceptions of role, and relationships with colleagues and with children. The arguments for the de-skilling and intensification of teachers' work or, alternatively, for enhanced professionalism in teaching are explored in the light of teachers' own perceptions of their work, and their senses of losses and gains in teaching.

The chapter will suggest that, overall, teachers' feelings of loss of the things they valued in teaching, of intensification, and of deskilling all became more marked between 1990 and 1992. In the later stages of the reforms, however, for some Key Stage 1 teachers, there was a decline in strong negative feelings about the impact of the National Curriculum and assessment and an increased sense of focus and clarity about their role. For others, the sense of a loss of control and of being submerged and taken over by the changes had not significantly lessened. What differentiates the two groups? Both the case studies and the statistical data presented here will attempt to shed light on this question and I shall identify the 'coping strategies' employed by a teacher who had successfully survived change.

4.2 TYPOLOGIES OF TEACHER RESPONSE TO CHANGE

At the end of Phase 1 of the PACE study, it was suggested that the response to change of our sample of teachers could be described in terms of five strategies. These strategies, which built upon Fullan (1991) and also had earlier roots in the work of Merton (1976) could be summarized as follows:

- Compliance: acceptance of the imposed changes and adjustment of teachers' professional ideology accordingly, so that greater central control is perceived as acceptable, or even desirable.
- Incorporation: appearing to accept the imposed changes but incorporating them into existing modes of working, so that existing methods are adapted rather than changed and the effect of change is considerably different from that intended.
- Creative mediation: taking active control of the changes and responding to them in a creative, but possibly selective, way.
- Retreatism: submission to the imposed changes without any change in professional ideology, leading to deep-seated feelings of resentment, demoralization and alienation.
- Resistance: resistance to the imposed changes in the hope that the sanctions available to enforce them will not be sufficiently powerful to make this impossible.

Most teachers at that stage adopted the strategy of 'incorporation'. There were relatively few 'resisters', but some teachers were 'compliant' (particularly those relatively new to teaching) and there were a considerable number of 'retreatists', many of whom were looking towards early retirement as a way out. However, a small proportion of teachers (about one fifth) were identified as having some of the characteristics of creative mediators, taking ownership and control of the innovations and working to develop new forms of practice in pedagogy and assessment while building on what they felt to be good about their existing practice.

Differences in teacher response appeared to be partly related to such factors as the teacher's age and years of experience, the existence of a collaborative and supportive school culture, and the social location of the school in which they worked. However, as the following short case studies of two teachers of similar age and experience working in the same school demonstrate, the pattern of adoption of one or another of these strategies can be considerably more complex than the statistics suggest.

4.3 CREATIVE MEDIATION AND RETREATISM: THE CASE OF SARA WILSON AND ELIZABETH WEST

Sara Wilson and Elizabeth West were highly experienced teachers who had both been working in the same infant school in the outskirts of a large southern city for well over ten years. Sara had been a teacher for 22 years and Elizabeth for 26 years. When I first interviewed them both in 1990, Sara taught a mixed class of Year 1 and Year 2 children and Elizabeth taught a Year 1 class. On the two occasions when I returned to their school to interview them again in 1992 and 1994 Sara was responsible for a Year 2 class and had become Deputy Head, while Elizabeth taught a mixed Year 1 and 2 class and had a point of responsibility (formerly A allowance) for special needs. Strikingly, in spite of many similarities in terms of their experience in teaching, their commitment to the children, and the same school context, the changes impacted quite differently upon them during the course of the four years.

In 1990, like many of the infant teachers I interviewed, both were feeling overloaded, stressed and anxious about the effect of the National Curriculum on the children in their class. They had considerable fears about how primary education would develop in the future and about the effect of national assessment on the quality of teaching and learning in their school.

Sara felt that the National Curriculum was quite adequate to meet the intellectual aspects of children's needs but that it didn't address children's social, emotional and physical development which, she argued, were of equal importance at this stage and which were tending to become overlooked. She saw overwhelming constraints operating on her compared with the past. As she put it:

> There is a huge body of knowledge to get through. Everything is so prescribed and detailed and specifically listed. It can lead to a tremendously pressurized feeling. You simply can't take your pace from the children any more or work at their pace.

Whereas her approach to teaching had always been to motivate the children by focusing on the things they can do, leaving the things they found difficult until later, she now felt that the demands of the National Curriculum made this difficult.

> [the National Curriculum] forces me to focus on the 'can't do's' although I'm still trying to concentrate on things they are good at. It's very difficult, because of the speed of change, to keep hold of good infant practice.

Nevertheless, she welcomed the general idea of a framework of guidance such as that intended by the National Curriculum, but she would have liked it to be more general and open in structure with a list of suggested approaches rather than a rigid set of prescriptions. In comparison with the past, her planning and organization had become very focused on covering specific areas of knowledge, and making sure that all attainment targets were covered.

The second teacher, Elizabeth, felt similarly that the needs of the slower children in her class were not being met by the National Curriculum, and that there had been a loss of spontaneity and fun in her teaching.

> There is so much to cover. I feel that we are trying to take it all on much too quickly. My teaching has narrowed down this year. Lots of fun things have gone. Things we've missed out on. I have tried not to come under pressure, but there's a feeling that I must get through this, I must see that every child has touched on this. It's not a good thing and it's the slower ones I most worry about. There's a feeling that there's no time to play. For example, when we did magnets, we wanted a lot of time to play with those, but we didn't get it.

She too felt that she had lost freedom of choice over how to teach as well as over the curriculum. She had had to change and become more formal in order to fit in covering every attainment target with every child, whereas in the past she could gear the topic to different groups of children. As she said:

> I know what [teaching methods] suit me, but I can't always do it now ... I find the organization difficult. I'm a bit of a perfectionist. Unless I can do it the way I want to I would rather not do it.

Both teachers felt over-burdened by the demands of record-keeping, checklists and paperwork, and both felt pressures on them to change their role in ways they were not happy about. As Elizabeth put it:

> In subtle ways, yes [my role as a teacher] has changed, though I don't want it to. I have lost some individualism. Children benefit from our individualism as teachers. I feel a pressure to become stereotyped, although it's a subtle one.

She identified her strengths as a teacher in caring and good relationships with children. She had enjoyed working with children, giving them an enjoyable school experience and 'a happy secure environment' and she felt that these strengths were being pushed aside by the National Curriculum, forcing her to tell children you must get through this.

When they were asked whether, if they had the chance to choose again they would still choose to be a teacher, there were noticeable differences in their responses. Elizabeth had serious doubts because of the effects of the ERA in general and felt that she would certainly be unlikely to recommend teaching as a career to others, although for herself her career was coming to an end and she wanted to move into other things. Sara, on the other hand, felt that she would still choose teaching because, at the moment, she 'could still continue to do things I think important and in a school where they are perceived to be important'.

It is notable that even in 1990, Sara was expressing a feeling that she could resist undesirable aspects of the changes or at least adapt them to fit in with what she felt to be 'good infant practice', and that she would get support from this from within the school. Elizabeth, on the other hand, almost appeared to be in the early stages of grief and loss at what she held to be most important in teaching. Nias (1989) has argued that it is not too strong to see this sense of loss amongst primary teachers in terms of bereavement. At the same time she felt compelled to implement the changes in what she herself termed a 'perfectionist' way, i.e. within the letter of the law, or at least exactly as laid down in the documents.

This difference between the two became distinctly more noticeable when I returned to interview them in 1992. Sara still felt that she had been able to hold on to her approach to teaching and was making determined efforts to integrate National Curriculum requirements rather than letting them take her over.

> I would say [my teaching approach] has become stronger and my determination to sort of hold on to it, I'd say, has become stronger. I've found there have been times when new documentation has been coming so quickly I've felt swamped and I've found myself into the dreadful, awful worksheet-to-meet-attainment-target thing and I've had to sort of fight it and in a way that's made me more determined to hold on to it. But I still haven't managed to integrate all the requirements into my practice. I am beginning to doubt if it's possible quite honestly, but ...

Sara still had a strong sense that children's classroom play opportunities were being restricted in favour of much more structured situations which had an end-product in mind. For example, she talked of the times that children's social and role play in the Home Corner had given her insights into their home situations and their development, and of the exciting ideas that had arisen from children's work in technology in the past. All these, she felt, were now having to give way to:

> artificial situations in which I want to have a product because I want to be able to say, 'Right, they've done that, tick,' and I feel that it's restricting their play very much. And I think that close activities is where they develop personally so much, whereas if all the activities in school are planned and you have got outcomes in mind, then you're losing a lot, the children are not developing the skills that they once did.

On the other hand, she also saw benefits in the fact that her planning had become much more rigorous and structured. She acknowledged that whereas before 'not all children in years gone by had all the experiences, now I have to make sure that all do it. I am accountable for that and that's a plus for the National Curriculum.'

In adapting to change she felt that she had derived a lot of support from being in a school with a strong, stable staff, and from her own temperament which she defined as calm and practical, enabling her to 'get hold of the changes and do them in the least damaging way, keeping hold of children's happiness and enthusiasm'.

However, perhaps the key point in Sara's response to the changes, and the one which most differentiated her from Elizabeth, was the emphasis she placed on the importance of taking control of the changes, and finding ways of making them part of her thinking rather than simply seeing them as external targets which had to be met. This is how she put it:

> I think that what I hope to do is to internalize myself as a teacher, internalize all this detail and to then be able to use it in good infant practice. Does that make sense? It's a funny sentence but I know what I mean because I know at the moment: the English, fine; the maths, mostly fine now; but the other subjects I'm still trying to get a hold of them into me, so that the approaches, so that the approaches, you know the historical questioning and reasoning, (I hope they are going to rewrite geography so I won't mention that); the science, the approach to science, I mean yes, a lot of it is rooted in good infant practice but

it's in a language and in a form which is hard for me, and I want to get it into me so that it's happening rather than me thinking, 'Oh, well I haven't done much on Attainment Target I, 2b,' rather than me thinking that, that it will be part of my practice.

Her striving after this internalization, taking control, and integration of new demands into what she defined as good infant practice are hallmarks of teachers whom we can identify as 'creative mediators', those who feel able to take active control of educational changes and to respond to them in a creative, but possibly selective way.

In contrast, in 1992, Elizabeth was feeling more and more submerged by the demands of the National Curriculum, although still trying to hold fast to her original priorities for the children. She explained this as:

To see that they're happy in school — to build a relationship with them and to see them building a relationship with each other.

She was finding it harder not to let these goals be taken over and admitted that:

Yes, they've taken a back seat. They are still there but other things have overridden them. I think it's showing. I do believe unless the children are happy and settled and relating well then the learning doesn't come so easily. It's a bit of a slog at the moment to be honest.

It was quite clear that she was unhappy about the way in which she had to change her teaching approach in order to 'fit everything in and trying to get every child to do everything. 'You've got 35 and you are now trying to get every child to do everything.' In consequence, she felt forced to do far more in whole class teaching situations than she would ideally have liked. Whereas, in the past, she had spent a lot of time doing practical work with the children working co-operatively in groups, and herself working with them, she now felt forced to spend more time recording and 'writing things down' rather than being with children and building on what they were doing.

She felt that the maths and science part of the National Curriculum were well suited to children's needs provided that they could be taken at the children's pace without the pressure to complete the work, which was 'subtly there all the time'. The same would probably be true of the PE, art, and music when they came on stream, but she was unhappy about the geography, history and technology requirements for such young children.

It was unsettling to see a clearly dedicated and committed teacher beginning to doubt her own abilities in a new situation. Clearly however, Elizabeth had serious doubts about the effectiveness of her own current teaching approach in raising the quality of children's learning, arguing that:

If you can take it at the children's pace and build around it (it's OK) but I think that's what I'm not doing. I'm trying to cover the curriculum rather than building around it and giving the children more experience ... There's just so much more pressure. Sometimes I wonder whether that's me, thinking it's got to be done, but I don't think it is because it has got to be done.

She felt de-skilled as a teacher, arguing that her particular strengths had always been building good relationships with children and doing things with them. However, these had been eroded in an adverse way by the changes, so that:

Whereas I used to find teaching much more enjoyable, and I know I was an effective teacher in the past, I'm not really sure I'm more effective now.

She was clearly operating under enormous constraints in terms of class size, and her responsibility for special needs children throughout the school made her particularly aware that such children were 'missing out' because the National Curriculum and the pace of work it demanded was ill-suited to their needs. Like Sara, she felt less free as a teacher than in the past:

> It's that subtle pressure of having to get through a certain amount of work. Somehow, if you don't do it there's that pressure telling you you've missed it.

As in 1990, both teachers were asked whether, if they had a chance to choose again they would still choose to be teachers. Elizabeth was far from sure that she would still enter teaching or that she would be prepared to recommend it to others, but Sara said that she still felt very enthusiastic about teaching and couldn't imagine doing anything else. For both teachers, one of the least rewarding aspects of being a primary teacher at this time was having to 'operate in a negative climate' in which both the media and the government seemed to be deliberately downgrading and 'rubbishing' teachers and setting out to make the public see schools in a detrimental light.

It is clear that by 1992, when the pressure of imposed change was at its height, these two teachers from comparable backgrounds and situations were beginning to respond quite differently to the changes. What was the situation two years later, in 1994, when for the first time for five years a more settled period for English primary education at last appeared to be in sight?

When I returned to interview Sara in 1994 it was evident that she felt that she had emerged from the difficulties of the last four years with a new sense of clarity and focus about her role and her practice. In terms of the teacher strategies discussed above she could certainly be seen as a 'creative mediator' who had taken active control of the changes and had responded to them in an imaginative, albeit selective, way. She was feeling positive about the way in which she was using the National Curriculum and assessment practices. She recognized that her approach to teaching had changed considerably and that it had become 'slightly more formal than it was before'. Although she couldn't be sure whether the results for the children were any better, she felt:

> I'm more focused when I plan an activity and because of the National Curriculum — this is a positive thing — I definitely do specify now what I'm intending the children to learn, whereas I think before I planned an activity and was open to see what the children learned. Now of course you still do have exciting situations where children do learn all sorts of things that you didn't expect them to and they show all sorts of knowledge, skills, etc. that you didn't know they had, which is good, and honestly I'm still looking for this. But I think that I'm far more able now to explain to somebody else in more concrete terms what I'm doing, which I think is a good thing.

So far as her own role as a teacher was concerned and in terms of the amount of freedom she felt she had in the classrooms, things had improved considerably. She felt particularly confident that she had acquired improved skills in assessment. In particular, she described how her practice had evolved to a point where she felt in control again:

> I definitely feel when the National Curriculum was first implemented and all the orders came through — we took them all on board — I felt very restricted. I felt under so much pressure. I felt it was an impossible task. I couldn't do it. I found myself doing lessons with the whole class that were completely unsuitable. I knew they were. I thought, 'Gosh, well I'd better do World War Two today,' you know. Ridiculous! Now — this is an evolved thing — now I feel that I've got to the end of finding out all the things that are in

the National Curriculum and the fact that the Dearing Report's come out and told me that it's going to be reduced, I feel far more in control now, and I feel, 'Yes, I can do this again.' It is possible, and I'll be able to gradually get back to focusing on maths and English and the other things being a very important enrichment. I hope — and I could be wrong when all these changes come about — but that's how I feel in me.

As a result, after a period when the rewards from teaching seemed to have declined, she was now feeling much more fulfilment:

Yes, I would say that [fulfilment] really follows the first one, to a degree, in that I love teaching. I really do. I still do but as the National Curriculum came on strength, I really ... the pressure was so great, it was spoiling my enjoyment of teaching and I felt that I wasn't such a good teacher. I felt that I was teaching lessons that were totally unsuitable. Now, that was my fault because the National Curriculum doesn't really force you to do that. It was just that the pressures were so great. The pressures were so great it was just — awful. But I feel now, as I said, that sort of ... I feel much more hopeful, much more positive.

Other things connected with her role as deputy, as distinct from her role as a classroom teacher, were now worrying her, particularly 'management issues, OFSTED, relationships with Governors and staff, the power balance'. But so far as her satisfaction in teaching compared with before the National Curriculum was concerned, she derived nearly as much as before, 'nearly! I've got great hopes, you know! Not quite, but nearly'.

Sara's emergence as a confident, post-ERA professional, who had successfully integrated the new requirements into her own identity as a teacher, contrasted with the unhappiness still felt by Elizabeth. Like her colleague, Elizabeth felt a greater 'awareness of what I'm teaching' although she did not use the word focus. But she did not feel that she had been able to preserve the exciting times referred to by Sara:

I've tightened up but also narrowed down. We are really missing the fun of the extra bits. As someone said in one of our staff meetings, 'It's like walking through a wood and keeping to a pathway, not seeing the interesting things on either side.'

She still derived far less satisfaction from teaching than she had felt before the changes, and she saw her role as a teacher as having changed for the worse.

For me the National Curriculum has narrowed my outlook as much as I have tried for it not to. There is still so much to get through and I still feel in a straitjacket. I do smashing work with the children and then I find it doesn't cover the Attainment Targets, so I realize that I still have all that to do ... It takes a lot of enjoyment from me. For me, teaching has always been a creative outlet. Now I'm constrained, I've lost a lot of creativity.

Even regarding her relationship with colleagues, an area where, as we have seen, many teachers felt positively about increased collegiality, she saw losses outweighing gains, 'The time constraint on us means less freedom to chat at lunchtimes. We have far less informal discussion now.' Her concern that the increase in formal, structured collaboration had resulted in a reduction of the more relaxed, informal occasions when teachers shared ideas, anecdotes about children, and humour is echoed in other research (Osborn and Black, 1994; Hargreaves, 1994).

Elizabeth's view of the effect of the changes on the children's learning was mixed:

Looking back, a lot of good has come out, but also a lot has gone. It's better that there is a wider curriculum and that teachers know more where they are going. Their aims are clearer and children move forward all the time. But it's worse in the sense that children's individuality is lost. They can't develop in the same way as individuals and lots of fun is gone.

However, when asked if she would still be a teacher if she had the chance to choose again, her answer was more positive than on previous occasions. 'Yes, I still feel the relationship with children makes it a worthwhile job. Having an influence in children's lives is still an important job, but I am near the end of my career now.'

In terms of the typology of teaching strategies, Elizabeth's response to change was closest to that of a 'retreatist' who had submitted to the imposed changes without any change in professional ideology, leading to feelings of demoralization and alienation.

4.4 DISCUSSION

These two teachers had emerged from a period of stress and turbulence for primary teachers with different views of their roles and their practices. For Sara the gains and rewards clearly outweighed the losses. For Elizabeth, on the whole there was still a continuing sense of loss. Her own identity as a teacher, her confidence, and her ability to be creative were still perceived by her to be under threat.

Since both teachers were at similar phases in their careers and had worked at the same school for a long period, an explanation for the difference in their responses must be sought elsewhere, in their personal biographies and their beliefs about teaching.

In a sample of middle- and high-school teachers studied by Huberman (1993), a key factor in professional satisfaction in the latter stages of these teachers' careers was a feeling of 'upward mobility and social promotion'. This characterized the career trajectories of many teachers who had remained the most energetic and committed. Another factor was the continuation of an enjoyable and good relationship with pupils. As we have seen, Sara had been able to move on to an additional role as a Deputy Head, which arguably gives her a broader view of the reforms, new challenges, and new motivations. Rather than feeling de-skilled, she had been able to make the new demands build on her strengths.

In contrast, Elizabeth's key 'satisfier' (Nias 1989) was her relationship with the children, which she perceived to be increasingly under threat. Her responsibility for, and concerns with, special needs children was particularly significant here and may be another factor influencing her response. Of the Key Stage 1 teachers in the 1994 PACE sample, 44 per cent saw the National Curriculum as particularly disadvantaging children with special needs. It was clear from Elizabeth's responses that she shared this view. Elizabeth's concern with caring and relationships and her particular strengths in this area made her vulnerable to a sense of loss as did her strong focus on the classroom teaching of young children. Her investment in her past role was such that, for her, losses far outweighed gains.

In primary teaching, there is a close link between the teacher's 'self' or sense of identity as part of the professional role and the 'self' as a person (Pollard, 1985; Nias, 1989; Cortazzi, 1991). In Elizabeth's case it appears that the changes threatened not only her professional identity, but also her sense of 'self' as a person, since for her it was the emotional response of the 'personal self' reinforced by her relationships which made teaching worthwhile.

Another key difference between the two women seemed to be in their ability to take control and make choices about how to implement the changes. Elizabeth was, by her own description, a perfectionist. She felt that she must conscientiously cover every attainment target with every child no matter what the cost. Sara, on the other hand, saw herself as able to say 'no' to new demands. She was able to avoid the over-conscientiousness which has been a characteristic of many committed primary teachers (Campbell, 1991). By 1992 she was talking about getting the best out of the National Curriculum rather than letting it drive her, and above all about internalizing its aims and integrating them into what she regarded as good infant practice.

In contrast, Elizabeth saw herself as having to give up good infant practice in order to implement the National Curriculum. She had not found a way of rationing the demands or of being selective in what she chose to carry out. She still felt that she must cover everything and was striving after perfectionist standards. Sara was mediating the demands to her own professional ends, while Elizabeth felt submerged and taken over.

Both these teachers had been working under many constraints, not the least of which were large classes. At the same time the school in which they worked provided a supportive environment in which teachers were encouraged to make their own decisions about how they selectively implemented change. The strategies which they evolved to cope with the constraints imposed by multiple change were influenced by their personal biographies and career trajectories, as well as their beliefs about teaching, and the level of satisfaction they continued to derive from their work. Both were highly committed and dedicated teachers, but one, by integrating and internalizing change into her own practice and by having the confidence to refuse to do what she considered untenable, had survived the changes and acquired a new sense of clarity and purpose. The other represented many teachers who appear to have lost confidence over the period in their ability to be creative professionals and who very much needed a sense of autonomy and purpose to be restored to them. The late 1990s will tell whether the 1995 changes to the National Curriculum and assessment have achieved this.

4.5 RESPONSES TO CHANGE OF THE WIDER PACE SAMPLE

The following section examines the responses of all the teachers in the PACE Key Stage 1 samples and suggests some more general patterns which set the responses to change of Sara and Elizabeth in a wider context. It is apparent from the data presented here that, like Sara, some teachers felt that a sense of loss in some areas was offset by a sense of gain in others. As we shall see, some Key Stage 1 teachers seemed to feel that they had been able to mediate the changes to professional ends and emerge with a creative response to changes. First, however, the evidence for a change in teachers' priorities and teaching approach is examined.

Teachers' priorities

Table 4.1 shows data gathered from interviews carried out with Key Stage 1 teachers in 1990, 1992 and 1994 as the impact of the National Curriculum and the multiple changes which followed it gathered momentum. In all three years, teachers were asked, 'What are your priorities in working with the children in your class?' The analysis of their responses indicates a clear shift over time, with a significant increase in the importance accorded to increasing basic skills (from 48 per cent in 1990 to 58 per cent in 1994) and an increase followed by a decrease in the importance of providing a broad, balanced curriculum (from 16 per cent in 1990 up to 44 per cent in 1992 and then back to 18 per cent in 1994). This striking shift seems to reflect the coming on stream of the curriculum orders in history, geography, art, music and technology in the middle years of the reforms, during which teachers were struggling to achieve wider curriculum coverage. The notable decline in emphasis since then may possibly be attributed to the Dearing Review with its promise of a cut in the number of attainment targets to be met in the core subjects and the dropping of standardized assessment in all subjects except English and maths at the end of this Key Stage. This may also be the explanation for the decline in the apparent importance in priority given to achieving National Curriculum attainment targets (from a significant rise between 1990 and 1992 from 3 per cent to 13 per cent and then a decline to 1 per cent in 1994).

Table 4.1 *Teachers' academic and non-academic priorities (percentages)*

	1990	1992	1994
Academic priorities			
Emphasizing basic skills	47.5	46.7	58.0
Developing individual potential	42.5	45.6	45.5
Matching work to children	32.5	22.2 *	26.1
Listening and communication skills	20.0	5.6 **	10.2
Broad, balanced curriculum	16.3	44.4 ***	18.2
Affective, creative curriculum	6.3	8.9	4.5
Achieving NC attainment targets	2.5	13.3 ***	1.1
Other	12.5	0.0	8.0
Not mentioned	9.1	3.2	3.4
Non-academic priorities			
Happiness, enjoyment in learning	65.3	53.8	54.4
Social skills, cooperative attitudes	41.7	32.3	25.0
Independence, autonomy	40.3	49.2	0.0
Moral, religious education	6.9	3.1	3.4
Other	5.6	4.6	8.0
Not mentioned	18.2	30.1	28.4

* Difference statistically significant p < 0.05
**Difference statistically significant p < 0.02
***Difference statistically significant p < 0.002
Source: PACE 1 and 2 teacher interviews
Sample: 88 Key Stage 1 teachers in 8 LEAs
Date: Summer 1990, summer 1992 and summer 1994
Note: Figures do not equal 100 per cent because of multiple coding of open-ended responses.

Over time, teachers also seemed to be attaching less importance to matching work to children (from 33 per cent in 1990 to down to 22 per cent in 1992 and 26 per cent in 1994) and to listening and communication skills (from 20 per cent in 1990 down to 6 per cent in 1992 and 10 per cent in 1994). It is important to make the point with all the figures cited here that they do not necessarily indicate that teachers actually wished to give less priority to a particular objective.

In coding teachers' replies we sorted the responses into 'academic' and 'non-academic' priorities, i.e. priorities concerned with the personal, social, moral, and general development of children. Whereas 82 per cent of teachers mentioned at least one non-academic priority in 1990, it was striking that this proportion declined to around 70 per cent in 1992 and 1994. In contrast, almost all teachers mentioned an academic priority in those two latter years. More specifically, fewer teachers in the later years gave a high priority to children's happiness in school and enjoyment in learning, although more than half still mentioned this as important. Similarly, there was a consistent decline in the importance accorded to social skills and to developing cooperative attitudes amongst children (from 42 per cent in 1990 to 32 per cent in 1992 and 25 per cent in 1994).

It is notable that teachers perceived their priorities to have stabilized to some extent in 1993 and 1994. In 1994 only 27 per cent said that they had been forced to change their priorities recently compared with over 50 per cent in 1992.

There appears to be quite clear evidence here that Key Stage 1 teachers had felt compelled to narrow their priorities to concentrate on basic skills at the expense of broader academic and non-academic objectives. In earlier reports on the PACE work (Pollard *et al.*, 1994; Osborn *et al.*, 1992) we documented the stress, work overload, and concerns about curriculum overload to which Key Stage 1 teachers were subject in the early phases of the implementation of the National Curriculum and assessment, and these concerns were echoed in other research, notably Campbell and Neill (1994). It seems likely that this apparent narrowing of priorities was a response to the extreme constraints imposed upon teachers by such overload. Teachers who had survived through a period of turbulence and multiple change may have been forced to be selective about their objectives in order to protect both themselves and the children. With an increasing range of educational objectives and obligations being imposed upon them (Pollard *et al.*, 1994), they appeared to have adopted as a 'coping strategy' (Pollard, 1985; Woods, 1977) the limitation of their goals to what was realistically achievable. By doing this they may have been able to preserve other aspects of their pedagogy which they valued, for example, protecting a positive relationship with children.

Related to this change in priorities, over half of the teachers in 1994 identified changes in their teaching approach and 98 per cent of these attributed the change to either the National Curriculum, or assessment requirements, or both. Overall, more teachers were using whole-class teaching as their predominant approach (20 per cent in 1994 compared to 10 per cent in 1992 and 13 per cent in 1990). Roughly the same proportion were using mainly individual work (25 per cent in 1994 compared with 48 per cent in 1992 and 21 per cent in 1990), but fewer were using cooperative groupwork as their predominant approach (11 per cent in 1994 compared with 52 per cent in 1990 and 23 per cent in 1992).

Changes in the teacher role

How far do English primary teachers appear to have moved from an extended to a more restricted conception of their role, or alternatively to have moved towards to a new mode of collaborative professionalism? As suggested in the previous section, the PACE data present a mixed picture.

What does emerge very clearly is that by 1994 close to half of all the Key Stage 1 teachers in our sample felt that their role had changed considerably. When asked for details of the ways in which their role had changed, 69 per cent identified more constraints operating upon them compared with only 6 per cent who identified more freedom. This represented a considerable increase over the past (5 per cent in 1992 identifying more constraints and 11 per cent in 1990).

However, fewer teachers in 1994 felt frustrated by unnecessary administration and paperwork (30 per cent compared with 64 per cent in 1992) and the proportion identifying large increases in time spent planning also declined (from 45 per cent in 1992 to 13 per cent in 1994) suggesting that teachers were now becoming somewhat adjusted to the new demands and that early gargantuan efforts to plan and to manage the paperwork had paid off and eventually resulted in a period of consolidation.

In 1994, a lower proportion of teachers than two years previously mentioned an increase in stress and anxiety in their work (25 per cent compared with 34 per cent in 1992 and 23 per cent in 1990). While 23 per cent said that they now felt less of a sense of enjoyment and fulfilment in their teaching, this was a declining proportion compared with the 35 per cent who felt this way in 1992. Moreover, it was noticeable that 17 per cent actually felt more enjoyment.

This suggests that in spite of considerable loss of autonomy, some teachers, perhaps those who have made a conscious decision not to allow themselves to be swamped by change, have found ways of developing their teaching and their professionalism within the National Curriculum. Indeed, it is arguable that by limiting their goals to what is realistically achievable in the circumstances and having a more clearly delineated role, these teachers may eventually achieve greater job satisfaction than those who, as a result of their wide-ranging objectives and their expanded conception of their role, may have set themselves goals which are impossible to achieve, leading to feelings of being overstretched, and of conflict and confusion about their role. Hoyle (1980) has suggested that an extension of teachers' roles may lead to loss of job satisfaction, and there is some evidence of this occurring amongst primary teachers in England prior to the 1988 Education Reform Act (Broadfoot and Osborn, 1988).

It is striking that over the four years of the PACE study, there was a steady increase in the proportion of teachers identifying closer cooperation and collaboration with colleagues as an important dimension of their changing role (from 34 per cent in 1992 to 44 per cent in 1992 and 52 per cent in 1994). Clearly this was a limited form of collegiality, since it mainly took the form of joint planning rather than joint work at the level of classroom practice (Little, 1990; Hargreaves, 1994). However, many teachers spoke very positively about this change in their role. Elsewhere, we have documented concerns about loss of a more informal relationship between teachers in favour of a more 'contrived' collegiality (Osborn and Black, 1994 and forthcoming; Osborn et al., 1992). However, only 2 per cent of teachers mentioned that they had experienced a loss of more informal relationships with colleagues. For most teachers it appears that collaboration with colleagues was becoming a significant focus of their work and a major support in coping with the consequences of change. In 1990 we noted the first signs of this important shift in teacher relationships but suspected that it could have been a response to a crisis almost 'wartime' situation for teachers in the face of multiple change rather than an enduring feature of the changes. The evidence of this trend over time suggests that, on the contrary, primary teachers have made a definite move towards a more collaborative professionalism.

In *Changing English Primary Schools?*, which dealt with the early phases of the implementation of the National Curriculum at Key Stage 1, we suggested that many teachers were pessimistic about the future of primary education and felt that current work and stress levels were unsustainable. They regretted keenly the loss of spontaneity in their work with the children and the difficulty of finding time to develop interests and topics introduced by the children. However, our most recent interviews with teachers in 1994 suggest that feelings of pressure, stress, and a threat to the quality of teacher–pupil relationships reached their height in 1992 and then declined. As Table 4.2 indicates, nearly 30 per cent of teachers still felt in 1994 that there had been some deterioration in teacher–pupil relations due to time pressures and stress on teachers, but this compares with far higher proportions in 1992 (58 per cent). In 1994, 41 per cent of teachers felt no change in teacher–pupil relationships, compared with 36 per cent in 1992 and 46 per cent in 1990. Fewer teachers in 1994 identified pressure on teacher time (27 per cent compared with 60 per cent in 1992) and teacher stress (22 per cent compared with 45 per cent in 1992) as a contributor to deteriorating relationships. This may be attributed to the change in climate brought about by the publication of the Dearing Report.

Table 4.2   *Effect of the National Curriculum and assessment on teacher–pupil relationships (percentages)*

	1990	1992	1994
Positive	9.1	6.5	17.0
Negative	30.7	58.1	29.5
Little or no change	45.5	35.5	40.9
Don't know	14.8	0.0	12.5
Comments on teacher–pupil relationships (percentages)			
	1990	1992	1994
Defended because so important	22.8	32.3	11.4
Not threatened	9.1	6.5	8.0
Pressure on teacher time	39.7	60.2	27.3
Feelings of stress	33.0	45.2	22.7
Affected by assessment	2.2	8.7	1.1
Other	6.8	1.1	20.5

Source: PACE 1 and 2 teacher interviews
Sample: 88 Key Stage 1 teachers in 8 LEAs
Date: Summer 1990, summer 1992 and summer 1994
Note: Figures do not equal 100 per cent because of multiple coding of open-ended responses

As the 'deluge' of changes began to subside into what might become a period of greater stability and consolidation it was clear that in some areas there had been considerable continuity. When asked what they considered to be the most important qualities of an outstanding teacher, most teachers still talked about personality, personal qualities and being good at affective relationships. The importance accorded to cognitive and management related skills declined from 1992, although an emphasis on 'professionalism' increased. Teachers were still seen as needing qualities of energy, enthusiasm and adaptability, and a sense of humour above all.

As Table 4.3 indicates, a majority of teachers in 1994 saw assessment skills, having clear aims, and subject knowledge as being considerably more important for a teacher currently than before the introduction of the National Curriculum. For most the relationship they had with children, knowledge of children, teaching skills, and maintaining order and good classroom organization had remained as important as they were before the National Curriculum. It is clear from this table that most of the stated 'qualities' of a primary teacher had either increased in importance or remained of similar importance for the teachers in our sample. Their perception was that to be a successful teacher in the 1990s required a stronger and wider range of skills and qualities than it had done prior to the 1988 Education Reform Act.

4.6 THE DE-SKILLING ARGUMENT

The policies introduced as a result of the 1988 Education Reform Act are seen by some researchers as leading to the de-skilling and intensification of teachers' work. Alternatively, they are presented by others as leading to the enhancement of the professionalism of primary teachers (D. Hargreaves, 1988). The enhancement argument

Table 4.3 *Qualities of a primary teacher: changes in importance (percentages)*

	More importance	Same importance	Less importance	Qualified post ERA/ No reply
Assessment skills	78.4	6.8	0.0	14.8
Clear aims	60.2	23.9	1.1	14.8
Subject knowledge	56.8	26.1	1.1	15.9
Classroom organization	43.2	42.0	0.0	14.8
Teaching skills	26.1	58.0	1.1	14.8
Knowledge of children	19.3	61.4	4.5	14.8
Maintaining order	15.9	68.2	1.1	14.8
Relationship with children	6.8	72.7	5.7	14.8

Source: PACE 2 teacher interviews
Sample: 88 Key Stage 1 teachers in 8 LEAs
Date: Summer 1994

sees professionalization resulting from the extension of teachers' roles through involvement in whole-school planning and curriculum development, new responsibilities as curriculum coordinators, an increase in collaboration with colleagues, and engagement in more rigorous assessment processes. In this view, teachers are seen as acquiring more complex skills and moving towards an extended or collaborative professionalism (Hoyle, 1992). It is also argued by proponents of this view that having an externally set curriculum may release teachers to be more creative in the way in which they present children with learning tasks. There is no doubt that examples abound both within the PACE research and elsewhere (for example Woods, 1995) of teachers working creatively within the National Curriculum.

However, the competing argument for the de-skilling and de-professionalization of teachers' work is a powerful one. In this account, teachers' work is seen as 'becoming more routinised and deskilled; more like the degraded work of manual workers and less like that of autonomous professionals ... Teachers are depicted as being increasingly controlled by prescribed programmes, mandated curricula, and step-by-step methods of instruction' (A. Hargreaves, 1994). Advocates of this view argue that professionalization is simply a strategy to get teachers to collaborate in their own exploitation as they take on more and more responsibilities while having very little real autonomy (Lawn, 1988; Galton, 1995).

In the volume reporting the first phase of the PACE study (Pollard *et al.*, 1994) we argued that although teachers' work had intensified considerably as a result of the National Curriculum and associated changes, and although there were perceptions of de-skilling amongst approximately half of all teachers in 1992, there remained a proportion of teachers (about one fifth) who saw the National Curriculum as complementing and enhancing their skills or providing them with the opportunity to develop them further. They saw themselves as able to appropriate the National Curriculum to support their own values and practice. What had happened to this sample of teachers by 1994 and how far had the last two years increased or decreased these concerns?

As Table 4.4 indicates, between 1990 and 1992, there was a considerable increase in the proportion of teachers who felt that their skills were being eroded by the National Curriculum, i.e. who perceived themselves as being 'de-skilled'. For example, 50 per cent of teachers in 1992 felt that their skills were being eroded compared with only 18 per cent who saw their skills being enhanced or complemented by the National Curriculum. However, in the intervening two years perceptions changed considerably. In 1994 30 per cent saw their skills being complemented and affirmed compared with 21 per cent who perceived erosion; 42 per cent saw no change. Perceptions of 'de-skilling' had become less and there was a definite sense in the 1994 teacher interviews that many of those teachers who had remained saw themselves as having acquired new professional skills and having developed creative ways of working and assessing within the National Curriculum. There was an increasing sense that it was possible to maintain their own beliefs and good practice and even to enrich their work within a prescribed curriculum.

Table 4.4   *Teachers' perceptions of the influence of the National Curriculum on their strengths (percentages)*

Perceived influences on strengths	1990	1992	1994
Complemented by NC	21.6	18.3	29.6
Eroded by NC	21.6	49.5***	20.9
No influence from NC	42.0	25.8	41.9
Possibly an influence in future/			
mixed improved and eroded	11.4	5.4	7.4
Other	3.4	1.0	0.0

*** Difference statistically significant $p < 0.001$
Source: PACE 1 and 2 teacher interviews
Sample: 88 Key Stage 1 teachers in 8 LEAs
Date: Summer 1990, summer 1992 and summer 1994
Note: Figures do not equal 100 per cent because of multiple coding of open-ended responses

One teacher of a mixed Year 1 and Year 2 class in the north of England described the way she and her colleagues combined National Curriculum requirements with what they believed to be a creative approach:

> We've worked very hard at taking the National Curriculum and looking at our beliefs and philosophy and what we believe is good early years practice and marrying the two. So we've worked very hard at not being swamped and panicking and rushing, you know. For us to step outside our beliefs would be to rush into worksheets and have the children sitting at tables all day trying to cover attainment targets, but we've tried to make it part of our philosophy to give the children firsthand experience and the chance to discover things, and everything's kept very lively. We don't feel we've lost out. As teachers, I think we some-times feel very pressurized. We're more straitjacketed, aren't we? ... But the National Curriculum has given us great width. We still do everything in an exciting way. The geog-raphy — we would go out and come back, make them tramp the streets and come back and make 2D maps and 3D maps and miniature worlds in sand, and we haven't lost any of our good practice.

This sense of increasing optimism is affirmed elsewhere in our interviews. For example, the proportion of teachers saying that they felt pessimistic about the future of primary education had declined considerably from 55 per cent in 1992 to 18 per cent in 1994. When asked whether they would still be a teacher if they had the chance to choose again, 71 per cent said that they would, compared with 51 per cent in 1992 and only 46 per cent in 1990. Teachers were also asked whether they thought that the children now in their class would have received a better or a worse education when they left primary school than they would have received seven years ago. Surprisingly only 5 per cent said that it would be worse; 35 per cent said that it would be better, while 24 per cent thought that it would be better in some respects and worse in others. It was thought by 11 per cent that the National Curriculum would make little difference, while the rest were unsure.

From these interviews, a picture begins to emerge which is quite different from that described in research carried out two years previously. While there is clear evidence of the continuing intensification of teachers' workload, classroom teachers themselves appeared to feel that they had emerged from the deluge with a new sense of professionalism. For them, over the four years, the gains had begun to outweigh the losses and they had emerged with more positive feelings about the future.

4.7 CONCLUSION

The PACE data appears to suggest that Key Stage 1 teachers' response to change was still in a state of flux in 1994, but with some indications of a trend towards more positive feelings about the future. It has been suggested that the publication of the Dearing Report (1994) played a part in this.

However, it could be argued that there are other potential explanations for the trends observed in the PACE data. It is possible that the rather different results for 1994 are the result of two factors. First, it is known that nationally, as a result of teacher stress and dissatisfaction with the changes, there has been a considerable drop-out of qualified teachers through early retirement, moves to other types of work, and teachers simply leaving without an alternative post. Secondly, there has been a steady flow of new entrants to the profession, trained specifically for the National Curriculum, and knowing no alternative. Both these factors could influence considerably the positive responses for 1994. In 1994, 26 per cent of our sample were in their first five years of teaching and therefore would not have taught before the National Curriculum began to come on stream. However, our case study data, and an examination of the responses of more experienced teachers in our sample, suggest that the positive trend was not confined only to the newer teachers in our sample. Like Sara, there were many experienced teachers who had adopted successful coping strategies to mediate change. They appeared to have internalized the changes in a selective way, ensuring that their practice was still consistent with their beliefs and values. Consequently they had begun to regain a sense of ownership and control in their work. The example of Sara and Elizabeth suggests that, even within the same teaching context, teachers of similar experience can vary in the extent to which they feel able to adopt a mediation role. Two key factors associated with the ability to mediate appeared to be a sense of confidence and self-esteem, and a continued satisfaction with some aspects of the teaching role. However, it is not easy to separate cause from effect here.

The evidence from the PACE study indicates that Key Stage 1 teachers have demonstrated a remarkable tenacity and ability to creatively adapt to change. If anything, our findings suggest that the 'front line' of change has been pushed back from infant schools and departments to further up the school. Above all, it is clear that there is a need for policy makers to recognize the importance of teachers' beliefs in influencing the outcome of reforms as well as the extent to which teachers' sense of self is closely bound up with their professional identity. It is vital to restore to teachers like Elizabeth a sense of confidence and of being valued for the work they do, as well as some flexibility to emphasize those aspects of their role from which they derive most satisfaction.

Chapter 5

Identity, Career and Change: A Tale of Two Teachers

Marilyn Osborn

5.1   Introduction
5.2   Key Stage 2 teachers' response to change
5.3   Case study 1: Peter Matthews
5.4   Case study 2: Kate Gill
5.5   Conclusions

5.1 INTRODUCTION

The importance of teachers' values, the understanding they share about their role, and the power or control that they have over their working situation are central to an understanding of how educational policy change may be translated into classroom practice. This chapter explores some of the influences on the formation of primary teachers' values and examines how teachers mediate the external pressures upon them through the filter of these values and their professional practice.

Using a case study approach, I will examine how these teachers' response to change has developed and how they have adapted or modified their beliefs, their practice, their views of children's learning, and the ways in which they work with other adults in the school. These teachers' values in relation to teaching are a result of a complex web of interacting influences in which social class, gender and the social context in which they work play an important part (Acker, 1995; Connell, 1985). Their stories show how, faced with the common recent experience of all English primary teachers of change imposed from above, they have mediated these pressures through their own particular values in relation to teaching. This has produced a particular, personal response to change which is evident in their professional ideology and their classroom practice.

First, however, I set this more qualitative approach in context by examining some key issues in the responses to change of the larger sample of PACE teachers.

5.2 KEY STAGE 2 TEACHERS' RESPONSE TO CHANGE

The PACE 2 project studied two different cohorts of teachers: the teachers of Years 3 and 4 (which is the stage our sample of pupils had reached) and Key Stage 1 teachers (who were revisited for a second interview following their initial participation in the PACE 1 study). This section draws principally upon the interviews carried out with the 92 Year 3 and 4 teachers in early 1994 and makes comparison where appropriate with the Key Stage 1 teachers (of Years 1 and 2).

Although, in many respects, the responses of the infant and junior teachers were strikingly similar, they differed in certain key respects which suggest that the full impact of the reforms was felt later by Key Stage 2 teachers and that, in 1994, unlike their colleagues at Key Stage 1, they felt relatively less reassured by the Dearing Review, and less positive and optimistic about the future. In a sense, this is not surprising since the full pressure of preparing for national assessment only made itself felt relatively recently so far as Key Stage 2 teachers were concerned while their infant school colleagues were the 'guinea pigs' who experienced the rapid pace of change and the constant revisions which characterized the first phase of the implementation of the National Curriculum.

A comparison of the interviews with the PACE sample of Key Stage 1 and Key Stage 2 teachers in 1994 suggests that both sets of teachers felt that their roles as teachers had changed considerably (Table 5.1). However, the Key Stage 2 teachers were more likely to have experienced a reduced sense of enjoyment and fulfilment in their teaching (31 per cent compared with 23 per cent of Key Stage 1 teachers). They felt less optimistic about the future of primary education than their colleagues at Key Stage 1 and were more likely to predict that the future held more constraints for teachers, a further loss of autonomy and a narrowing of role (Table 5.2). In contrast with the revisited sample of Key Stage 1 teachers, they were more likely to see a deterioration in their relationships with pupils and to mention pressure on teacher time (42 per cent compared with 30 per cent of Key Stage 1 teachers) as a result of the introduction of a National Curriculum and assessment (Table 5.3).

Table 5.1 *Change in role as a teacher (percentages)*

Overall response	Y3/4	Y1/2
Considerable change	50.0	45.5
Moderate change	16.3	26.1
Little or no change	12.0	9.1
NA: qualified post-ERA	18.5	11.4

Source: PACE 2 teacher interviews
Sample: 88 Key Stage 1 teachers and 92 Key Stage 2 teachers in 8 LEAs
Date: Spring 1994

When the Key Stage 2 teachers were asked whether, if they had the chance to choose again, they would still choose to be a teacher they were slightly less likely than their colleagues at Key Stage 1 to say 'yes' (61 per cent compared with 77 per cent of Key Stage 1 teachers). However, to set this in overall perspective, this did, of course, represent the majority of teachers in both year groups. It was also notable that 39 per cent of junior teachers and 35 per cent of infant teachers thought that when the children currently in their class left their school they would have had a better primary education than in the past. Roughly one quarter of both sets of teachers had mixed feelings about this, arguing that in some ways children's experience would be better and in some ways worse (Table 5.4). It was striking, however, that the junior teachers were more likely to argue that children's experience under the National Curriculum would be worse than before (14 per cent compared with only 5 per cent of infant teachers).

Table 5.2 *Expectations of primary education in next five or ten years (percentages)*

	Y3/4	Y1/2
Overall response		
Optimistic	17.4	27.3
Mixed	39.1	15.9
Pessimistic	25.0	18.2
Unsure	17.4	34.1
Specific expectations about the changed nature of teachers' work		
More teacher collaboration	4.3	4.5
More reflection, review of own practice	5.4	13.6
More teacher stress, frustration, drop-out	9.8	9.1
More constraints, loss of autonomy,	33.7	19.3
narrowing of role personal fulfilment	4.3	2.3
Other	8.7	2.3

Source: PACE 2 teacher interviews
Sample: 88 Key Stage 1 teachers and 92 Key Stage 2 teachers in 8 LEAs
Date: Spring 1994

Both sets of teachers felt that it was even more important now than in the past for a primary teacher to have skills in assessment, clear aims and subject knowledge, and both cohorts of teachers felt that a good relationship with children was of the same importance as it always had been. Very few teachers overall seemed to feel that any aspect of a primary teacher's work had become significantly less important. Indeed these interviews lend further weight to our 1992 findings that primary teachers were attempting to achieve even more objectives than in the past, and that they were unwilling to give up the expressive and affective dimensions of their role.

Table 5.3 *Quality of teacher–pupil relationship: change in recent years (percentages)*

Overall response	Y3/4	Y1/2
Positive	14.1	17.0
Little or no change	32.6	40.9
Negative	42.4	29.5
Don't know	7.6	12.5

Source: PACE 2 teacher interviews
Sample: 88 Key Stage 1 teachers and 92 Key Stage 2 teachers in 8 LEAs
Date: Spring 1994

In general the Key Stage 2 teachers, looking back over their own practice, were saying that they were tightening up in the classroom, allowing less child choice, and having fewer activities going on at the same time. They were doing more whole-class teaching or teaching in larger rather than smaller groups and doing less art and creative work than in the past. Many of these changes were also true of Key Stage 1 teachers in 1992, but to a lesser degree. It seems from the above comparisons that children's experience of curriculum, pedagogy, and classroom organization was likely to have changed

Table 5.4   Evaluation of quality of education received by children when they leave, *compared with those who left primary school seven years earlier (percentage)*

Overall response	Y3/4	Y1/2
Much better	28.3	23.9
Slightly better	10.9	11.4
Mixed: better in some ways, worse in others	26.1	23.9
Little or no difference	8.7	11.4
Slightly worse	9.8	1.1
Much worse	4.3	3.4
Unsure	7.6	19.3

Source: PACE 2 teacher interviews
Sample: 88 Key Stage 1 teachers and 92 Key Stage 2 teachers in 8 LEAs
Date: Spring 1994

considerably as they moved from Key Stage 1 to Key Stage 2. However, there were some important continuities. In particular, the emphasis placed by all teachers on the importance of a good relationship with the children.

In summary, the responses of the Year 3 and 4 teachers and the Key Stage 1 teachers were similar in many ways, but they also differed in certain key respects, suggesting that the full impact of the reforms was felt later by Key Stage 2 teachers. In particular these teachers felt less reassured by the Dearing Review of the National Curriculum and were less optimistic about the future. They felt the curriculum for older primary school pupils to be particularly overloaded and were concerned about new assessment requirements.

These statistics give an overall picture of teachers' responses to recent education reforms. They do not tell us about the differences between teachers in the way they respond to or deal with change. The reforms are likely to impact differently, for example, on teachers working in different socio-economic locations, on more experienced and less experienced teachers, on men and women, and on those from different social-class backgrounds.

In addition, there has been a tendency in much of the recent research on teachers to focus on school experience alone and to ignore other important aspects of teachers' lives, to present teachers as having neither a past nor a future, as being without life beyond the classroom (Lightfoot, 1983; Acker, 1995). This chapter aims to redress a possible imbalance in the existing PACE work on teachers as well as much other recent work on the impact of the National Curriculum by portraying some of the complexities and contingencies in the lives of two quite different teachers. In particular the two case studies presented here illuminate the effect of the teachers' own social class backgrounds, gender, and the social contexts in which they work on the formation of their values and beliefs about teaching and their identities as professionals.

5.3 CASE STUDY 1: PETER MATTHEWS

Since Peter moved up with his class from Year 2 to Year 3 over the course of the PACE study, he was in the position of participating in the study over the course of four consecutive years. I first interviewed Peter in April 1991, when I spent several days in his classroom as part of our observation of the first SATs to be carried out in England.

Late in 1991 he was interviewed as part of the second round of PACE survey interviews, and subsequently I spent a week in his classroom in March 1992, a further few days observing the second round of SATs in June 1992, and a further classroom study week in June 1993. He was interviewed for the last time in November 1993 as part of the final round of survey interviews with Key Stage 2 teachers.

When he was first interviewed Peter had been at his school, St Anne's, a large Catholic primary school on the outskirts of a Northern city, for 9 years, and had been a primary teacher for 21 years. He was settled and very well established in St Anne's, where he felt highly valued by the head and where he was a very popular teacher with both parents and children. St Anne's was located in an extremely disadvantaged area, where the majority of parents were unemployed and where there was a very high take-up of free school meals. Many children came from families under stress. Several were living with grannies, relatives or friends, rather than their own parents, and a number were being closely supported by social services.

However, the school had a very caring, close-knit family ethos, deriving in part from its Catholic philosophy, and this was reflected most of the time in the children's behaviour and the way they related to each other and to adults. Most children were responsive and affectionate towards to their teacher and towards visiting adults such as myself.

Both the social class context in which he worked and his own family background seemed to be crucial in the formation of Peter's values in relation to teaching. He had a very firm set of beliefs about teaching and a highly distinctive teaching style, which derived from his own experience as a child in a large Catholic family and as a pupil in a tough area of the same Northern city where, as he put it, you had to either be 'fast on your feet or be able to talk your way out of a situation' in order to survive. He believed strongly in providing a firm structure and guidelines for the children, something which he felt was largely lacking in their home lives. At the same time, he wanted to make school enjoyable and aimed to keep the children's attention as much as possible through turning many lessons and even the SATs into games and competitions in which the children competed either in teams or as individuals for house points which eventually might earn them small prizes or commendations read out at assemblies.

This meant a high concentration on whole-class teaching and an unusual teaching style which appeared to be highly successful in involving the children and keeping their attention, and in achieving results. In terms of David Hargreaves' typology of teaching styles (Hargreaves, 1975), Peter could be described as an 'entertainer' who ran lively, game-like whole-class sessions rather in the style of a television quiz-master or a circus ring-master. Children enjoyed being in his class and responded with lively interest. His relationship with them was full of warmth and humour. Most children described their teacher as 'just brilliant', 'dead good'; 'He's so handsome. I love him,' as one little girl put it, and most parents were keen to have their children in his class and to keep them there as long as possible.

In terms of the teacher strategies outlined in Chapter 4, Peter was very clearly a 'creative mediator' who was filtering the demands imposed from above by the National Curriculum through his own values (which in turn were influenced by his own social class, gender, and the school context in which he worked), to produce a particular teaching style which was protective of the children yet nevertheless aimed to give them an entitlement to a wider set of experiences than they would otherwise have had access to.

Peter saw the National Curriculum as a 'very middle-class, Southern sort of curriculum' 'assuming a lot of cultural background which the children don't have' and 'making use of inappropriate reading texts and materials in science which were not easily available in the children's homes'. Although he did not use these words, his argument was that the National Curriculum, although intended to ensure equal entitlement for all children, nevertheless required a certain amount of 'cultural capital' which was not available for some children's families (Bourdieu, 1970; 1977) and certainly not in the families of the majority of children in his class. He was very clearly aware of the dilemma posed by the National Curriculum's emphasis on equal entitlement in a situation where he felt that nevertheless there was a need to find a starting-point which was relevant for the children. He was therefore concerned to build bridges between the children's experience and the demands of the National Curriculum and to mediate some of its 'middle-class' effects.

The effect of the National Curriculum had been to make a typical day in his classroom 'far more loaded and more structured and rigid'. Nevertheless, he felt he had been able largely to protect his relationship with the children through making a game out of learning and even, when he was responsible for Year 2, out of the SATs. As he described it, 'You dress it up with stories and a bit of a joke and make a fun and game out of it …' so that '… half the time they don't realize that they're working'. Similarly, he felt that he had been able to mediate the demands of the National Curriculum to meet some of his own expectations, so that it had been possible to take up those things he felt to be most valuable and important and 'prioritize the rest to meet the children's needs'.

Although his teaching of the basics was largely by whole-class methods and he felt that the only way he could cover the whole curriculum was by increasing the use of workbooks in maths and English, the pedagogy was enlivened by the use of games and competitions. Outside the basic subjects his approach to topic work involved the children more in experiential learning and independent activity. For one science topic on waste and recycling the children were collecting cans and newspaper and raising money for the class. Peter described how for another science topic on weather he had taken the children outside on a very foggy day, even though it had meant missing assembly:

> We just sent our apologies, and we went out and just stood in the middle of the field, in the middle of a thick, thick fog bank, because that's the only way to experience weather like that, and they came in shivering and covered in frost. They had a tremendous time and they knew exactly what it meant, they saw melting and thawing and what have you. But I would like to have done that even if it hadn't been a National Curriculum target, I was just lucky it happened to fit in.

When Peter was interviewed in both 1991 and 1992 he was feeling 'deeply unhappy' with teaching as a job and felt he would be unlikely to choose it if he had the chance to choose again, even though he acknowledged that 'I've realized what is upsetting is that I'm good at it. I've sort of found what I was meant to be, and the fact that we're not allowed to enjoy what we're doing is very disheartening.'

By his own admission, Peter was a perfectionist in his teaching. This posed particular pressures for him in terms of covering the National Curriculum in the depth and breadth required and in carrying out the record-keeping and assessment requirements. He described himself as 'obsessively organized' and easily stressed if his planning and organization was disrupted, to the extent that he was sometimes told to 'ease off' his hard work by the headteacher, who was also a long-term colleague from college days.

Peter was very committed and hard-working but, in spite of his role as curriculum co-ordinator for English, relatively autonomous and isolated in his own classroom. He rarely went into the staffroom and did most of his planning and preparation alone. Whereas most teachers were now working more collaboratively, he found himself working more and more alone and resenting time spent in meetings or group sessions which took him away from a concentration on his own teaching. As he put it:

> I like to shut my classroom door and get on with it ... My relationships with my colleagues are almost non-existent. I just don't seem to have the time. I've certainly got no social life at school, if we could use that term ... I don't feel there's enough hours in the day when I'm at work.

In the autumn term of 1992, Peter had moved up with his class to Year 3, and when he was interviewed the following summer he was deriving more job satisfaction from the change of year group and the new challenges this presented. Nevertheless he felt keenly that the constraints on his teaching were increasing and, in particular, that it was almost impossible to cover the whole curriculum.

> I feel the curriculum gets between you and the children. I don't know whether that's more the case because I've gone into the junior department and moved out of the infant department. But it's become more mechanistic, our relationship, more concerned with getting through quotas and lessons, not even trying to get through topics any more. It's more lessons. You know, I've got a geography lesson to do, I've got a history lesson.

In addition to the barrier imposed by curriculum coverage and the pressure to teach subjects in a separate rather than an integrated way, he felt that he had largely given in to the pressure to resort almost entirely to whole-class teaching and for all children to do the same activity even when they were working as individuals. Nevertheless, he argued that in some ways he found it easier and more manageable being able to say

> Oh right, I've got to do this for history, this for science this year. It's kind of automatic. And I don't have to worry about whether I have analysed it all for myself. ... I know I've got to work in the context of 'invaders and settlers' or 'explorers' or 'ancient Egypt'. Great! I've got a focus now and I didn't have a focus in the infant department.

In a way, he felt that the restriction on choice made his work easier and gave it more clarity, enabling him to concentrate on teaching creatively.

> Being nailed down to one area in history, to use that as an example, means you can start saying 'Now, how am I going to teach that? What am I going to do, what technological elements, what social elements, what English and maths elements can I bring into it?' So it frees your mind for that activity.

Although he was aware that the degree of child choice and the number of activities going on in the class were now even more severely restricted, in the light of Peter's beliefs about the needs of the children he taught and the importance of structure in their lives this did not seem so difficult to live with for him as it might have been for many teachers. Once again, the influence of the social-class context and his own childhood experiences on the formation of his values about teaching was very apparent.

> I think that especially for children from round here, school is probably the only time in their lives that they do get some sort of structure, some sort of reliability. They know that it's Tuesday, so they're going to do PE. It's Monday, so they're going to do singing, Wednesday so they're going to watch a TV programme. Because you get the feeling from between the lines, or even from direct observation, that they go home, they don't know if

they're going to be let in, if they're going to be outside, if they're going to be fed tonight, or if they've got to go over to Gran's.

It was clear through all the discussions with Peter how deeply his own background and his perceptions of the needs of disadvantaged children had influenced his approach to teaching. It was particularly important to him to build up children's self-esteem and self-confidence, but at the same time, to introduce them to a wider set of experiences which included literature and, as he put it, 'to bring some poetry into their lives'.

By the late autumn of 1993, the last time Peter was interviewed, he was definitely feeling more relaxed and happier about teaching and about the effect of change on his working life. By then, the interim report of the Dearing Review had been published, following an intensive round of consultations, and it was becoming clear that the work-load involved in the National Curriculum would be reduced and that the scheme of assessment would be overhauled. The prevailing policy climate was changing to the extent that teachers' concerns with the unmanageability of the National Curriculum appeared at last to be taken seriously in government circles.

This was clearly reflected in the way in which Peter talked about his classroom prac-tice. Although he continued to describe his teaching as having become 'more formalized, more structured and strictured', he also found that he had relaxed into a mixed approach which combined a 'number of topics, and a number of subjects approach' and had found that 'the sky hasn't fallen in and we are meeting National Curriculum targets as well'. He had been able to make his approach more thematic than the year before and had found that he could meet a large number of National Curricu-lum attainment targets that way. Compared with a year ago, he could see a sort of 'underground movement' among teachers towards some sort of solidarity over how they implemented the National Curriculum and how they carried out the SATs.

He was far more confident now that he could break out of any constraints imposed by the National Curriculum. As he put it, the National Curriculum was now exercising less constraint because

> The whole atmosphere from the profession seems to be one of, 'All right, we've tried it, now we're finding that we can actually break out and push against those constraints, and we're not all being dragged into court or sued for breaking our contracts.' And once you realize that, it's going to be the case that this constraint is actually an illusion. It's not so constraining. You start to experiment like we've done and say, 'Well, what's this? Bend it a little bit. Be a bit more flexible. Cover things. Not leave them out. But go back to being a bit more imaginative. Regain a bit of that freedom.' Maybe, to be fair to the National Curriculum, that was always the intention and we just misread it.

In this apparently changed post-Dearing policy climate the possibilities of mediating the curriculum to one's own professional concerns seemed to him to be greater. There was a sense of a greater solidarity with other teachers who might be seen as acting collec-tively as 'practitioner-policy-makers' in their own classrooms (Chapter 2) regaining the ability to maintain and promote their own interests and beliefs within an imposed curriculum. Compared with a year or two earlier, Peter's sense of satisfaction and fulfilment in teaching was greater, and this was still derived primarily from his relation-ship with children and the children's response to teaching. If he had any doubts about satisfaction from the job, he felt that these were caused not only by the educational reforms, but also by his own circumstances and phase of the life-cycle as a teacher. He still would not choose to be a teacher if he had the chance to choose again, but this, he argued, was because he had been teaching for 21 years and was beginning to feel that he needed a change and was 'getting into a rut'.

There was also a feeling of being close to reaching burn-out, which, he argued, was due only in part to the effect of the education reforms, but also to his phase of the life cycle as a teacher. However, his references to the intensification of teachers' work as a result of the reforms suggested that he saw this as a key factor making it more difficult for older teachers to continue to retirement age.

> I mean, you're asking me at a stage in my career now, where I'm starting to think of, in the next few years, paying off the mortgage and stopping full-time teaching, because I seriously do believe it is a physically very difficult job and nobody at the moment could possibly consider doing it until 65. At the present level and pace it would kill you.

Peter's life as a teacher during a period of extreme turbulence for primary education illustrates how deeply teachers' beliefs and values in relation to teaching are rooted in past experiences, both in childhood, social class and family background, and developed in relation to the social context and particular constraints within which they work. In this view of teaching, a teacher's individual biography, training and professional experience intersect with constraints such as those imposed by the Education Reform Act. These constraints may delimit perspectives but they can also be creative (Woods, 1995), leading teachers to become mediators, developing new ways of working, of enlivening learning and arousing children's interests within a prescribed curriculum. Peter's values and beliefs filtered out the effects of the reforms which he deemed to be undesirable for the children in his class and led him to develop his own unique methods of delivering the curriculum and, in particular, of carrying out the assessment tasks.

In Peter's career it was also evident that his personal and his professional 'self' were closely fused so that there was a heavy investment of self in his work as a teacher (Pollard, 1985; Nias, 1989). In order to maintain this integrity between his beliefs and his professional identity, he had worked incredibly hard, but had also isolated himself in his own classroom, sacrificing the informal collaboration with colleagues which might have helped to sustain or to reinforce or 'renew' him (Woods, 1995). Five years after the implementation of the reforms, although he was feeling more positive than he had initially about the reforms, he felt close to burn-out and was beginning to think about the possibilities of early retirement. For him, this might be a new beginning, but it would be a loss to education of a committed and creative teacher.

5.4 CASE STUDY 2: KATE GILL

Kate Gill worked in a very different kind of school and with quite different kinds of children from Peter. Like Peter, however, she was unusual in the PACE sample of teachers in that, because she taught a mixed-age class, she participated in the study over the course of four years between 1990 and 1994. When I first interviewed her in the summer of 1990, as part of the larger round of PACE survey interviews, she had a mixed-age class of Years 2, 3 and 4 with a very few Year 1s. For two successive years I was in her classroom when she administered the SATs; I also spent a week in her class in November 1991 and another week in, respectively, summer 93 and summer 94. During that time the composition of her class changed, when the school acquired a fourth teacher to take all Year 2s. Kate then became responsible for a mixed class of Year 3s and Year 4s only, whereas previously she had been required to cope with the very wide range of needs presented by children aged from six to nine.

At her first interview, Kate had been at her school, Orchard Primary, a small rural school in southern England, for seven years. She had been a teacher for nearly twenty years, although with some gaps for child-rearing. Her own career was very different from Peter's. When she left school she had not immediately chosen teaching, but, at sixteen had taken office and then laboratory work until, having spent some time helping in an infant school, she decided to apply for training college. Within seven years of taking up her first teaching post she had become a Deputy Head, but subsequently left to start a family. On returning to teaching, first on a part-time supply basis, and eventually full-time, she had, like most women returners to teaching, not been able to come back at the level at which she had worked earlier and had to gradually work her way into a permanent full-time job as a classroom teacher. Throughout the current phase of her career she had been aware of the need to balance the demands of teaching with the needs of caring for her own young son, who was also of primary school age. This had prevented her from actively seeking to return to deputy headship.

Acker (1995) emphasizes the fragmented, accidental quality of the 'careers' described by many of the women teachers she interviewed as well as the extent to which many older women often blamed themselves for not following a more consistent progress through the career structure. The influence of gender was evident not only on Kate's career as a teacher but also in the way she drew upon her experience as a mother in her approach to teaching the children in her class.

Orchard was in an attractive village occupied mainly by professional and business families, most of whose children attended the school, although many of them went on to independent secondary education. The school was also attended by a number of children from local farms. It was a happy, pleasant environment and Kate knew most of the children's families, and a considerable amount about their personal lives. She described herself as 'middle-aged and middle-class' with a 'firm but fair' approach towards the children. She felt that most of the parents, like herself with her own son, had high expectations and that she had to be fairly tough with children about producing a good finished product within a certain time period.

As in the case of Peter, both her own social class and family background and the social context in which she worked had shaped Kate's values as a teacher. She acknowledged that her own beliefs about teaching were influenced not only by her experiences as a parent but also by the high expectations of the many professional and middle class parents in the school. These were evident in the way she responded to the demands of the National Curriculum. She planned and prepared meticulously to cover National Curriculum attainment targets in a thematic way, and was particularly imaginative and enthusiastic about the science work she introduced to the class.

On one of my early visits to her class, the children were doing the 'weather' as a topic, and were making wind-gauges and weather-gauges, according to their year group. These were tested in the playground and results recorded. Many other activities were centred round this topic, including much of their English writing and maths work. Kate coped with the three-year age range by adapting the one topic to the needs of each age group, so that, for example, in a science topic, younger groups of children would do more practical work, such as going out into the playground on successive occasions to measure the size of a puddle in order to understand the process of evaporation, while older groups might do library research tasks based on the same topic.

Kate's planning of a topic had increased considerably as a result of the National Curriculum and she worried that 'We are now being asked to do far more than we ever did before, and to cover far more areas.' As a result she felt that 'In some areas we are glossing over rather than getting depth.' She gave frequent verbal feedback and assessment of children's work and had very high standards. Children frequently had to redo their work if it was unsatisfactory and some regularly had to stay in at break and lunchtime to finish work if it was not completed within the reasonable time period allotted.

Probably as a result of their parents' high expectations as well as Kate's own, the children in her class worked in a highly competitive way and showed considerable awareness of where they stood in a hierarchy of achievement. Children often vied with one another to be 'best' and to complete their work first, as the following extract from field notes suggests.

> Anna, a Year 3 child, has spent too long on drawing her picture and has not yet started her writing. Kate calls to her, 'Anna, you must have written at least four lines before you go out to play.'
>
> John, sitting nearby, comments, 'She spent half an hour on that picture. I could have done it in five minutes.'
> Larry, another Year 3 boy, adds, 'She's always the slowest'.
> Ben calls to Harriet, 'Laura's finished.'
> Harriet says, 'Yes, well I finished before her. I'm checking mine now.'

It was clear from such exchanges, which occurred frequently throughout the week, that the children, as well as the teacher, were feeling the pressure to achieve targets within a set period.

In terms of her classroom organization, Kate had responded to the earlier demands of the National Curriculum by grouping children by both age and ability far more than she had in the past, when she felt she had been able to work more with individuals. She normally spent the first part of a morning talking to the children all together, grouped in the book corner, outlining what she expected them to achieve that day. Then, while she worked with a group for either maths or language, the other groups had a chance to choose the order in which they would do the activities she had presented, always on the understanding that all the tasks had to be completed.

On the whole she felt that the National Curriculum met the needs of most of the children in her class fairly well and that she still had plenty of scope for using her own ideas and imagination. This was characteristic of many of the teachers working in schools in middle-class catchment areas within the PACE sample (Pollard *et al.*, 1994, p.98), and contrasted with the argument of teachers like Peter, based in working-class areas, that the National Curriculum was not well suited to the children's needs.

Although the way Kate organized her work had had to change to accommodate the National Curriculum, her approach had always been relatively formal and structured, and she did not feel in 1990 and 1991 that she had fundamentally changed her role or her beliefs about teaching. Even at that stage, however, she was not sure that she would still choose to be a teacher if she had the chance to choose again. Family commitments and demands intersected with the pressures from curriculum overload, record-keeping and assessment. There was no longer a sense in which teaching could be seen as a career which dovetailed well with family commitments. As Kate argued:

> Before I had my own family I enjoyed it far more. It's a strain when you're teaching all day and you go home to your children.

By early 1993, Kate was finding it harder to face the effects of the reforms with equanimity. The constraints now imposed by the National Curriculum and the coming on-stream of further subject areas such as geography, history, art and music were forcing her to teach more either in large groups or with the whole class together, even though the evidence she was deriving from assessment suggested to her that the children did not learn so effectively this way. She was finding the curriculum 'too wide and unwieldy' and that 'You're constantly checking back on yourself, "Have I done this? Have I done that? Have I covered the other ...?" There's this constant feeling of pressure and tension all the time because you never feel that you're doing a good job.'

The pressures of assessment also had negative as well as positive effects. She was less able to enjoy children's learning:

> I'm far more aware of where they are now. I think I've said before I'm looking for things that they can't do. I think probably that's the wrong approach. I do try and praise where it's due, but I don't do that as much as I used to. Sort of really just enjoy what one child has produced for its own sake, the fact that they've worked very hard. I'm always looking for weaknesses and how they can improve.

The pressures of curriculum coverage also meant that Kate had narrowed down her classroom approach to only one or two activities going on at one time, compared with three or four in the past. There was far less music and less creative art activity taking place now than in the past, and she was able to allow less child choice of activity.

By the end of 1993, Kate was describing her teaching as 'more directive' and 'more subject-based' although she still tried to keep a balance between single subjects and topics.

> I don't give the children anywhere near as much free choice as I used to and the 'play activities' have virtually sort of ceased to be in existence. I tend to plan much more rigidly and plan for my teaching, I think, perhaps rather than the children's learning, and although we're still doing project work, it's much more tightly knitted together and so each thing passes on straight after the one before it.

She felt less close to the children than in the past, and doubtful about the wholehearted benefits to children's learning of the National Curriculum. While she felt that the children would have a far better general knowledge than in the past, she doubted that they would be as self-directive or independent in their learning.

When I returned for a final classroom study visit in 1994, the strictures of continued change were such that Kate described her teaching as more rigid, giving less freedom of choice to children, with a resultant effect on her relationship with them. She felt far more stressed than in the past and was aware that the whole nature of her job had altered with the rigours of time pressure and the need for tight classroom management. Consequently, she felt conscious of imparting knowledge to children far more than in the past and directing the children far more. In addition, she had concerns about the children's sense of success and self-esteem because of the rigours of assessment. She felt that she was constantly pushing them to improve and to achieve a little bit more rather than simply accepting a piece of work for what it was and offering praise.

> I am constantly looking for what a child can do to improve his or her work, so the poor

children never do anything that's perfect ... I think that with the National Curriculum, the feeling is that infinity is the ultimate and therefore they never actually reach the level one would expect them to reach, and I do feel that questioning and then questioning again to see more and more understanding is perhaps not what I want to do. There is a limit to how much they can cope with.

The pressures to pursue excellence even at the risk of children's sense of self-esteem were making themselves felt particularly strongly in a social context where parents had very high expectations of their children's achievement. In addition, the expectation of an OFSTED inspection in the near future was dominating the school's planning and management and there was a corresponding need to collect constant evidence. Both at school level and at the level of the individual teacher, planning was taking place in much more depth than previously. Kate felt that this was necessary and fruitful in some ways, particularly as planning was beginning to take place across the Key Stages as well as within them, so that continuity was strengthened. Nevertheless, she argued that it did mean that there wasn't the ability to 'digress, to go off at a tangent if a child's interest tends to take them that way. You keep drawing them back to what you want them to learn rather than what they might want to learn.'

However, a really positive boost was the strengthening of relationships with colleagues and the sense of working very much as a team. There was a shared feeling of responsibility and 'as a result of that we've grown closer together. Everybody feels they're in this together and you can't really just go your own way any more.' In Kate's working life as in that of many of the other PACE teachers there was a constant tension between the need for autonomy and the pressure towards collaboration. Loss of autonomy in the classroom meant that the freedom to digress (see above) was diminished and that choice of topic work was no longer an individual matter, yet team collaboration also had many benefits in terms of support, reduction of individual workload, and warmer relationships.

In Kate's case, collaboration had extended both within and beyond the confines of her own school. Like the curriculum, her own responsibilities in the school had expanded during this period. She was at once special-needs co-ordinator, maths co-ordinator, and IT co-ordinator and also had a budget responsibility. In addition, she had an incentive allowance as administrative co-ordinator for the cluster of primary schools of which Orchard was one.

Teachers across the cluster worked together for maths, sports, science and art in order to share expertise. For example, one art teacher had organized a range of activities for all the children in a particular year-group in the cluster of schools. Children went to the local secondary school to do the activities. Joint policies had been developed in special needs and the arts, and joint policy statements were being prepared for able children, equal opportunities, and PE. The cluster schools had also collaborated to issue a joint statement opposing the publication of the SATs and refusing to release the results to the LEA, although reporting them to parents.

For teachers like Kate, working in relatively small schools, cluster activity gave opportunities for professional development and collaboration far beyond what could be found solely within the school. Collaboration with others also enabled her to 'consolidate' her perspective on the National Curriculum (Woods, 1995) and to join with a wider body of teachers in a strategy of 'resistance' to the publication of SAT results.

However, in spite of developments such as the cluster activities, Kate no longer derived the fulfilment she had originally obtained from teaching. She felt that her enjoyment had slumped over the five years since the introduction of the National Curriculum. The feeling that 'you can't just take time out to stand back and assimilate' was destructive of her satisfaction in the job, but she also attributed some of the loss to getting older and 'because I'm not as tolerant as I was when I was a young teacher'. She admitted to feeling 'a bit burnt out' and, although she very much enjoyed working with the new Head she thought she might make a move to some other type of work in the next two or three years. There were strong parallels here with Peter's argument that, in the context of rapid change, primary teaching was no longer a job you could do for life without reaching burn-out. Similar points were put by many of the older and more experienced teachers in the PACE sample.

Kate appeared to have moved from a period of reassessment (Huberman, 1993) as a result of the National Curriculum, during which she was initially very optimistic and creative in her response, to a phase of self-doubt and undoubted exhaustion. She was no longer sure that even if the opportunity presented itself to become a Deputy Head once again she now wanted the post. Family responsibilities and pressures as well as work pressures made it all seem less desirable. As in the case of Peter, Kate's sense of self was strongly bound up with her professional identity as a teacher. Although she derived some support and 'renewal' from her collaboration with other teachers in the cluster and with the new headteacher, her continued effort to mediate external demands in line with her values and beliefs as a teacher had taken a toll on her energy and enthusiasm. As for Peter, the reforms had created for her a 'critical career phase' (Sikes *et al.,* 1985) during which she had sustained her commitment to certain values and beliefs about teaching, but at some personal cost.

5.5 CONCLUSIONS

The careers of these two teachers during a period of extreme turbulence for primary education suggest that the relationship between the imposition of change from above and its implementation in classrooms is a far from simple one. In many ways these teachers' stories are a cause for optimism since they demonstrate the power of individuals to maintain their beliefs, their integrity and their personal and professional identities in spite of the changes imposed from above. However, this was not achieved without struggle and personal cost.

In terms of the teaching strategies outlined in Chapter 4, both these teachers were 'creative mediators' and both had a strong professional commitment to doing the best for their children and protecting them from what they perceived as the worst effects of change. In particular, their stories illustrate the importance of teachers' personal biographies and the influence of gender, social class and social context in the formation of values and beliefs about teaching. As Figure 5.1 illustrates, these teachers' values intersected with the effects of policy change to produce a particular personal response which was evident in their professional ideology and their classroom practice.

As the careers of Peter and Kate suggest, the phase of the life-cycle reached by a teacher may also influence their response to change. Huberman (1993) argues that it is possible to identify particular phases or stages of teaching in which teachers may perceive themselves differently at different moments of their career. He identifies

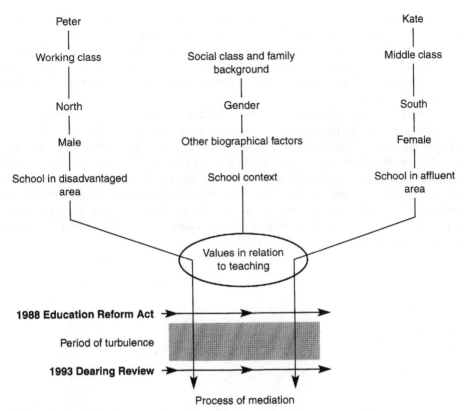

Figure 5.1 *Teachers' careers, values and the mediation of change*

phases such as 'initial exploration', followed by 'stabilization', and 'consolidation', and subsequently 're-assessment' followed by either self-doubt or a period of renewed optimism, and a final phase of 'disengagement' involving a search for balance between professional and personal lives.

Of course, these teachers did not participate in the study over their whole life-cycles, but it is arguable that in a period of extreme turbulence where individuals are undergoing intense pressure to change in a relatively short period these phases may have considerable relevance. Both Peter and Kate appeared to have changed their view of teaching as a career over the last five years, and these views were partly bound up with the reforms and partly with other biographical and life-cycle influences.

Compared with their colleagues at the infant stage, Key Stage 2 teachers appeared to experience the worst and most stressful effects of the changes slightly later. An initial phase of accommodation, a feeling that the changes could be incorporated within existing patterns of working, was followed by a period of much greater stress during which both teachers experienced a tightening up and pressure to change their teaching methods or to fight harder to avoid doing this (either adaptation or resistance). This was followed by a reassessment when the Dearing Review seemed to promise a more settled period for primary education, and ultimately by either self-doubt (in the case of Kate) or a more optimistic feeling and a sense of relative satisfaction (in the case of Peter). After the 'reassessment' period both teachers, in different ways, talked of the need to retrieve a balance in their lives and both seemed to be entering a period of disengagement, of becoming more detached (not actively seeking promotion or career advancement) and perhaps looking towards either early retirement or a change of career. Significantly, both mentioned that they felt near to a stage of 'burn-out', which they perceived as an effect both of the National Curriculum and of their phase of the life-cycle as a teacher.

These teachers' stories underline the many influences on teachers' thinking and practice which are outside the control of policy-makers and show the possibilities for mediation and manoeuvre between policy-making and its implementation in the classroom. For both Peter and Kate, their own childhood experiences, their family background, their gender, their phase of the life cycle as a teacher, and the background of the children they taught had a profound effect on their beliefs about teaching and consequently on their response to educational change. Their stories also raise policy issues which urgently need to be addressed concerning the prevalence of burn-out and stress amongst committed and experienced teachers.

Chapter 6

Do We Really Need to Write it All Down? Managing the Challenge of National Assessment at Key Stage 1 and Key Stage 2

Patricia Broadfoot

6.1 INTRODUCTION

The discussion of teacher assessment at Key Stage 1 in *Changing English Primary Schools?* is prefaced by the general comment arising from the data that primary teachers' views of and practices concerning assessment are explicitly ideological, reflecting the broader professional ideology held by the teacher. Thus, in talking about the role that they felt assessment ought to play in infant classrooms, teacher responses typically reflected their more general ideas concerning how learning can best be facilitated and supported. In brief, it was found that professional practices could be analysed in terms of three main dimensions: frequency, purpose and mode. The typical approach in infant classrooms involved a constant but intuitive, almost at times unconscious, monitoring by the teacher of both the individual child and the class as a whole in order to provide ongoing encouragement and/or guidance in the spirit of formative assessment. In reporting teachers' views of the changes they were perceiving with the implementation of National Curriculum assessment requirements, the book reports a pressure experienced by teachers to move towards a different set of priorities in terms of mode, purpose and frequency, namely the use of more overt, intermittent and formalized assessment procedures, the purpose of which is accountability as much as pupil learning. The book goes on to report the chagrin felt by many teachers about these changes and, at the same time, how successfully they felt themselves to be grappling with the new assessment requirements in terms of teacher assessment.

Whilst the PACE 1 project also deals extensively with the impact of SATs on infant schools and teachers, clearly the PACE 2 project is not dealing with the end of a Key Stage. Thus the impact of SATs is a great deal more marginal for these teachers and does not figure prominently in the current analysis. In what follows, we discuss findings from the teachers studied in PACE 2 by means of conversations and observations in the nine schools in which we have conducted our detailed longitudinal classroom studies, as well as data drawn from interviews with teachers in our larger sample of 48 schools. The overall aim of the paper is to document how far teachers in Key Stage 2 manifest the same understanding of and attitude to the role and purpose of assessment in their classrooms and how they in turn are reacting to the new pressures and requirements on them. By so doing, it is hoped both to present a descriptive picture of current practice in this respect among teachers in Years 3 and 4, and also to draw out any comparisons that exist between Key Stage 1 and Key Stage 2 teachers in this respect, including the particular issue of the use of assessment in the transfer between Key Stages.

6.2 TEACHERS' FEELINGS ABOUT ASSESSMENT IN YEARS 3 AND 4

It must be said that, as Table 6.1 shows, a significant number of the KS2 teachers studied were generally negative about the teacher assessment they are required to do.

Table 6.1 *'How do you feel about the teacher assessment you are now required to do?' (percentages)*

Generally positive	15
Neutral	11
Generally negative	45
Mixed likes and dislikes	29

Source: PACE 2 teacher interviews
Sample: 92 Year 3 and Year 4 teachers
Date: Autumn 1993

The explanation of these feelings — shown in Table 6.2 — makes clear that it is the issues of extra workload on the one hand and the perceived lack of utility of tick-box type records on the other that are the principal bones of contention.

Table 6.2 *Feelings about teacher assessment (percentages)*

Too much writing	61
Useful, constructive	22
Prefer narrative comments	25
Becoming easier with practice	11
Useful but should be reduced	34
NC criteria difficult to use	27
SAT reporting unreliable	8
Other	13

Source: PACE 2 teacher interviews
Sample: 92 Year 3 and Year 4 teachers
Date: Autumn 1993
Note: Percentages add to more than 100 since up to three replies could be coded.

As Table 6.3 shows, most of the teachers, like their Key Stage 1 colleagues, were engaged in assessment activity of some kind virtually all the time.

These data show clearly the mixed meaning that the word assessment still has for Key Stage 2 teachers (see also Osborn and Black, 1994). For most, it is the ongoing monitoring which is inseparable from teaching itself. For a few, it is the more explicit summative activity designed to produce formal results. The amount of regular classroom testing is also worthy of note.

Table 6.3 *'How much time do you feel you are engaged in assessment activity when you are working with the children?' (percentages)*

Virtually all the time	76
Very little time	11
Only during formal assessment	5
Listening to groups at work	13
Working with pupils one-to-one	7
Regular classroom testing	26
LEA choice of tests	2
Other	4

Source: PACE 2 teacher interviews
Sample: 92 Year 3 and Year 4 teachers
Date: Autumn 1993
Note: Up to 3 responses coded.

6.3 TEACHERS' APPROACHES TO ASSESSMENT IN YEARS 3 AND 4

Frequency

The Key Stage 2 teachers shared many common features in their approach to assessment with their Key Stage 1 colleagues. As far as the frequency of assessment is concerned, the sentiments expressed in the following quotation are typical of the emphasis given to ongoing minute-by-minute monitoring and individualized decision-making.

> Interviewer: So, for example, this morning you were going round from group to group looking at what they'd done in their workbooks and so on. Were you actually assessing ...?
> Teacher: Oh, yes, because in a case like that, that's a very unique way of assessment. I don't know how you could formalize that because you're looking at what they've done and you've got to make an instant decision, 'Can they go on to the next element of this work? Do they need to mark time? Do they need to do more examples of this activity?' That's, I think, where assessment really works, because you're making a spot decision and it's no good writing that down, 'Today so-and-so didn't do very well on their algebra. They need to do more work.' You need to know there and then now, otherwise that morning's wasted. So I would regard the time taken to formally assess them then as wasted time.

Similarly, other teachers interviewed drew the distinction between the more formalized approach to assessment, aimed at producing externalized evidence of achievement or need, and the constant, almost intuitive assessment discourse which is almost synonymous with the process of instruction. For example:

> Teacher: Yes, rather than isolating a little period and saying, 'I'm now assessing,' which I know some courses I've attended says that you really should put your assessment hat on and sit back and observe. I don't find that easy ... I think [I'm doing assessment] all of the time. It's so integrated, it's so overlapping, it's continual really ... I think I'm very, very aware of assessment now but I really feel — if I think deeply about it — I've been assess-

ing all of the time but not perhaps putting the word 'assessment' on it.

Interviewer: I know.

Teacher: Just again, as most teachers have done for ... since time began ...

Interviewer: It's labelled now.

Teacher: Yes, it's labelled. And we know at the end of the year that the assessment must form part of the report that we will write on the child.

Interviewer: Oh, those reports, yes.

Teacher: Yes, great difficulty and very time-consuming, and perhaps that's the period when you actually can spend 10 to 15 minutes just sitting thinking about the particular child, looking at books. Again, it's a good thing in that it focuses your attention totally on that child without any intrusion for a certain length of time, so that is great assessment in itself.

Mode

The same similarity with Key Stage 1 teachers is evidenced in terms of the mode of assessment, that is, the way evidence is collected.

Assessment's always gone on because it's part of the diagnostic procedure. It's going on with everything you do. When you're speaking to a child you're finding out what they can and can't do, and having done that, you're then taking it one step further thinking what you're going to do next. So assessment's always gone on. I think it's just that it's become a different kind of assessment under National Curriculum and the fact that there has to be evidence. And also in that teachers' assessment doesn't seem to be valued and yet that's what every teacher always has and always will do but there has to be evidence now to show outside people and it's not ... sometimes things happen off the cuff and I think if ... you build in assessment into your everyday practice. I think National Curriculum really has formalized it and it's given a lot of concern and worry to a lot of teachers ...

It's going on all the time, but I think it's ... the formalization of it has become the problem that you're forever thinking how it can be shown as evidence, how it can be made tangible for other people to see it and how to record it that it will be useful to another teacher. Because I think, you see, if you've already got a good team you don't need all this formalization and paperwork, because we've always talked to each other and every member of staff knows every child in the school, not just by name but we know their talents and we recognize them and I think it's almost as if National Curriculum's come along ... it's like there are poor drivers on the road and therefore you can only drive the same speed as the slowest, and yet if you were already there and discussing children and informing the next member of staff as to what's going on, it was already happening, but it's become formalized, it's turned into red tape and I think it's unnecessary when everything was in place and in motion and working.

Purpose

The emphasis that these Key Stage 2 teachers put on the pressures they are experiencing to externalize the process of assessment, in what these teachers, at least, regard as an unnecessary way, relates to the third element which characterizes their assessment discourse: this concerns the purpose of assessment as well as these previous comments on mode. The way in which the National Curriculum is constructed, as well as its emphasis on recording achievement, stresses a form of assessment discourse in which the purpose of assessment is to provide a record of where each child is at in their learning. For the teachers, however, there is a rather different kind of assessment discourse. This embodies a much more dynamic and formative set of notions which have built into them a diagnostic commentary which allows the teacher to make ongoing pedagogic decisions. This is evidenced in the following example.

> Victoria, yes. Well, yes, because Anthony is an outstanding child in ability terms, and the instructions for the game were actually there in language that he could understand, and I think that it is typical of his problem, which again, yes, I did assess that he hadn't taken the time and the trouble to apply an ability that he has, which is to read and understand. And Victoria, who has less ability, had at least made the effort and yes, that's a kind ... this goes into your memory bank as to the nature of his problem and how to try and do something about it. You see, Anthony needs challenges, but then, when you give him one, he can't be bothered with it, even though in theory he enjoys them and wants them.

For this teacher, simply to have recorded the achievement of a particular level or attainment target would not have provided her with the dynamic, interpretative knowledge she needs to make suitably individualized pedagogic decisions, and it is partly for this reason that teachers seem to be impatient with the formal recording aspect of assessment because it cannot encompass this kind of dynamic, holistic knowledge of the child as a learner with a particular set of metacognitive needs.

As well as this ongoing intuitive discourse concerning individual children's needs and characteristics, there is a parallel concern with the needs and characteristics of the class as a whole, as exemplified in the following statement:

> I think it always crosses your mind that there is something that I want to cover, possibly with the whole class. Just working this morning for instance, I did think as I was looking round, some children are making their sentences so short, 'They did this,' 'They had that,' 'They had to do — the other,' but really they do need a session on sentence links which are other than 'and then', to make their work flow better and that I could work on that more as a grammar exercise than ... So, I think you're always looking for ways of improving their work but I tend to look far more generally than at the individual child ... How I can help a group within the class rather than each individual child which perhaps I should be doing.

These examples illustrate a consistent pattern among nearly a hundred Key Stage 2 teachers interviewed which stresses the purpose of assessment as being to inform teaching decisions, whether this is with regard to an individual child, a group or the class as a whole. There is very little evidence in their assessment discourse that the teachers are convinced of the need to communicate more systematically, whether this is with colleagues, parents or, least of all, government and the public for accountability purposes. It is interesting to note that while this was equally true of Key Stage 1 teachers when the PACE project was studying them in detail between 1990 and 1992, recent repeat interviews (spring and summer 1994) with Key Stage 1 teachers in the same schools indicate the beginnings of a change in this picture, with the teachers after their now quite substantial experience with teacher assessment and SATs, as well as the associated training, evidencing a much greater facility in talking about assessment and equally a more explicit awareness of the positive potential of other assessment purposes, as the following response from a KS1 teacher illustrates.

> Interviewer: Could you describe the assessment procedures you use? Thinking of things from spelling tests, listening to children to self-assessment.

Teacher: Well, when I make my plans I actually write in — I plan an activity and I write in what I'm hoping to assess in that activity and so the way I assess it is obviously teacher observation, looking at the children's recorded work afterwards and my own impressions, I mean of a child, are very hard to quantify and so that's one thing.

And then when it comes to the basic skills bit again I do have a particular spelling test which is weekly. I assess pure number, computation of number, on a little worksheet with each group, I would watch every half term, something like that, just to make sure that what I thought was true is true. Do you see what I mean? I sort of focus on each group in turn and watch them do it, as opposed to sending them away to do it.

When it comes to the process skills in science and all those other subjects, then some of those I can assess from their recorded work. I also take teacher observation notes as they're doing activities with me. And I look at end results. I mean in science if they were setting up a little test I obviously look at the end result and question them about it. In technology you can look at what they've actually made and question them about it.

I find it quite difficult to get them to do their own self-evaluation and their own assessment of what they've done. I find that very difficult with six- and seven-year-olds. A few children are ready to do that but I find that most of them are not. And on every child we keep evidence, we keep the teacher's notes, however scribbled. I've got things that nobody else could read but here I needed those notes to explain why I had assessed a child at a certain level. It is all there. But I'd need my two weeks to get it all up together, I can tell you!

Equally, there is some indication that teachers are more explicitly separating teaching from assessment as in the following example:

Interviewer: How much time do you feel that you are engaged in assessment activity when you are working with the children?

Teacher: Well, that's interesting because ... It's very hard, isn't it, that? Teaching and assessing, you know, it's hard to say, hard to separate the two sometimes because ... how much time am I spending assessing the children? Do you mean as a percentage?

Interviewer: No, more ... unless you can, I think that's very hard to say ... but ...

Teacher: OK. Well, let's say ... what about a particular activity? So, what did I do? I did an activity with eggs and science. Now, I set that up specifically to assess where they were in certain aspects of science that came in Attainment Target 1. So I was assessing all the time during that activity. So that was a total assessment activity because I planned it like that.

Now, what other activities have I done? I taught them, read them the story of Jesus going into Jerusalem. I asked them to go away and do a picture and label the picture about it. Now, during that activity when I was teaching I wasn't assessing, while they were doing the activity I wasn't assessing; the only assessment, if I did any, would be looking at the finished piece of work. Is that helpful?

Interviewer: Yes.

Teacher: I'm not quite sure how to explain it because it's so ...
Interviewer: Yes. And, as you said, it's so hard to separate because in a way you're assessing, you're making observations, even if you didn't plan to.

Teacher: That's right. And then, for instance, in a maths activity doing something like a maths addition work card. Off they go and do it, back they come with it. Now sometimes I say, 'Did you use counters?' and then I'll scribble at the bottom of the piece of work 'Unaided', 'Used counters', 'No apparatus used', 'Very quick'. Do you see that I mean? So I write little sort of assessment comments on the piece of work so that when I come to do my final teacher assessment of something or think about the next piece of work I'm going to give them I've got a clue — because you can't remember with all the third years who did what. There's hundreds of things. Millions of things.

and from another teacher:

> How I teacher-assess? Well, when I've taught something, and I don't mean once, I mean taught them for a period of time, for two weeks, say, on a concept or something like that, I give them a sheet but they have help to finish it, to actually reinforce what we've done, like at the end of a section or something. And then, this is with several things, not all things, when I go to the next topic in the next half term, I try and get the same concept in there and see who can tell me, by relating back to that knowledge, what they've got from it. Some children will say, well for instance in this topic it goes weekly and children are now saying to me, 'All the woodwind instruments have got keys,' like they've got that. I mean that's not an attainment target but they've sorted that one out. So I did keep all that and record that and mark those off. If they actually prove to me at a later date I don't teacher-assess them at the time that I've introduced it because they can all achieve it on that day so I tend to keep it until later and see if they can prove it in other ways and then I do make notes of that. And then in my record book if I feel that they've demonstrated something like that I tick it off and then I transfer it to the profile, if need be. If I don't feel that the child's demonstrated any of that, which is another thing, sometimes I'll ask questions to see what they say. I hardly ever do recorded, child-recorded assessment. I do write things down, there, that they say.

6.4 PRESSURES FOR CHANGE

Externalizing assessment

Three major themes emerge as characterizing the changes Key Stage 2 teachers feel are impacting on them concerning assessment at the present time. The first of these is the felt need to externalize and formalize the assessment process, indeed, the fact that the attainment targets of the National Curriculum have provided a language with which to do this. For example:

> I think the difference is with this awareness of assessment is that they've actually put it into language and you've done things without ... My difficulty is getting things across in a language. Words elude me and it brings ... it really frustrates me because I'm searching in the air for a word, but the ... I've discovered that in effect what I've been doing is what they're aiming for on the whole. It's just the way they would justify it, qualify it, describe what I'm doing.

Or:

> There's so much more pressure to deliver the goods and once the pressure is on, you feel that you're not really doing anything very well. One's constantly looking at the children and thinking what they can't do, rather than what they can. That's one of the effects of assessment. You look at things that they haven't done yet and sort of plan for that rather than enjoying the things they can do ... I'm far more aware of where they are now. I think I've said before I'm looking for things that they can't do. I think probably that's the wrong approach. I do try and praise where it's due but I don't do that as much as I used to. Sort of really just enjoy what one child has produced for its own sake, the fact that they've worked very hard. I'm always looking for something else.

Changing assessment methods

As well as being more aware of the need to formalize their assessment procedures and to express them in terms of the National Curriculum language, teachers are actually in the process of trying to change their methods of data collection for assessment, although this presents some difficulties, partly because it is an unfamiliar practice and for some, regarded as an unnecessary practice.

> I'm sure it is helpful for people just coming into teaching. It's only through experience that you can store all this in your mind ... You see, I'm sure I do assess and I'm not really aware of the fact that I'm assessing.

Many teachers in trying to approach assessment more systematically clearly experience both professional and practical difficulties in introducing these new kinds of systematic assessment activity, especially observation, into their day-to-day practice.

> Assessment is one of the areas that I find most difficult, but that's a personal assessment in the sense that you've got to stand back and assess a child for ten minutes. I always feel that's taking ten minutes out of teaching time which is very, very wrong, I realize that. I think assessment takes a very important part in any class but my assessment is very often covered from looking at pieces of work, looking for something specific within the work on that day or perhaps they have been set a special task where the demand has been made and assessing afterwards, whereas I know there's special emphasis on the observation of children.

and another teacher:

> I think the thing I find most difficult when I'm doing an assessment with a group is actually keeping the other children away. It's organizing everybody else so that I've got the space, the length of time to concentrate on what I want to look at. I'm thinking particularly about maths investigations and being able to assess what the children are doing there, which always means that you've got to stay there quite a long time to see who's leading the group and how they're thinking and question them as to how they understand it, and then if everybody's sort of coming up to me and saying, 'What do I do with this?' and 'Where do I put that?' ... It's getting them trained not to do that.

Contrast this with the comment of one Key Stage 1 teacher who appears to have mastered these practical difficulties and to relish a much more explicit assessment role:

> You're just continually assessing, aren't you really. If I work with a group, I continually write down ... Like if I work with a group and it's a special-need child, I jot down the times and what they've said and whether they've got it right or wrong and ... I have a on-task, off-task for my child who can't sit still and I have a running list for a child who I feel is a very special need. I do try to get to those children who are able because I feel they're the ones who suffer when you teacher-assess because you know that they can do it and they actually need pushing forward. But I would say you spend a fair amount of time watching children. I'd like sometimes just to stand back. I'm working with an observational drawing group. I give them their input and say a few things. You know, 'Look at the detail. Does that really look like that?' but all the time I'm there, I'm actually looking at one or two children and actually watching what they're doing and trying to gauge where they are. I like that. I could do that as a job actually.

Changing whole-school approaches to assessment

The third theme in the change process in terms of teacher assessment concerns the developments taking place in whole-school approaches to assessment. Asked if they had a school assessment policy, 24 per cent replied in the affirmative with 22 per cent not having one and 52 per cent significantly saying one was being developed. A number of the respondents referred to initiatives in their school concerned with building up portfolios of typical work as a benchmark to inform the awarding of levels for teacher assessment. Others referred to the use of Records of Achievement and the involvement of children themselves in selecting and assessing their own work. The elements of such policies which were mentioned are shown in Table 6.4.

Table 6.4 *Elements of whole-school assessment policies (percentages)*

Children's portfolios of work	32
Regular formal testing	16
Use of standardized tests	9
Negotiation with children	4
Follow LEA policy	13
Other	19

Source: PACE 2 teacher interviews
Sample: 92 Year 3 and Year 4 teachers
Date: Autumn 1993
Note: Up to 3 responses coded.

There is a clear distinction drawn between various kinds of evidence and the recording of it in a systematic way. On the one hand, many teachers refer to their own personal records, idiosyncratic and couched in the same individualized diagnostic discourse that is used for the ongoing intuitive, pedagogic decision-making of the classroom.

> I've always been one for having records, my own particular records, and very detailed they are as well. I keep records of my markbooks from the point of view I can look at my markbooks and tell you exactly where a child is in most areas. I keep child profiles — so a general social behavioural study, any problems. I keep that and always have done, but added to that we have got these relating to the National Curriculum documents and you've got ... we have the one document which is a class record — and then we have individual sheets on which you fill in all the attainment targets. You wouldn't believe how time-consuming it is, and it doesn't really tell you anything in the end.

The tone of a Key Stage 1 teacher's response to the same question, 'Could you tell me whether you have a school assessment policy?' is rather different:

> Well, we've got record books which show achievement rather than assessment, but I mean in order to be accurate about that you have to have done the assessment first, and we're setting up folders which contain particular examples of how you've assessed a particular piece of work and what you've assessed it to be, which is very useful. These are usually sort of done through staff meetings and discussions so that at the end of the day you know there's a general agreement on what constitutes, say, a Level 2 piece of English story-writing or something like that.

6.5 PROBLEMS IN USING ASSESSMENT INFORMATION

The utility of different kinds of records comes out most strongly in the context of the transfer of children between teachers, and particularly between Key Stages 1 and 2. Forty-two per cent of teachers interviewed felt the transfer from Key Stage 1 to Key Stage 2 raised important issues, mentioning, in consequence, their close contact with the Year 2 teacher (28 per cent). Only 13 per cent mentioned the use of National Curriculum records as against 15 per cent using other records. Portfolios of work were used to provide curriculum continuity by 13 per cent of respondents, with most relying on the content of teaching — in the form of a planned sequence of topics (36 per cent) rather than assessment information — to achieve this. Not surprisingly, continuity was markedly more difficult between Key Stages 1 and 2 (16 per cent) than between years 3 and 4 within Key Stage 2 (7 per cent). Despite providing for progression having been a key element in the impetus behind the introduction of the National Curriculum, there was very little evidence among the teachers studied that the existence of national assessment information had facilitated this process at all. This was for a number of reasons.

Lack of accuracy

First, and most importantly, was the perceived lack of accuracy in the information coming from Key Stage 1 assessments. One of the more obvious reasons for this is differences in standards being applied between teachers in the same school and between different schools despite the provision of moderation to counteract this.

> I found last year that they were being assessed as I thought they were going to be, so that was fair enough. I have been getting children from another class that I didn't actually assess, and I've found that in that case I've treated them sometimes under ... as under-achieving what they can actually do because of their assessment. Whether it's the summer holidays that's made a difference or a new teacher's made a difference but they've been assessed at say — take an arbitrary figure — Level 1 and really they're Level 2, or by the time they got to me they were Level 2 ... I think there's teacher's natural caution not to have put them at a higher level because you're going to get rumbled later on and to say, 'Oh, well, there may be one or two but I'd better put them at 1 and then they'll look as if they've improved,' ... well, no, that sounds very cynical, but the room is there for improvement in the right direction.

Levels too broad

There was a general view that the SAT information coming from Key Stage 1 colleagues was not helpful, partly because the levels were too broad.

> This is certainly a very delicate subject and I wouldn't like to insult my colleague in Year 2 who does a tremendous amount of work, in fact over and above the call of her, testing; but as the receiving teacher I don't think it gives me any more information than C would have passed on in half an hour discussion or on little pieces of paper in the natural assessment between teacher and teacher because I have noticed that each of these levels are so wide. In fact again I was focusing in on them when I was writing my reports because I had each child's folder in front of me and I was astonished occasionally to see that perhaps five different children were all Level 2 on maths, or science or whatever, and the variety of levels within that level! This is where it's very, very vague.

Real differences in achievement

But the problem of different schools using different standards and different teachers using different standards, potentially reducing the utility of summative assessment information, already limited in its usefulness as a pedagogic guide because of being too

broad, is much less significant than what would appear to be real differences in achievement of the children concerned. As one teacher put it:

> The National Curriculum's all about recording, and yet all the records I've ever had up to
> now, when they've come through, have never related to the attainment targets that I'm
> working with ... And then each year the parameters have changed on the SATs. But that
> apart, where things have come through, for instance the maths has changed very little and
> children have come in at Level 2, then in theory I should then begin work at Level 3 and
> I've found that invariably they couldn't cope with Level 3. I don't dispute that they haven't
> got the Level 2 but this goes back to what I say about they know it on a day but after a
> summer holiday and a period of SATs ... But there hasn't been the breadth, in the rush to
> assess everybody and get something down, which I understand, because I find myself
> rushing, but the breadth doesn't go in and therefore you can't begin another level because
> the understanding's not there in the rush to get through these assessments.
>
> So, I'm not very happy and it's not been very useful to me at all, but legally I'm
> supposed to begin Level 3 after Level 2, but I find I have to do lots more work at Level 2,
> which is no criticism of any particular person or ... I just feel it's ... whereas I looked
> forward to National Curriculum, thinking well, I'll know now where these children are
> when they come to me from a separate building and they are unknown children, but I find
> that my own judgement is the best one at the end of the day. These statistics on paper are
> not very helpful. They are an indication, but that's all they are, of what's gone on before
> rather that where they are at that moment. I think you have to bear in mind that the infant
> school is a separate school under a separate Head in a separate building on a separate site
> and I looked forward to having some kind of knowledge about the children before they
> came but it's a bit 'pie in the sky'.

Another teacher also refers to the different world of the infant and the junior school and
the impact of this on children's performance:

> And also I think it's forgotten that the actual transfer from an infant to a junior school has
> such strong psychological effect and that a child who has struggled in the infant school
> because of a relatively wide age difference ... this is starting a new book for a child, and a
> child who struggled in the infants may suddenly take off in the juniors.

The problem essentially is not one of measurement but one of real differences in
achievement as children are affected by the particular learning context they find themselves in.

> Most of them — the previous teacher's assessment on the work-rate ability is pretty accu-
> rate, but it's some sort of thing ... the biggest problem with assessment anyway, all
> you've found out is what the child was like on that day or even at that hour of that day and
> by the following day or the following week, and in some cases you're talking six months
> later, they're a totally different child. They could have had the 'flu or been under the
> weather that day as well.
>
> I know it's not just based on one day's SATs. It's on one year's continuous assessment.
> But then it's personalities; do they work better for a man or a woman, or ... as they get a
> bit older? I've certainly noticed maturation in a lot of the children this year. Really fulfilled
> the potential that we hoped that they would.

These comments and many similar ones from teachers reflect the feeling that summative
assessment of this kind is almost inevitably flawed.

> Also, to me these assessment tasks are a bit artificial because you can set a task and you
> know, in your heart of hearts, that the child knows that there and then, and they do, and
> they do well on the assessment, but I mean, you ask someone three months later a question
> about that unit of work and they might not know the answer, because it's like swotting for
> an exam. You can take the exam and pass it and then really you can't even remember

learning it three months later. So it's a very artificial ... it only shows what a child knows at any one particular moment in time.

This view is echoed in a very similar comment from a Key Stage 1 teacher:

Teacher: It's easy for them all to achieve when you've done it. It's whether they actually retain it. I know that's not actually what the National Curriculum is about.

Interviewer: But you think it's ...

Teacher: But I think that that's a true assessment. Because some children who can take away today won't be able to do it next week, so I feel when they demonstrate it, you know, I say that they've achieved it and other teachers might not work that way but ...

Assessment and teaching

Fundamentally, however, the issue is not one that centres on the inaccuracy of an assessment but rather its lack of utility in the business of being a teacher. It is quite clear from all the data presented in this paper so far that when primary teachers discuss their assessment practice they are thinking predominantly in terms of their own needs as teachers and to an extent the needs of pupils for formative guidance and encouragement. This is well summed up in the following comment on the utility of the traditional type of test used in the primary classroom.

Teacher: Where they're at has been decided by a formal spelling-type test, but even within that you see, I would say that although it gives me an indication, it only gives me an indication of a certain type of spelling memory ... so that's given an indication of how strong they are at spelling but not necessarily how they learn their spellings and how they can remember them ...

Interviewer: Yes. You told me that a lot of children did much better when they were writing words in context than on that one-off word test.

Given that the assessment discourse of teachers is essentially a pedagogic one, an internal personal discourse private to the teacher and at times the subject of professional discussion between teachers, it will be interesting to see the final impact of the various initiatives towards more whole-school support for systematic assessment and recording. Our interviews documented a number of instances in which schools as a whole or year group teachers had initiated a regular meeting, at which the staff brought in examples they felt exemplified particular kinds and levels of work and the teachers looked at them across the whole school to see if they could agree a level. This is typical of a growing pattern of staff collecting children's work and storing it as an evidential record — a pattern which again, our data suggest, is very much more in evidence in Key Stage 1. It may be that, when established, the existence of this evidential record will provide the basis for the kind of interpersonal idiosyncratic assessment discussion which teachers say they value, whilst at the same time providing a degree of structure and objectivity in terms of evidence to provide for communication to others, such as pupils and parents. Alternatively, this process may become part of that repertoire of assessment obligations which do not integrate with the pedagogic discourse of assessment and so become separated from classroom practice.

Meanwhile, teachers are remarking several effects on their teaching. There is a widespread feeling that there are more constraints and more pressures:

More pressure on you to, I think, feeling you should be producing results, having something to show, some evidence that the children have done it. I think maybe before, I wasn't so concerned about having something on paper which is, I feel, more now because we're having to annotate stuff, because we're having to have evidence to show something's happened, is different. It's a different emphasis.

Or another teacher:

[My teaching is] it's even more organized. I didn't think it would be possible. I used to get teased for being so organized it wasn't true.

The price of this increased organization, which many teachers report as part of the process of becoming more explicit and formal about assessment activities, is the tension with spontaneity and creativity in learning.

I think you're always thinking of a task at the end of the unit of work that will provide this evidence and then ... and the children then have to do this on their own whereas you ... as the unit's progressing you're wanting them to talk to each other, to learn from each other. Then ... they have to work in isolation otherwise it's not purely their work but I think it's the production of the evidence. You're always looking for a task that will fit in with the statement that you're assessing, and of course trying to slot it in at the end of the unit of work.

These more formal attempts to record both curriculum coverage and pupil achievement in relation to particular attainment targets take various forms for different teachers: sometimes they're individualized, sometimes for a particular group, or indeed, for a whole class, and even a whole year group in at least one of the schools studied. However, they share a common rationale as an attempt to generate comparable and explicit summary information about pupil achievement. Very frequently they are a source of tension since they are out of kilter with Key Stage 2 teachers' preference for ongoing cumulative assessment. In the PACE 1 study, as reported in *Changing English Primary Schools?*, classroom practice is related in the first instance to the teacher's own professional ideology, itself a construct resulting from a blend of personal biography, training, professional experience and national professional traditions, which is mediated by professional discourse. This professional discourse embodies the teachers' fundamental ideas about how education should be conducted but is mediated by the experienced reality of a sometimes conflicting network of obligations and practical constraints. This relationship is summarized in Figure 6.1.

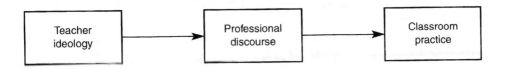

Figure 6.1 *Factors in classroom practice*

In this case the increasing emphasis on a strongly classified curriculum and strong pedagogic framing is matched by an increasingly explicit categorization of achievement in place of the invisible assessment which is such an integral part of child-centred pedagogy.

6.6 IMPACT ON CHILDREN

However, it remains to be seen what the significance of these currents is in terms of their impact on children's learning and indeed their attitude to their learning. Most teachers (52 per cent) felt children were largely unaware of assessments — that many enjoyed it (27 per cent) and very few were nervous (4 per cent) — partly because the teachers deliberately kept is low key (21 per cent). Nevertheless, many of the teachers studied (39 per cent) were convinced that the children in Years 3 and 4 were quite well aware of their differences in achievement, with 25 per cent feeling they were largely unaware — a finding that was borne out by our interviews with the children themselves — 35 per cent of teachers, however, felt that children were more conscious as a result of National Curriculum assessment. More important perhaps was the feeling that what might change was not children's awareness of such differences but the interpretation they placed on the significance of these differences, that children might begin to become anxious and react to level labels as the meaning and significance of such labels became more a common currency. Both Key Stage 1 and Key Stage 2 teachers seemed very aware of the potential dangers of children becoming too aware of differences in achievement levels and have developed a variety of strategies for preventing this, especially keeping assessment 'low key' (45 per cent) and/or routinized (14 per cent) and stressing positive achievement (54 per cent).

> Teacher: I don't think the National Curriculum *per se* does anything about a sense of failure or achievement. I think that comes down to the individual teacher who delivers it and responds to the children's work.

> Interviewer: I was also asking about assessment procedures. What about them?

> Teacher: Yes, that was the bit I was going to come on to. Assessment procedures could do, but again it's if they're handled sensitively. Like last year, I don't think, I hope, the children knew that they were being assessed or tested. Proof of that, if proof were needed, is that parents kept coming to me afterwards and saying when are we going to start testing, and I could say, 'We've done it.' You only communicate or develop a sense of failure, I think, if you come into the classroom ... well, I would feel this if you came into the classroom one day brandishing a sheaf of papers and saying, 'You, you and you, I tested you last week. Haha, you've failed. You're awful.' Because I like to think that the children just feel that they've either satisfied my requirements or not satisfied my requirements or they've felt themselves they've done the best for themselves and that's as far as we go in terms of success or failure in the classroom.

> Interviewer: Yes. Last year you made most of the SATs into a competition or a game or something, didn't you, and they ...

> Teacher: Which is the ethos we have in the classroom most of the time anyway. You've got to keep a competitive element there, otherwise some children just won't get stretched, and that's it. No more intense or serious than that. At the back of it all ... I mean, they don't see behind the scenes where you're grading them to an A, B, C, D grade or whatever. I don't think that it's necessary that they need know that. They have enough problems if they're not succeeding, without being labelled as well.

> Interviewer: Are there any things that you do specifically to address this issue? I mean you award points for a lot of things like progress and so on, rather than just comparing their achievement so that everyone gets a chance to get points?

> Teacher: You've got to be aware of that. I remember one school I was at when the Headmaster at the end of the year used to give out certificates to everybody and there was one

child and we thought, 'What's he giving a certificate for?' and in the end he called this child out on to the stage and we were waiting to find out and he said, 'For the best child at going to the toilet and coming back without making any fuss and taking the least possible time.' In the whole school! The moral is they've all got something to contribute. I mean maybe that's a Christian ethic but you've got to be always aware of that, to help them to develop their own self-esteem and to maintain their own sense of value. And all these little competitions and tricks and gimmicks and throwing hundreds of housepoints out, they think they're housepoint millionaires but at the end of the day it's meaningless, because they're only in competition with each other. They're all getting the same volume. And other teachers say, 'Well, why are you giving hundreds of housepoints like that. I only give two.' And I say, 'Well, it's alternative values. Your two is my hundred. It doesn't matter. It's like a foreign language.' But they feel, 'All right, I'm no good in school but I can collect more newspapers than anybody else and help my team to win.' And you've got over the biggest problem a lot of them have, I mean of saying, 'What's school for me? How does it fit my requirements? Why should I bother with it?'

Interviewer: So there's lots of ways in which they can contribute to the classroom without ...?

Teacher: Not least academically. I mean that comes up all the time. You saw that performance today and this week with maths groups as well. They were in competition table against table and got a lollipop, God help us. But you couldn't do that with older children because they'd just sneer at you but while they're like that — and they don't realize they're sort of cut throat at each other just for a lollipop! — what they're doing is pushing themselves that bit further.

Interviewer: Yes. They do seem to actually enjoy the competition itself, in a way, don't they?

Teacher: Yes. I wouldn't do it if there wasn't any enjoyment there because it would be miserable for all of us.

The teacher here is typical of many in seeking a way to convey to the children that all different kinds of achievement will be valued and that what matters is to keep the level of competition high so that everybody continues to try hard. The following examples express a similar sentiment:

Well, a lot of children can work much quicker than others. That's how I usually put it, that they can work quicker, and often I put work for all of them on the board and I say, 'Now, when you've finished the work on the board, you can do this work that I'm going to put on a paper,' and I put work up on a sheet of paper which is a continuation of the work that everybody has done, and it is, in fact, it is the quicker workers who then go on to the harder work but I don't think the poor achievers realize this.

and:

Yes, it's my policy, my philosophy I guess, that the child is travelling the route and that in the same way that a child grows at different heights at their own pace, they will learn at different paces, and I say that to the children that sometimes somebody will go fast and sometimes have a little spurt and some others are a little bit slower, 'But you just get there in your own time.'

6.7 CONCLUSION

Assessment and recording continue to figure prominently as a key area of the experienced changes in their working lives imposed on teachers by the 1988 Education Reform Act.

When teachers were asked 'Has your approach to teaching changed in response to the educational developments of the last few years?' these obligations figured prominently in their responses, as is shown in Table 6.5.

Table 6.5 *Changes in approaches to teaching (percentages)*

Content of curriculum	53
Nature of assessment	19
Nature of record-keeping	11
More involvement with colleagues	9
More planning	21
More aware of own practice	17
More structured	27
More creative opportunity	0
Less creative opportunity	7

Source: PACE 2 teacher interviews
Sample: 92 Year 3 and Year 4 teachers
Date: Autumn 1993
Note: Up to 4 responses coded.

It is not surprising therefore that assessment skills are identified as one of the areas that have gained most in importance in teachers' work in recent years. Table 6.6 shows teacher responses to a question about changes in the importance of different aspects of their work, giving clear evidence of the increasing importance of assessment.

Table 6.6 *'Do you think that each of the following are more or less important for a teacher's work now than in the past?' (percentages)*

	No response*	More	Same	Less
Clear aims	12	67	21	–
Teaching skills	12	37	51	–
Assessment skills	12	84	5	–
Subject knowledge	12	73	16	–
Classroom organization	12	45	44	1
Knowledge of children	12	16	69	4
Relationship with children	12	11	72	7
Maintain order	12	15	71	2

* including teachers who qualified post-ERA
Source: PACE 2 teacher interviews
Sample: 92 Year 3 and Year 4 teachers
Date: Autumn 1993

Indeed, Table 6.6 raises a host of important questions about how the Education Reform Act has affected the perceived priorities of teachers. Firstly there is evidence of 'intensification' — very few aspects of the job are regarded as less important than formerly. However, it is clarity of aims, assessment skills and subject knowledge which have figured most prominently as requirements of change. Against this, teaching skills, knowledge of and relationship with children, maintaining order and, to a lesser extent, classroom organization, have stayed as constants in the core of teachers' work. Thus there is little evidence as yet of any shift from a child-centred ideology of teaching. Rather, a reconfirmation of the findings of PACE 1 that teachers will add new practices to their repertoire as required by law but, in the short term at least, will seek to mediate the goals of these new practices to support their existing understanding of what primary teaching is and indeed their values concerning what it should be. The initial analysis of Key Stage 1 teachers' views and practices concerning assessment which have been presented in this chapter suggests that, in the longer term, the effect of struggling with the required changes in practice — in this case assessment — may lead to changes in understanding concerning the nature of primary teaching — if not, as yet, of its core ideology as espoused by teachers in this country.

Whether the same pattern eventually characterizes assessment at Key Stage 2 is currently a much more problematic question. The draft orders (July 1994; confirmed by an announcement from Gillian Shephard, Secretary of State for Education, 6 September 1994) for external marking of Key Stage 2 SATs provide little or no money for assessment training for teachers (Munby, 1994) and much less requirement for teachers to integrate formal assessment obligations into their practice. Black (1994) quotes American experience in this respect:

> When given sole responsibility for the public certification of their pupils, teachers used their own summative methods and did not explore the development of formative assessment as the state planners intended. (Butler and Beasley, 1987, cited in Black 1994, p. 201)

a finding which prompts Black to pose the question, 'What should be the optimum relationship between the formative and summative functions of teacher assessment?'

In the terms of this paper, we ask: Is the shift from constant, intuitive, formative assessment to more systematic, planned and recorded semi-summative assessment which is taking place in Key Stage 1 and seems likely to take place in Key Stage 2 likely to result, as some teachers feel, in more carefully targeted, planned and individualized teaching? Or rather, will it move assessment to a largely summative role, where its explicitness and public language inhibits the fluid immediacy of a genuinely formative, learning-oriented assessment discourse? The findings of PACE 1, as well as a number of other studies (e.g. Archibald and Porter, 1994) argue that teachers will always decide when and how to follow policy when it comes to day-to-day classroom practice. Such decisions are informed by their professional values and their understanding concerning the practices that best serve those values. Power therefore operates not through coercion but in a more insidious way through the re-structuring of such understanding — and ultimately, values — through changes in discourse. Whether this will happen and what its consequences may be for children's learning are questions which it is too soon to answer. We can, however, already be clear that the monitoring of teachers' assessment discourse as the example below illustrates, will provide insights into the more general fundamental characteristics of primary teachers and their teaching in this country and of the significance of this for children. This is the goal that the PACE project will continue to pursue. The final quotation in this paper provides an illustration of the way in which teachers' assessment discourse articulates their underlying pedagogic philosophy and values and hence, the importance of studying such descriptions.

> Well, I think when you're not explaining something, a task, to them, or you are not actually explaining something that you know is new, then most of your talking with the children, unless it's organizational, is actually assessing what they understand, what they know. I mean, when you're looking at the books and marking it ... you're just assessing it and you've got different criteria in your head as to what you're going to say for different children. For instance with David, who is one of the children you've been looking at, I'm trying to get him to slow down and check before he brings it to me.

Chapter 7

Teachers and Pupils: Expectations and Judgements

Dorothy Abbott

7.1 INTRODUCTION

Few teachers will be able to approach a class with a completely open mind about their pupils; even in a new school the screen will not remain blank for long. If a colleague says, 'Oh, you have Nigel — poor you!', or 'Alexandra's an absolute joy; wait until you read her stories,' it is difficult to believe that one's views of Alexandra and Nigel will not be influenced. This does not necessarily mean that there will be negative consequences for Nigel, for he may receive particularly warm support, being considered to deserve every chance to redeem himself, but images of those children are likely to linger in their teacher's mind. In most school situations teachers will have much clearer bases for their judgements: records are passed from class to class and staffroom conversation is frequently concerned with pupils, their behaviour and their achievement levels. Do such preconceptions matter?

In many cases it has been claimed that they matter a great deal, that children may be approached differently, and possibly unfairly, by their teachers because of such issues as class, gender, race or received information on attainment levels, and that their future achievement may be adversely affected by such treatment. In other words, children expected by a teacher to be academically successful may unintentionally be given more encouragement or more positive feedback on performance than those perceived to be at the other end of the spectrum, and this treatment will in itself *lead* to higher achievement in those pupils. Ominously, of course, the reverse will apply; teacher expectations lead to a self-fulfilling prophecy for failure as well as for success.

Is this true? One aim of the PACE research project was to examine teachers' opinions of their pupils. (We avoid the term 'expectations', in case this is seen as implying prediction. Teachers were interviewed at different times in the school year, sometimes as late as June; at this stage their perceptions of children would have been consolidated by experience, and could not be described as expectations.) It was no concern of the project to judge these judgements, to measure them against any doubtful 'objective' assessments of children's achievements; rather, other questions were considered.

Did the views of different teachers, year on year, of the same pupils, remain consistent from class to class? If so, was this because teachers used the same criteria for their opinions, and applied them reliably? Or did an individual pupil enter each new class with an achieved status, whether as a 'star' or as a nuisance or as a struggler, in which case did that status become reified, allowing little chance for improvement or other change? Were teachers' views of pupils' behaviour reflected in the conduct recorded through systematic observation, and were they related in any way to the views expressed by children of their teachers and of their own curricular strengths, weaknesses and preferences?

This chapter focuses on some of these issues, beginning with a review of some previous research and debate. It goes on to describe the methodology of the PACE study of this area and to outline teachers' perceptions of their pupils' attainment and social behaviour. It then summarizes the levels assigned by teachers to individual pupils, year by year, and continues by attempting to relate these perceptions to children's socio-economic backgrounds and gender. (In only one of the classrooms studied in detail were children from ethnic minorities included in the random sample of pupils, and no evidence related to ethnicity can be presented here.) Finally, comments made on individual pupils are examined in more detail, and an attempt is made to relate these to children's own perceptions.

The central argument here is that teachers taking part in this study were considered to have based their evaluations of pupils' attainment and behaviour on observation and experience in the classroom and the school. Their explicated judgements drew on detailed knowledge of the work produced by their pupils and of their relationships with teachers and classmates; we found no evidence that social class, gender or socio-economic backgrounds were linked to low expectations of attainment and thus to polarization.

7.2   PREVIOUS RESEARCH

Rosenthal and Jacobson's study, *Pygmalion in the Classroom* (1968), set out to show that teacher expectations did have an effect. Teachers were told, untruthfully, that predictive tests showed that certain pupils were likely soon to make great academic gains, although, in fact, the pupils were randomly selected. When tests were carried out some months later, these 'bloomers' had strikingly higher test scores than those of their classmates not so designated; in the words of the authors: 'a significant expectancy advantage was found' (p. 176). Teachers probably watched their special children more closely, and this greater attentiveness may have led to more rapid reinforcement of correct responses with a consequent increase in pupils' learning. However, the design and methodology of this study have been severely criticized: Boydell (1978) outlines some of its flaws, among them the use of inappropriate IQ tests, the lack of standardization in administering these, inadequate statistical processing of data and researchers' failure to follow up children lost to the study. Moreover, teachers questioned later were unable to remember the names of most of the children named as future high attainers.

Few expectations are based on such specific information from an outside source, however; teachers form their own opinions of children's potential and behaviour and these perceptions have important implications for pupils' future careers in school. Hargreaves *et al.* (1975) outline the links between the self-fulfilling prophecy theory and labelling theory, the latter suggesting that a pupil who commits a deviant act may be labelled as a deviant, experience problems as a result of such labelling and continue to act in a deviant manner in an attempt to deal with these problems. Typing of pupils may thus be reinforced, although Hargreaves *et al.,* whose study was based in secondary schools, show that such views of pupils need not be fixed. Teachers may change their minds — although they are likely to assume that pupils have changed, rather than that their initial judgement was at fault.

Clearly, a teacher who observes that a nine-year-old child cannot spell three-letter words or read simple books will conclude that this pupil has learning difficulties; there will be obvious grounds for such a judgement. Frequently, however, it has been asserted that teachers' expectations are not well founded, but are based on assumptions related to class, race or gender.

Sharp and Green (1975), for example, argued that the infant teachers they observed differentiated among and stratified their pupils, attributing to them such qualities as being, in the case of a minority, 'difficult', 'dim' or 'really peculiar'. The identities of such pupils were thus reified; they were 'problems', in contrast to the majority of 'normal' pupils, described by Sharp and Green as bright, biddable and easily controllable, and in contrast to 'the elite of the social structure ... the few "bright" children':

> This sort of pupil fits the teacher's ideal for children 'from a good area' or a 'middle class' district. This type is bright and articulate, interested and interesting ... [and] ... most approximates to the teacher's own ideal of what school children should be like (p. 123)

The teachers observed, it was claimed, devoted more time and attention to these children, who thus became more successful, apparently confirming the self-fulfilling prophecy theory.

Other studies have seen the situation as more complex. In his study of infant schools, King (1978) found that, although middle-class homes were more often assessed favourably, teachers' judgements were related less to class — parents' occupations were frequently unknown — than to the degree of parental interest displayed. Teachers in one school in a socially deprived area did indeed explain pupils' low achievement in terms of their family-home backgrounds. King, however, is sceptical of self-fulfilling prophecy theories, finding that these explanations *followed* appraisals of low achievement rather than preceding them. What is more:

> the manifest and purposeful consequences of this definition were attempts to improve their

levels of progress through remedial reading, speech therapy and the adjustment [special needs] class. (p. 133)

King's later study of junior schools argued that the typification of pupils by teachers was a complex process, involving not only homes and families, but also perceived learning capacity, friendship patterns, health and behaviour (1989, p. 72). The analysis following in the ORACLE study, of the relationship between social class, achievement and interaction, showed that pupils from middle-class backgrounds reached, on average, higher achievement levels than those from working-class homes. Interestingly, however, this large-scale study using a systematic, pre-coded observation system:

> found differences in attainment between middle-class and working-class pupils, and differences in rates of progress. But it did not find differences in treatment which would account for these … it is very unlikely that, in general, the poorer performance of working-class pupils compared with middle-class pupils attending the same school can be explained by reference to conscious or unconscious unfairness on the part of teachers…. the present analysis makes highly questionable some explanations for social class differences in school performance that have … been gaining credence … (Croll, 1981, p. 129)

Similar debates have taken place on teacher expectations based on gender or race stereotypes, and again the picture is complicated. Tizard *et al.* (1988), a study of children's progress and behaviour in 33 infant schools, found that at the pre-school stage there were few differences between ethnic groups in early reading, writing, vocabulary and maths skills. At this level, however, and indeed throughout the infant school, both black and white girls had superior writing skills to boys. At the end of the infant school black girls were ahead of all other groups in reading and writing, while black boys were furthest behind. At maths, white boys made most progress, while all boys were ahead of girls; in reading, however, girls were well ahead. White boys were found to be most work-oriented and to be happiest about going to school, while black boys were more often — although still quite seldom — observed to be 'fooling about' and were more often seen to receive teacher criticism. Social class differences played very little part in this study, as the children were largely working-class. The differences in progress were found hard to explain; teachers did seem to have higher expectations of boys than of girls, especially in maths, but there was no evidence of ethnically related differences in expectations. Behaviour problems were not related to progress when other factors, including teacher expectations, were taken into account, but it was thought possible that behaviour problems could have influenced those expectations; the interaction between gender, race, behaviour and progress was regarded as too complex to be analysed further with the available data.

Moving up the age scale, Mortimore *et al.* (1988) considered teacher expectations of children in London junior schools in terms of age, gender, social class, ethnicity, perceived ability and behaviour. Children from non-manual backgrounds were usually more successful in cognitive assessment tasks and in academic progress, but they were also likely to be more highly rated in terms of 'ability', irrespective of their academic performance. These pupils, however, did not receive more teacher attention; on the contrary, pupils from manual and unskilled backgrounds, and particularly those whose fathers were absent, received more supervision of their work.

Girls were found to have slightly higher attainments in mathematics by their third year, and significantly higher attainments in reading and writing throughout the junior school. They were also rated more highly by their teachers in their achievement levels, attitudes to work and behaviour, although ratings of boys' ability was slightly flattering, compared with their cognitive assessments. Boys received more teacher contact, but this was chiefly related to comments on behaviour; they also received more work supervision and feedback, but girls received more praise. Both sexes were heard reading with similar frequency.

It has been claimed that teacher expectations have been influenced by negative stereotypes of different ethnic groups; the Rampton Report (1981), for example, suggested links between such low expectations and the academic achievement of ethnic minority pupils. Carrington and Short (1989) approach the question from another angle, suggesting that teachers' experience of ethnic groups in classrooms might have influenced their expectations, rather than the reverse. The Junior School Project found that teachers' perceptions of children were not related to their ethnic backgrounds, but were strongly related to attainment levels, which were in themselves lower for African–Caribbean and some Asian pupils. African–Caribbean pupils were considered to have more behavioural problems, and it was suggested that this might have accounted for the extra time teachers gave to hearing these pupils read, and to non-work related conversations with them. Work-related discussion, supervision and feedback were similar for all ethnic groups.

These are difficult issues to analyse; in their meta-analysis of research on the bases of teacher expectancies Dusek and Joseph (1983) concluded that, among other factors, conduct, race and social class were related to teacher expectancies, but that gender and the number of parents at home were not. The authors pointed out, however, that it is important to consider the context of teacher expectancies, that most research examined had been cross-sectional, taking no account of longitudinal changes in teachers' views as they become more familiar with their pupils through the school year, and that more research was needed on multiple/interactive, rather than on single, influences. Moreover, they suggested that expectations 'may be based on reasonable and appropriate information and may ... benefit the student'. In a similar overview of research literature, Brophy concluded:

> that a minority of teachers have major expectation effects on their students' achievement, but that such effects are minimal for most teachers because their expectations are generally accurate and open to corrective feedback. (Brophy, 1983, p. 631)

The debate has clearly been intense, and few questions can be said to have been answered definitively. It must be stressed here that most of the information on which this chapter is based has been drawn from what teachers said in interviews. Long-term ethnographic research (Pollard and Filer, 1996) demonstrates that children's school progress is related to self-image and a sense of well-being; these develop through a complex web of influences. Pupil–teacher interaction is only one factor in this structure; parent and sibling relationships, friendships and physical circumstances are all involved

7.3 PACE RESEARCH METHODS ON TEACHER TYPIFICATIONS OF PUPILS

During the full week of classroom studies which took place in each of nine schools in each year, from 1990/91 to 1993/94, teachers were asked to describe their pupils. All pupils in the year group of the cohort were discussed briefly, while the six randomly selected target pupils in each class were described in more detail; this chapter focuses on these target pupils, who were systematically observed and were themselves interviewed. Broadfoot (1979) discusses research which appears to demonstrate that 'non-cognitive assessment is at least as important as the more obvious academic evaluations of the classroom', and that most teachers find it virtually impossible to separate the two areas. In the PACE interviews, however, teachers' attention was drawn to the distinction between academic attainment and social relationships and behaviour. Teachers were asked to allot children to one of five attainment levels, 1 being highest, and, separately, to describe social relationships open-endedly. These descriptions were then used retrospectively by members of the research team to allocate behaviour grades in the same terms as the attainment grades. This required careful consideration, although extremes of attainment and behaviour were easier to recognize, but, after moderation among team members, grades were matched to descriptions as follows:

1. Always sensible, kind, friendly, hard-working, well-behaved and popular.
2. Popular, usually amiable, occasional arguments, no real problems, usually tries hard.
3. Quite amiable, sometimes 'moody', mixture of effort and laziness.
4. Can behave quite well, but can upset other children; makes an effort sporadically but does not work to perceived ability level.
5. Very quarrelsome, aggressive, lazy, unpopular.

Obviously, there were variations within each of these categories which necessitated the use of considerable judgement; a child might be graded as 3 or 4 in terms of relationships, not because of aggressive behaviour but because of what was seen as excessive timidity or shyness. While recognizing these limitations, an average was calculated of each pupil's attainment level and relationship level over the four years of the first and second phases of the PACE study. For the analysis of continuity below, the original five point scales are used and reflect assessments at specific points in time. However, for the analysis of socio-economic group differences the central categories have been collapsed to give a three point scale of 'high', 'medium' and 'low' with regard to averaged assessments and averaged assessments, are also used in the analyses of gender and ethnicity.

7.4   CONTINUITY IN TEACHER ASSESSMENTS

The longitudinal design of the PACE study means that the same children were described by their teachers on up to four occasions. In order to look at continuity between teacher assessments, Tables 7.1 and 7.2 consider paired assessments for attainment and behaviour/relationships respectively. The 103 entries in the tables are paired descriptions separated by one year and, in the great majority of cases, made by different teachers. The descriptions come from a total of 35 teachers and were made of 41 pupils for whom descriptions on at least three occasions were available. For example, an entry in the top left hand cell of a table represents a child who was rated '1' by a teacher in one year of the study and rated '1' again in the subsequent year.

The patterns revealed in Tables 7.1 and 7.2 suggest that extreme variations in different teachers' views of pupils year by year were relatively unusual. Of the 103 entries in each table, ascribed attainment levels varying by more than one grade occured in only twelve cases and the same applied for behavioural levels. But it is also clear that teacher perceptions of pupils did not typically become an ascribed identity which was taken over by subsequent teachers. There is considerable variation in teacher ascriptions at the extremes as well as in the middle of the scales. There is some support in the tables for the view that 'high' ascriptions are more permanent than 'low' ones. The majority of pupils in the 'top' category in one year remained there while this is not so for the 'bottom' category.

Table 7.1   *Continuity in teacher assessment of attainment levels*

Early assessment	Later assessment				
	1 (high)	2	3	4	5 (low)
1 (high)	13	7	–	–	–
2	5	4	12	–	–
3	4	9	13	4	2
4	–	2	3	7	4
5 (low)	–	–	4	6	4

Source: PACE 1 and PACE 2 Classroom Studies
Sample: 35 teachers, 41 pupils
Date: Autumn 1990 and 1991, summer 1993 and 1994

Table 7.2   *Continuity in teacher assessment of relationships and behaviour*

Early assessment	Later assessment				
	1 (high)	2	3	4	5 (low)
1 (high)	15	6	1	–	–
2	3	3	13	5	–
3	1	7	9	10	1
4	–	2	7	12	2
5 (low)	–	–	2	4	–

Source: PACE 1 and PACE 2 Classroom Studies
Sample: 35 teachers, 41 pupils
Date: Autumn 1990 and 1991, summer 1993 and 1994

7.5 PUPILS' ATTAINMENT AND THEIR SOCIO-ECONOMIC BACKGROUNDS

To examine the relationship, if any, between pupils' social class and teachers' views of the children, the PACE project used the abbreviated version of the ILEA Educational Priority Data scale: 1 (non-manual), 2 (skilled manual) and 3 (unskilled). Parental occupations were classified according to this scale using information which was initially provided by teachers. These are very broadly based groups, but it is not clear that a more finely graded scale could have been used as it became clear that many teachers were vague about the occupations of their pupils' parents; what they said frequently had to be clarified by further inquiries in the schools.

There must be some reservations then, related to the knowledge teachers had, or did not have, of pupils' backgrounds, and the accuracy of what they said, and to the limitations of the coding system. Accepting this, we found that the 41 pupils present for at least three years of the study were classified as shown in Table 7.3. This table shows that the proportion of high-scoring pupils was higher among non-manual families but there were high attainers among the lowest socio-economic group, and one low attainer in the highest. Nothing here suggests an automatic linking of pupil evaluations to the occupations of their parents.

The interviews often mirrored those in King's 1978 study of infant schools; teachers were more interested in the relationships parents had with the schools. Thus at one extreme we were told: 'I don't know his social background, but I've met Mum many times, because she comes in every week to hear reading.' and; '... a lovely family; they've all been superb at creative writing, poetry, stories ... They're a really nice family...'. In strong contrast were the comments on the situation of Moira, '... I don't think father's around; various men seem to come and go... Mother is very fond of her, over-indulgent. She has an elder sister whom I met under very unfortunate circumstances. One afternoon Moira said, "There's Mummy", so I let her go; then a distraught teenager came in, swearing madly at me for letting Moira go when Mummy was not really there. Oh, it was a ... we had to call the police. Yet Moira herself is lovely; I wonder how she copes so well ... Mummy did come to see me after the incident ... she said she didn't think the sister was on drugs, but it could have been drink.' Moira herself, then, was highly regarded by her teacher; unfavourable impressions of other members of her family appeared not to influence this. Unfavourable judgements on families were occasionally made, but these were usually associated with admiring or sympathetic comments on the pupil. Daphne's family was apparently well known to social workers in the area, who liaised with the school. Her Year 1 teacher said:

Table 7.3   *Pupils' perceived attainment grades related to their socio-economic backgrounds*

	Attainment		
Socio-economic group	High	Medium	Low
High	6	9	1
Medium	1	10	2
Low	2	7	3

Source: PACE 1 and PACE 2 Classroom Studies
Sample: 35 teachers, 41 pupils
Date: Autumn 1990 and 1991, summer 1993 and 1994

> She often comes in with no breakfast. Her mother doesn't get up in the morning; she gets herself up. The family home is apparently strewn with dirty clothes, pets, etc. Daphne is left to fend for herself; she's the youngest of four children who all have the same problem — their clothes and their hair and their general appearance — which affects other children's reactions to her. She's isolated because of her appearance; children pass comments on it.

However, Daphne's clearly unfavourable home circumstances did not adversely affect her teacher's opinion of her:

> She is a low achiever, partly through many absences for no particular reason, but she is actually quite bright, imaginative and talented ... quite talented in her art work. She's showing signs of a good memory ... She's a delightful child, a lovely personality, always kind.

It was clear from this and later interviews, and from observational notes made during visits to the school, that Daphne's teachers worked hard to improve her relationships and that, although little changed in her home, many of her classmates improved their attitudes towards her.

7.6 PUPILS' ATTAINMENT AND GENDER

It appears, then, that PACE research did not support claims that working-class children are generally viewed less favourably by their teachers than are their middle-class peers. Similarly, little evidence was found to support any theories that connect teacher expectations with gender. Although random selection procedures resulted in roughly equal numbers of boys and girls in the PACE sample, the 41 children who took part in the study for at least three years included 23 girls and 18 boys. Girls averaged 2.58 in their attainment grades, while boys' average was lower at 3.02; behaviour grades were remarkably similar, with girls averaging 2.84 and boys 2.8. Girls were therefore viewed rather more favourably in terms of attainment, while differences in behaviour grades were virtually absent. The relatively small numbers here make it difficult to draw meaningful conclusions, but our findings seem to accord well with those of, for example, Tizard and Mortimore, cited earlier.

7.7 SOME INDIVIDUAL PUPILS

Tables 7.1 and 7.2 suggested that there seemed to be a fair degree of consistency in teachers' descriptions of pupils' achievement and relationships. Accepting the limitations imposed by the numbers involved here, there seemed to be little evidence to link this pattern to stereotyping of children, to early categorizing which was passed on from teacher to teacher and became reified. No teacher referred in an interview to a child's school record or reputation; nor, perhaps surprisingly, was National Curriculum assessment through SATs mentioned — even in the school year following these. Comments were usually based on descriptions of what teachers observed in their classrooms, as the following cases of individual pupils may illustrate.

Yasmin, for example, at the inner-city school, Meadway, was consistently rated in the lowest attainment group. Her Year 1 teacher said that Yasmin was 'an underachiever', suggesting that she did not receive support at home, while the next teacher described her work as poor. Yasmin, she said, seemed to have no idea of the purpose of school, had no reading or writing skills and was only a little more successful at maths. In Year 3 Yasmin was said to have 'great problems'; she was successful at art and her handwriting was neat, but there had been very little progress in the 'basics'. Her attitude was described as 'laid back'; she was apparently happy to be at school and unworried by her low achievement. It may be considered that these comments sound like views based on observation and knowledge of a pupil, rather than on an ascribed identity; it is difficult to believe that Yasmin's teachers' opinions would have been affected had they taken part in Rosenthal's self-fulfilling prophecy experiment and been told that she was predicted to be a high achiever.

Taking into account what her teachers said, Yasmin's own comments offered few surprises. In her first, Year 1, interview, she claimed to enjoy and to be good at maths, reading, writing and science, although she was unable to explain what science was. When asked what she liked about some specified activities, however, Yasmin was unable to articulate her reasons, answering, 'Cos that's why — I just did.' When she was asked what she enjoyed most at school, her response was as follows:

Yasmin: Writing.

Interviewer: Really?

Yasmin: No, not really; I like dressing up and building.

In Year 2, Yasmin was asked to describe a group activity with her teacher, in which she had taken part; this had included weighing objects and testing for floating characteristics. The interviews were structured in that questions were pre-specified, but there was scope, within time limits, to probe children's answers more fully. Pre-specified questions are marked * in the following extract:

Interviewer: What were you doing with the tank of water and the balance?*

Yasmin: We had to do things like — the cup is heavy and the cubes are getting heavier and down.

Interviewer: And after that?

Yasmin: We see if some was sinking.

Interviewer: Did some things sink?

Yasmin: Some; the marble went down and the cup — no — yes, it did, but them two things, the ball and the — the marble — um...

Interviewer: Why do you think some things sank and some floated?

Yasmin: Some things are light and some are slow.

Yasmin still claimed to be 'good' at all subjects, but her artistic skills, mentioned by her Year 3 teacher, were already important to her:

Yasmin: I like doing painting really slowly ... paintings are good, and we don't muck up our clothes; we wear aprons.

By the next year, Yasmin had developed a less confident assessment of her own achievement; painting was still important to her: 'Painting is nice; you make something with it.' However, she had not enjoyed a maths activity because it was 'too hard for me', and although she still claimed to be 'good at writing', she later named 'writing hard words' as an area where she was not successful. 'I get them wrong', she explained, 'and I can't spell words; the others learn more'.

There may be further evidence that the PACE teachers did not rigidly typify their pupils in the record of Tom at Greenmantle. His Year 1 teacher placed him at Level 5 in attainment, saying that he was immature, had good general knowledge but poor manipulative skills and was 'not especially clued in' to routine; he would happily do nothing. In Year 2, Tom was said to be in attainment group 4; he needed special help for writing and his average attainment was still low, but his reading was improving. He was described as positive, enthusiastic, 'not unintelligent' and likely to improve in the following year. The next teacher did re-grade Tom as level 2 for attainment; his handwriting was still below standard because of poor motor control, but the content of his writing was said to be 'quite good; above average' and he read well. In the final year of this period, Tom had moved back down to attainment level 3. His Year 4 teacher again focused on the presentation of Tom's work as a weak point, in spite of the efforts he made, while describing his other work as average and his general knowledge and retention of facts as good:

> His handwriting's really, really bad. His pencil holding is poor and his whole presentation ... We can talk about what we've done or something we did last week and he'll remember all those things, but his handwriting's so poor ... he'll start and take an awfully long time and it still looks bad, so he kind of gives up.

Again, Tom's record suggests that his teachers made up their own minds on their pupils' attainment levels and were able to provide explication of their judgements. It was also clear that Tom was not blamed for the poor presentation of his work; he tried hard, his mother supported him, and his teacher, while trying various strategies, admitted to feeling perplexed.

Tom himself showed some awareness of his motor control difficulties while he was still in Year 1; he was, he said, 'not very good at drawing around stuff'. In Year 3 he seemed to have gained some confidence, while still focusing on the same skill, saying that when he showed his work to his teacher he felt, 'happy, because if I've done my neatest writing, I think she'll say, "Really good."' During his next interview, in Year 3, Tom expressed pleasure in maths, sports, using modelling toys and 'making things'. However, Tom now saw painting as an area of failure, 'because I can't think of what to paint and I don't know what colours to use', although pleasure in creativity was evident: 'at home I've got loads of modelling toys, and I make stuff ... islands and boats, out of papier maché and pipe cleaners'. In contrast, handwriting was named as the activity Tom liked least.

Oliver received the most consistently high ratings of any target pupil, both in terms of academic attainment and of behaviour, having been rated through the four years of the study as 1, 1, 2, 1 for the former and as 1 in each year for the latter. Comments on his academic achievement included:

> Very, very good in all areas ... an all-rounder ... (Y1)

> Very, very able ... picks up new things very easily ... most able in all class subjects ... he likes school and brings in information ... a wonderful memory ... (Y2)

> Above average ... very capable and works very hard ... a very good attitude ... (Y3)
> [This was the only teacher who placed Oliver in the second attainment group.]

> In the top ten ... in the top six, in fact ... a very good attitude to school ... (Y4)

Oliver was a diabetic, and his responsible and stoical attitude was much admired. All teachers reported that he was aware of when he needed a sweet drink to raise his blood sugar level, and that he dealt with this, as well as carrying out his own insulin injections, quietly and unobtrusively. His parents' socio-economic group was unknown to three of the four teachers, although they all described the family as supportive and interested. The Year 3 teacher, however, thought that Oliver's parents were not 'in the professional area ... We think that this is perhaps where Oliver loses out, in that often there aren't enough experiences outside school to support the ability that this child has.'

Oliver, even in Year 1, clearly thought in terms of a hierarchy of attainment. When asked how well he read, he replied, 'Good. I'm on 4a now, I think. I'm good, but Tracy, Helen and Jason are in the lead, I think. We watch each other and see how we're getting on.' To a similar question about writing, he said, 'Good; I've got a word book. It's only the ones that are really brainy that get them. I can write on my own when I know some of the words.' Oliver had clear ideas on the most and least successful pupils in the class, but his explanation did not imply any superior innate ability:

'Some people don't talk so much — and they think.' He continued through the next three years of the study to rate his achievement level as 'Good' in most areas, but his views seemed to be based on careful assessment, rather than on self-satisfaction. In Year 2, for example, he thought that he was 'OK; just alright,' at science, while in Year 3 he said of his writing: 'It's not that tidy; I've always had a problem with my writing' and added that he found geography rather hard. In Year 4, Oliver differed from some of the pupils interviewed in distinguishing clearly between the appearance and the content of his written English. He liked writing stories, he said, because 'I have good ideas in my head', and he would not be satisfied with a piece of work, 'if it looked scruffy and I hadn't done much and if it didn't have good ideas in it'. In this Oliver differed from pupils observed by Bennett and his colleagues (1984) whose perceived criteria for high quality writing centred on neatness.

Although a pupil's words can be quoted, it is difficult to characterize an attitude other than impressionistically. It did seem, however, that Oliver, while confident about his school work, was fairly nonchalant; he had no reason to worry about his achievement, but nor did it delight him. If he had been over-confident or boastful, it seems unlikely that he would have been selected, as he frequently was, as a child with whom his peers liked to play.

In the same school, Eliot was placed in the mid-range of attainment by each teacher, but, after being described as seeming to be 'alright with other children — no problem' by his Year 1 teacher, received glowing reports in the next two years on his social relationships and general behaviour. His Year 2 teacher said:

> He's beautiful ... He loves coming to school ... He comes in smiling ... He's fine with the other children, very popular ... I can't really fault him ... a class of Eliots would be a dream...

and his Year 3 teacher supported this:

> A very popular little boy, very nice-looking and popular ... a charming personality ... certainly no aggression ... He's got a lovely attitude to school.

His Year 4 teacher saw Eliot as a 'charming little boy', who was perhaps a little immature, but whose attitude to school was 'very good indeed'. What is strongly contrasted in Oliver's and Eliot's cases, however, is that Oliver was consistently popular among his classmates, named by several pupils in each class as one of the children they liked to play with, as well as one of those who were 'good at their work'. Eliot, however, after being nominated as a friend by one child only in each of the first two classes, received no nominations at all in the third and fourth years — and this in a large class, consistently well over thirty. What is interesting is not that teachers' opinions of pupils may not match those of children, but that occasionally teachers seemed to misjudge peer popularity so noticeably; all thought that Eliot was well liked.

However accurately or inaccurately, teachers' views of Oliver and Eliot were fairly constant over the four-year span. At Audley school, on the other hand, two children who were consistently highly evaluated for attainment showed different patterns for their behaviour ratings. Both Mandy's and Brian's attainment levels were: 1, 1, 1, 1; but Brian's behaviour was rated: 1, 2, 3, 4, and Mandy's: 1, 2, 2, 4. Why, when these children received the highest academic rating in the class from each teacher, did their behaviour seem to deteriorate? In Year 1, Brian's social relationships were described as 'fine', although in Year 2 he was thought to have been formerly 'a bit clinging and attention-seeking', but to be 'improving'. In Year 3, however, Brian was described as attention-seeking and as :

> very much like Jekyll and Hyde. He can be absolutely horrible when he decides to be, and then he can be lovable. The other children see him as naughty ... they think he's babyish ... they find it hard to reconcile that he's very clever and yet seeks the amount of attention that he does ... He's also found to have been involved in stealing ... He's **so** advanced mentally in one way and yet he's so retarded emotionally ...

In his next class, Brian's teacher said of him:

> If he doesn't want to do something, then that's it; he won't do it. There's no argument — 'I don't want to do it; that's that.' He's not good with the other children; he's very argumentative with them — even with his friend, Daniel, there's falling out and he hits him now and then. If anyone says anything to him, it's all: 'Right, you're going to get done now — you're going to get done!'

In the last two teacher interviews, details about Brian's background emerged which could well be seen as relevant to his behaviour. Born to a 'very young mother', he had been adopted after going into care and living in a series of children's homes and foster families — 22, according to his Year 3 teacher. No previous foster parents had been prepared to adopt him, and his adoptive parents were regarded by this teacher as 'being very brave, because he'll either be very rewarding or a disaster'. Yet the disturbance in Brian's background seemed to have no adverse effect at all on his academic performance. In Year 1 he was described as 'fine ... no problems ... ', and in Year 2 as 'bright — one of the best academically in the class'. His Year 3 teacher said that he was 'more than exceptional at maths, bordering on the brilliant ... absolutely logical ... he has a fantastic vocabulary ... his reading ability is very, very good'. This opinion was reflected in the comments of the Year 4 teacher: 'He's exceptionally bright. He really is. Especially in maths. Very, very bright.'

What does Brian's record tell us about teacher expectations and self-fulfilling prophecies? It seems unlikely that a teacher who heard about his difficult first years would have predicted a bright academic future for Brian, and no teacher ever attempted to claim credit for his performance. His background was used to explain, and by implication to excuse, at least partly, his obstinacy and aggression, but, like Oliver, he seemed to be seen as having innate 'ability'. Nor did his behaviour pattern fit Sharp and Green's suggestion of a teacher's ideal pupil, described above as 'bright and articulate, interested and interesting ... the teacher's own ideal of what school children should be like' (1975, p. 123), and who, it was claimed, thus became more successful. It is possible to speculate upon Brian's apparently worsening behaviour as he moved up through the school and to relate this to his insecure beginnings, or to the possibility of boredom through insufficient challenge. What does seem clear, however, is that his reported disobedience and quarrels had no adverse effect on his academic progress nor on his teachers' estimation of this.

Brian's self-assessment was consistently quite high; his Year 1 answers were laconic; he was 'quite good' at everything. In Year 2 he thought his reading was 'very good; only Samantha has got as far as me', but that he was 'OK' at maths. The interviewer queried this, saying 'Just OK?', and Brian qualified his answer: 'Well, I suppose I am good really; we are the top group.' In the same interview, Brian again mentioned his group's achievement level: 'We're the cleverest.' By the Year 3 interview, Brian's confidence seemed more firmly established; responses included: 'Good; she mostly gives me stars,' 'Good; first in the class,' and, 'I can do it better.' Success was still important; he did not like painting: 'cos every time I paint I always get the colours running'. In addition, though, and unusually in these interviews, Brian seemed to seek in his work not merely success, but challenge and stimulation too. In Year 3, he described a maths task: 'taking away, adding and graphs ... it's really boring, 'cos it's too easy'. Brian's high opinion of his achievement was sustained in Year 4, when some of his responses included:

... basically, I'm good at everything.

[Maths?] Excellent — nearly the highest in the school.

I like sport a lot. I've got the muscles and things for it. I'm going to be in the sports for running, I think.

I can beat practically anyone in chess.

It may be hard to warm to such apparent immodesty, but it does not seem that Brian's high self-assessment was simply conceit. His teachers' evaluations of his attainment supported his own, and there are probably relatively few Year 4 pupils who would answer a question about an observed activity, as he did, in this way:

We were doing geography, reading questions and answering them, and drawing maps, eight squares by eight — two cm per square, if you want precise details. Yes, I liked it, because you can get better at things; doing maps was quite a challenge.

Brian's circumstances were clearly unusual. Mandy, however, belonged to a stable family; her father was a self-employed businessman and both parents were described as interested and supportive. Again, teachers' views of Mandy's achievement were consistently favourable, although below those of Brian; all four placed her in the top attainment group. In Year 1, her teacher estimated that she would probably reach junior school level in most curriculum areas, describing her as especially good orally. The Year 2 teacher at the school thought that Mandy's attitude was very positive; she was about average in maths, but 'one of the top children in terms of language'. Mandy's Year 3 teacher also placed her as average in maths, but considered her to be conscientious and very clever — 'excellent on the English side ... top in the Junior 1 reading sweep', and the Year 4 teacher described her as 'an all-rounder, really — very near the top'. However, views of Mandy's social relationships and attitude to school were more variable. In Year 1 Mandy was said to be very positive and enthusiastic, a 'very good, caring child ... with no problems'; this seemed to justify a Group 1 rating. In the following year Mandy's teacher described her as an ordinary, pleasant little girl, saying that her relationships were generally good, but that she could be shy and 'hard to get to', while in Year 3 her teacher said that she got on quite well, would help others and seek help herself; she could be 'argumentative, but not seriously'. These views suggested that Mandy's behaviour grade should be moved to 2 for both of these years, but in Year 4 she was graded at 4 because of such comments as these:

She's very argumentative ... very catty, causes a lot of arguments and fall-outs ... It's exactly the same in the playground ... 'I'm not being your friend' sort of thing; she causes a lot of arguments between others. She can be a bit argumentative with me; she doesn't like me telling her off at all. She's not happy with that; she's been known to pull faces when you do tell her things.

Again then, children did not seem to be viewed as permanently fixed in one behaviour pattern. Further remarks made by the same teacher suggested that what could be seen as a deterioration in Mandy's relationships might be contextually based. She apparently sat with a group of girls who were seen as 'very catty':

> They're all actually on one table. I think if I'd been here at the beginning of the year [when this teacher was on maternity leave] I might not have put them all together, but they sit there because they're of similar ability.

What of Mandy's judgements of her own progress? She answered only briefly in her Year 1 interview; she thought she was 'good' at maths, reading and writing. In Year 2 her responses were more cautious:

> Interviewer: What about maths?
>
> Mandy: I'm in the best group.
>
> Interviewer: So you are very good — are you one of the best?
>
> Mandy: Not really, not always. I am not as good at maths as I am at reading; maths is not as interesting.
>
> Interviewer: Is there anything else you're good at?
>
> Mandy: Writing stories and drawing and making things.

In Year 3 Mandy was again hesitant in her claims. Her reading, she said, was 'OK', her writing was 'sometimes neat', at science she was 'good — a bit good', while of maths Mandy said, 'I'm OK, but sometimes I get stuck.' The appearance of her work had now become important to Mandy: she liked, but with reservations, showing her work to her teacher: 'sometimes, when it's nice writing ... sometimes I think, "Is she going to say it's messy?"'

  The formation of a pupil's identity is clearly part of a complex process; a single child's social relationships are not solely in the control of that child. The data and space available do not permit a deeper analysis of the factors affecting Mandy's social development, but it is possible to speculate that her father's illness, mentioned by her Year 3 teacher, the change of teachers within the year and clashing personalities in her classroom might well have contributed to this. On the other hand, another child might have reacted in a quite different way to similar conditions; we can attempt to explain retrospectively, but this is very different from starting with a child's circumstances and predicting outcomes. The complex network of factors interacting to influence children's development can be only hinted at here. More valuable and informative analysis would require much longer-term and much more detailed ethnographic research; Pollard with Filer (1995) provides such an investigation. The model of children's learning offered in that study integrates such factors as family, as well as school, relationships, and learning challenges, strategies, opportunities and outcomes, both formal and informal, to demonstrate the complexity of education in any full sense.

7.8 CONCLUSIONS

On the whole, the evidence here seems to suggest that pupils' self-assessments were usually fairly consistent and that they did not diverge radically from their teachers' judgements. It could, of course, be argued that children simply absorbed and accepted their teachers' estimations, but this seems unlikely; pupils frequently assessed, apparently carefully and realistically, their own performance in recently completed tasks, not yet seen by their teachers. Although there is no room here for detailed accounts, observers were usually able to see, and often to collect samples of, work completed by different children, which suggested that teachers' and pupils' judgements of higher and lower attainers were well founded.

Further tentative conclusions are that pupils' attainment and behaviour patterns were described in similar terms by different teachers. Variations were frequent enough, however, to indicate that teachers based their judgements on what they experienced, rather than on previously acquired pupil biographies, and that attainment levels normally seemed to be judged independently of behaviour patterns. Even when low attainment and behaviour grades were fairly closely matched, this does not in itself mean that children were 'labelled', with the result that they were expected to, and therefore did, perform badly. 'Commonsense' suggests that, other factors being equal, a pupil who 'plays' for most of the day would be less likely to achieve high standards than one who concentrated on work. However, the accounts reported above of Brian's high attainment, combined with his difficult behaviour, seem sufficient evidence alone to cast doubt on Sharp and Green's arguments linking favourable teacher assessments of attainment to acceptable behaviour.

PACE data seemed to provide little evidence that social class, gender and race were in themselves linked to teachers' expectations and typifications of pupils. It is emphasized above that our numbers of children in minority ethnic groups were too small for generalized conclusions, but within the limits of the one school where different ethnic groups occurred there was no evidence of stereotyping and expectations based on ethnicity. There were no meaningful differences in teachers' assessments of boys' and girls' attainment; if anything, girls' slight perceived edge in attainment grades, and both genders' evenly matched behaviour levels, work against the usual preconceptions. In terms of pupils' socio-economic backgrounds, and teachers' differential treatment of pupils in different groups, the very fact that teachers were so often vague about parental occupations throws doubt on suggestions that children of working-class parents are neglected, or that teachers expect little of them. In this the PACE study supports the views of King, Croll and Mortimore, cited above.

It has already been mentioned that teachers seldom, if ever, referred to formal assessment, including SAT testing. Nevertheless, in response to other questions, and in other interviews, teachers have demonstrated a growing awareness of assessment as an ongoing process, referring to a close and analytic focus on each child as a positive outcome of the changes associated with the introduction of the National Curriculum. Comments on individual pupils' attainment and behaviour suggested, in most cases, that PACE teachers 'knew' their pupils very well; their explanations drew on detailed descriptions of children's work and relationships, rather than on generalizations. As Chapters 4 and 5 point out, teachers feel more constrained in their work, and Key Stage 2 teachers are particularly worried about pressure of time and its effect on their relationships. Even so, their accounts of their pupils suggest that their professionalism and care for the children in their classes have not diminished.

Chapter 8

Lessons from Lessons: Constraints on Teaching and Learning

Dorothy Abbott

8.1 Introduction

8.2 The class and the teacher

8.3 Instructional objectives: Closed questioning

8.4 Expressive objectives: Open-ended questioning

8.5 Classroom relationships

8.6 Groupwork and the Zone of Proximal Development

8.7 Prescriptions for teaching?

8.1 INTRODUCTION

The introduction of the National Curriculum in itself implied dissatisfaction with what was happening in schools previously; the rising tide of criticism and subsequent government action are documented in the first PACE book (Pollard *et al.*, 1994). Schools were frequently stigmatized as failing, but success and failure are strong and emotive terms, in classrooms as elsewhere. Presumably no teacher would deliberately plan a bad lesson; who would willingly bore children, waste their time or present them with tasks well beyond their capacity? Yet most teachers would recognize that all of those things have happened in their classrooms at one time or another, so what intervenes between planning and execution? How, in fact, does a teacher, or anyone else, form judgements on what is successful in teaching and learning? How do the effects of successful or unsuccessful lessons manifest themselves? And what are the factors influencing success?

Whatever shortages teachers may have suffered recently — of ancillary support, resources, space — advice has not been among them. On the contrary, they have been lavishly supplied with advice, instructions, government communications, courses, LEA guidance, HMI criticism, research findings and media censure. It might be assumed by the general public that if only teachers followed the guidelines with which they are so generously supplied then every pupil would receive a faultless education, and the

National Curriculum has often been hailed as at least a step in the right direction. Classroom shelves contain National Curriculum documents, specifying exactly what children should know of each 'subject', and school files containing detailed plans for imparting this knowledge, whether through integrated topic work or in discrete blocks. As all schools receive the same material it might be expected that what goes on in different classrooms would converge, become homogenized, that classrooms in different areas would be organized in generally similar ways. However, PACE observation suggests that variations are still noticeable. Teachers not only adjust their practice to individual local circumstances, but also mediate centrally imposed requirements through their individual philosophies and priorities.

If teachers were required to analyse and to communicate in writing before each lesson exactly what their aims were for the following forty minutes, and were further expected to differentiate all these aims for pupils of varying achievement levels, it not only would require a high degree of self-awareness but would be an impossibly complex and time-consuming task. Nevertheless, teachers will usually be aware of different kinds of purpose; Eisner, for example, distinguishes between instructional and expressive objectives. The first are used in a predictive mode, the teacher knowing specifically what knowledge or skills the pupils are hoped to acquire: how to add tens and units, for example, or how to record a night's rainfall. Evaluation, deciding whether or not the competence has been acquired, is thus fairly straightforward — although, of course, the retention of knowledge is another matter. Expressive objectives are related to the process, rather than the product, of learning; they could include interpretations of a poem or making clay models, and here evaluation needs to be open-ended and enquiring.

Children bring into their classrooms widely varied experiences and social formation; teachers will allow for this spontaneously during individual interactions, but class teaching, which teachers have been advised to increase, (e.g. Alexander *et al.,* 1992) is more complex, needing open-ended discourse from the teacher, to which children may be able to respond on different levels.

The purpose of this chapter is not to make judgements on the success or failure of any particular lesson or teaching style; it is not to criticize or praise. Rather it is to use a focus on one class to examine the complexity of the teaching situation in the primary classroom and the difficulties faced by teachers, first in planning activities, delicately balancing class and individual needs, then in adjusting, developing or even abandoning those plans in response to contingencies, to the unexpected, and finally in their evaluation of what has taken place.

Focusing on some of the events observed in one class during one week may make it possible to consider some of the 'dilemmas of teaching' which Pollard and Tann (1993), draw on:

> When practicalities, teaching competence, personal ideals and wider educational concerns are considered together, the job of rising to the challenges and reconciling the numerous requirements and possible conflicts often seems to be overwhelming. (p. 5)

My suggestion is that teachers do need to be aware of research findings, developments in curriculum knowledge and guidelines, that they need to plan with these in mind and to reflect on outcomes, but that this, not surprisingly, will not make teaching problem-free. Teachers will constantly have to draw upon their own reserves of ideas, flexibility and experience in their teaching, on what Pollard (1994) describes as their repertoires of teaching approaches, skills at diagnostic and formative assessment, and subject expertise. At the final stage of evaluation — although 'final' is misleading, as we are talking about a circular process here — then theories, ideas, may again prove their value, providing a structure to help teachers question their practice.

8.2 THE CLASS AND THE TEACHER

The focus here is on a teacher, much admired by the researcher who spent time in her classroom, to demonstrate that teaching does not fit a one-way, input – output model, but is a human situation. Pupils always add variables to the teaching process, and what happens is not totally dependent on the teacher, nor on the advice and professional training she receives. However scrupulously she plans, she may well be faced during the day with the need to make countless rapid decisions, judging whether to continue with or to change a strategy, to react to or ignore an interruption, to choose between two possibly conflicting aims.

The class discussed here contained seventeen Year 3 and eleven Year 4 children, in a five-teacher school in a midlands commuter village. Their teacher, Leonie, the school's science co-ordinator, frequently attended courses, read widely on developments in primary education and was keen on breadth, integration and interest in the curriculum, and on good relationships in the classroom and the school. Her informal conversation frequently touched on government philosophy as well as its practice, and on the moral and cultural aims associated with different views of the curriculum. Leonie could be described, in Hoyle's terms (1974), as an extended professional, a teacher whose thought and practice go beyond the immediate concerns of the classroom. Her teaching could be measured by the principles once seen by HMI as essential to effective education: a curriculum offering breadth, balance, relevance and differentiation (HMI, 1985).

Leonie encouraged open-ended discussion, welcomed contributions from children and took careful note of individual pupils' needs and stage of development. She paid great attention to planning and recording; her overall plan for the spring term during which she was visited consisted of thirty handwritten pages, supplemented by daily and weekly records and notes. Her teaching style was largely thematic, linking different curriculum areas. Using Bernstein's terms, it belonged in the integrated code, having weak inter-disciplinary boundaries, rather than in the collection code, where subjects, some given higher status than others, are strongly separated. Bernstein describes the degree of separation of subjects as classification, using the concept of framing to refer to the context of the teaching, the range of options open to teachers and pupils in selecting, organizing and pacing activities, fewer options meaning stronger framing. There are also variations in the strength of boundaries between educational and everyday non-school knowledge. Leonie preferred to link areas of the curriculum where this could happen without unnaturally forced connections, but her planning covered discrete subjects, noting the National Curriculum programmes of study and Attainment Targets to be covered in each field. The plan was detailed and ambitious, providing no suggestion of a narrow curriculum focusing on 'basics' at the expense of breadth, nor of merely skimming the surface of the broad curriculum at the expense of depth. Leonie also varied her teaching styles; pupils were provided with one-to-one support when this was possible, and was thought helpful, but groupwork also took place, and there were times when class teaching was considered appropriate.

As an example, the following illustrates one of Leonie's planning pages for history:

History

AIM: To cover the following:
Core Study Unit: ANCIENT GREECE

1. City State — Athens and Sparta
    Citizens and Slaves
2. The Economy — Agriculture and Trade
    Sea Transport
3. Everyday Life — lives of men, women and children; sport
4. Greek Religion and Thought
    — Gods/ religious practice
    — Myths and Legends
    — Scientists and Philosophers
5. Arts — Architecture, art,
    —drama and literature and how they reflected Greek Society
6. Relations with Other Peoples
    — Persian Wars
    — Greece and Rome
7. Legacy of Greece
    — language, politics,
    — sports and the arts

ATs1, 3 a,b,c, 4 b,c
2, 3a, 4a
3, 3a

Objectives: Children will

In study groups of 2 or 3 create research trail for peers, based on 20 questions
As individuals, create Ancient Greece Activity Book to incorporate:

Word Search	Maze
Dot to dot	Crossword
Illustration to colour	Mask
Jumbled words	Any other pages of own choice

(to be photocopied and given to peers for completion)

Children to complete Research Trail created by other groups, presenting information via one of the following as chosen by group:
i.   Information book
ii.   Comic Strip
iii. Frieze
iv.   Display
v.   Radio
vi.   Any other to be discussed

In addition, as mentioned above, Leonie made notes each evening, both planning in detail, and with timing, for the following day and recording her assessments of the previous day. Leonie's awareness of the needs of individual pupils is demonstrated by her plan for a morning's work for a classroom assistant whose support was available twice a week:

9.00   Prepare new number cards, 1–30; A–Z
9.30   Take Lee, David, Laura; spelling (introductory Level, SME)
10.00   Return to classroom
         Time game with group Year 3 children
10.20   Children in assembly; planning meeting with Leonie
10.45   Break
11.00   One to one with Wayne; hear him read/ maths game
11.20   One to one with Alan; hear him read/ discuss maths work — weight
11.40   One to one with Ken; hear him read/ help with maths — time pages, SPM
         Time dominoes

The page concluded with notes on activities which had been altered, Ken's absence and so on — in other words, responses to contingencies.

Were National Curriculum requirements helpful in teaching this mixed age class? Leonie explained in an interview:

> What they've asked for isn't anything more in a way than what we were doing before; it's just that it's so structured, and whereas before we were creating our own structure, now it is so clearly defined and makes life far more difficult in some respects ... We begin with the National Curriculum ... in the old days you went by topic and brainstormed a single topic and it gave you that freedom ... that flexibility ... these days you allow for a certain degree of flexibility, but in the end your anxiety is whether you are covering the attainment targets. I've always been able to start at a certain point and open out, but now I've got various points. It's like having ... whereas before it was one torch and the beam broadening out as you opened up, now you've got several torches parallel and the beams crossing and you're interlinking and it makes life awfully difficult.

There was ample evidence in Leonie's records of her plans to provide extra support for lower-attaining pupils, and an extract from an interview demonstrates her consciousness of the need to nurture children's self-esteem:

> Interviewer: Am I right in thinking that you try not to differentiate among the children by giving them different activities, but that you prefer open-ended tasks so that differentiation is by outcome?
>
> Leonie: Very much so. It's not always possible; when I was doing the subtraction activities on the blackboard this morning some children were going on with their SPMG maths books work, but as often as I can I give children the same work so that nobody feels they've been given specially easy things to do.
>
> Interviewer: You're thinking of their self-esteem?
>
> Leonie: Yes indeed — and if you noticed: the children going on with SPMG this morning were mixed. Jenny was using it because it would have wasted her time to follow the subtraction exercises, but David had something else to do because he couldn't have followed it.

This professionalism in planning and knowledge of children's needs might be expected to lead to lessons seen as successful by any observers and, more importantly, by Leonie herself. In fact, she often expressed deep disappointment; as Eisner points out, objectives entail prediction, and human situations are never totally predictable. Many of Leonie's lessons demonstrated the significance of other factors for the quality of learning possible in different circumstances, and the difficulty of allowing for accidental determinants.

8.3 INSTRUCTIONAL OBJECTIVES: CLOSED QUESTIONING

The week began with a session whose objectives were indisputably instructional. Written on the board were the date in full, a question: 'Are these correct? Copy and check,' and several easy tens and units subtraction sums:

19	85	79	66
−7	−12	−32	−36
11	73	46	30

Leonie explained what was required: 'Of course, one good way of checking subtraction sums is to add; if you add the answer to the bottom line, the answer should be the same as the top line. When you've checked these, I'd like you to make up six of your own. Let's check these first, though: right, Year 3, nineteen take away seven leaves eleven. As I just said, to check we can add the second line to the answer. What do seven and eleven make?' The answer was offered generally: eighteen. Leonie continued: 'So is that sum right? No, it should have a little cross by it, shouldn't it? '

This was clearly much easier work than one would expect to find being presented to Year 3 pupils, but Leonie's aim was not to introduce simple subtraction. She went on to draw a five-square grid on the board and copied one or two sums into it, stressing the importance of place value and of writing figures in correct alignment, reminding the children that '1' could mean one unit or one ten, according to its position, and continuing through the sequence; one hundred, one thousand, ten thousand. Leonie urged the children to use 'material' — Diene's apparatus was available — or to draw diagrams as she had demonstrated.

When the children had worked on the maths for a minute or two, Leonie stopped them, saying: 'I know a lot of you have hurried through these sums, thinking they're dead easy. Well, they are dead easy; I've deliberately made them dead easy. But I do want you to use material or to draw diagrams; you must show me the working.' There were groans from the children at this, and Leonie went on: 'Yes, I know I'm horrible, but you'll see why later; I'm building up to something, and you'll find this system very useful when we move on to harder work.'

At first, Leonie's pupils had clearly misunderstood her purpose, thinking that the point of this activity was to subtract tens and units, while Leonie's aim was to introduce a new system, as she briefly explained. It was striking that none of the children had expressed any surprise when they were given an unexpectedly easy task, as it had first appeared; their attitude was one of acceptance — this was what they had been asked to do and they would do it. In an interview later, Christopher seemed to demonstrate that he did understand Leonie's explanation. 'We were doing easy sums, but we had to find out how they're really set out, because it will help us later on.'

Nevertheless, comments overheard among the children suggested that 'getting sums right' and speed in working remained their overall aims. 'All right! Dead easy!' was a typical remark; no pupil was heard to comment with pride on aligning digits correctly, or on successfully using diagrams or apparatus. This raises questions about differences in pupils' and teachers' interpretations of the meanings of tasks: the advice of HMI is relevant here:

> The value of clear objectives for each lesson, and the need for pupils to understand these objectives, are often demonstrated. Where pupils understand the teacher's objectives for a

lesson, and know why they are doing what they are doing, they are able to participate more actively and intelligently. (HMI, 1985, para 21)

Leonie had clearly explained the long-term objective of this activity, but it seems likely that children's priorities — getting things right — overrode those she defined. Nevertheless, the purpose of this activity was fairly clear-cut, and most children did demonstrate their awareness of place value and their ability to fit the numerals into a grid. However, it is less clear whether they absorbed the broader aim of developing more advanced strategies for solving mathematical problems.

8.4 EXPRESSIVE OBJECTIVES: OPEN-ENDED QUESTIONING

The next session was more open-ended, planned to develop children's abilities to match different writing styles to different purposes, again an aim commended by HMI (1984). Leonie reminded the children that they had recently produced cartoon strips of Greek myths, when they had needed to convey information through pictures and through very few words; today they would write the story of Pandora's box as a newspaper story, complete with headlines, so writing would have to be concise and vivid.

> Leonie: No, we're not going to do it individually today; we'll do it as a class. This will be the story of how, according to the Ancient Greeks, troubles came into the world... Let's look at these newspapers; what do we call these? [Leonie pointed at some headlines.]
>
> Answer: Big letters.
>
> Leonie: Yes, they are big letters; what do we call big letters in newspapers?
>
> Answer: Big letters in newspapers. [Much laughter]
>
> Leonie: Yes, but they're called headlines, and what is written underneath is called an article. [She wrote these words on the board.] Why do people buy newspapers?
>
> Diana: Because they have Bingo in the Sun and that's what makes papers interesting; you can win thousands and millions of pounds.
>
> Richard: It's boring — why don't they read Teletext?
>
> Jane: I know why my father reads it — to look at the page 3 girl. [She mimed goggling at the paper; again much laughter.)
>
> John: You can find out things, like what's dangerous.
>
> Leonie: Good; what else?

This led into a discussion of the concept of news. Other responses included: 'To find out what's on the telly.' 'The weather.' 'My dad looks at it because he's bored.' 'To look for jobs.' By leading and responding to children's suggestions, Leonie compiled a list: to find things out, competitions, games, free offers, cinema and theatre programmes, advertisements, weather forecasts, crosswords, sport, page 3 girls, car sales, house sales. However, the conversation was then side-tracked into a discussion of the benefits of Teletext; Leonie tried to lead the children into a recognition of the advantages of newspapers, their portability, for example:

> Sharon: You can carry it.

Leonie: Thank you, Sharon; one advantage is that you can fold up a newspaper and slip it into your bag or a pocket ...

Richard: But you can carry a portable TV.

Lee: But they don't have Teletext.

Richard: But they could have...

Sharon: Papers are cheaper.

Leonie: Good girl.

Derek: But if you add it all up newspapers are just as dear and they get out of date and Teletext doesn't.

Anne: Let's have a vote.

Leonie: No, we won't have a vote; it's a matter of personal choice. But let's make a list of pros and cons for newspapers and Teletext.

Compiling the table took about twelve minutes. Richard then asked about share prices, which he said were available on Teletext but not in newspapers; Leonie explained that they were printed in some papers, and the argument about Teletext broke out again. No-one pointed out the total lack of realism in Richard's vision of commuters carrying portable television sets in order to read the news.

Leonie: Well, we had an interesting discussion about that and you did it very well; now ...

Hannah: Can we have one team point each?

Leonie: That would rather defeat the object. Let's get back to the article: if they had newspapers at the time, what would have been a good headline with punch?

Diana: Trouble Invasion

Mark: Troubles In The World

Leonie: Imagine if I'd said that aliens had landed ... no, no, calm down, please, we ... don't need all this noise and excitement ... what could headlines be then?

When Leonie had settled the class, suggestions included: Aliens Have Come, Flying Saucer Spotted, Aliens Invade, Aliens Attack.

Leonie: Come on, we've been talking for a long time and I can tell you're getting bored, but we're nearly there. Now: 'Aliens Attack'; you see how these words begin with the same letter — newspapers often do that in their headlines to add a bit of punch.

Nora: Watch Out, Aliens About.

Leonie: Good! Yes, that's something else often used in headlines: rhymes. Now, you see, you found that quite easy to write about aliens; now all we have to do is to replace 'Aliens' with 'Troubles'.

Leonie then read some of the revised headlines, and the lesson, which had begun at 11.05, ended at 12.10. Leonie had expected to have finished work on a first draft of an article with headlines in thirty minutes or so. Leonie's dilemmas during this session, of which, of course, there is room here for only short extracts, are obvious. She had a clear idea of what she hoped to achieve in the period and had prepared thoroughly, providing a selection of local and national newspapers to stimulate the children's interest, as well as illustrations of the Pandora myth. Although Leonie had planned the general content of the lesson, she did not want to dominate it with prescriptive teacher direction, but the open-ended dialogue she encouraged led in unexpected directions. Leonie allowed this, and responded with an unplanned activity, the table of comparisons of print and electronic media. Her disappointment was evident; she said later that she half-wished that she had closed off the discussion about Teletext to reach the content of the article much sooner, but in doing so she would have had to be more directive than she had hoped.

In the event, Leonie adjusted her weekly plan and returned to the activity four days later, to produce a jointly written version of the article, reminding her pupils that 'next time' they would write individually. Comments made by some children revealed that they had been paying attention to newspapers in the meantime; they had noticed reporters' bylines, for instance, and asked Leonie about the use of columns.

8.5 CLASSROOM RELATIONSHIPS

During this session there had been distractions of a different kind. Alan had clearly been disturbed earlier that morning, when he had flatly refused to join in a spelling activity; Leonie was conciliatory and said that he could try it on his own with the teaching assistant later; for now, he could continue with his maths pages. Alan proceeded to wander around, looking at other children's work, waving his ruler around, 'fencing', tapping his neighbour's head and calling out; all of this Leonie ignored, except to say, 'Don't draw two lines on your page, Alan, just one please.' Alan's loud response was 'I always draw two lines.' During the newspaper session, Alan joined in, suggesting as a headline, 'Everything was fine yesterday until a box came.'

> Derek: No, Alan, it's got to have punch.
>
> Ken: Yeah, punch.
>
> Alan: You come here and I'll give you a punch.
>
> Derek: Let's put, 'Woman gets splattered.'
>
> Joan: I think Derek is a sexist pig. All the men are heroes and a woman opens the box of troubles.

After contending with political correctness, Leonie had to deal with further interruptions. When a messenger came to ask whether Leonie had received a form, Ken called out, 'I ate it! I thought it was waste paper,' after which he laughed loudly, with no response from his classmates other than weary sighs. A little later, Joan was in tears:

> Joan: Alan called me a fat pig.
>
> Leonie: Alan, do you remember the other day? We were saying that some people don't mind being teased, but that others do ...
>
> Alan: But she called Derek a sexist pig.
>
> Joan: But he's not crying!
>
> Leonie: No, but that doesn't necessarily mean that you didn't offend him; people can feel upset without crying.

Pupil behaviour is a sensitive area to discuss; teachers have been accused of employing a deficit model of children's home and family backgrounds to account for deficiencies in their behaviour or academic progress and thus to absolve themselves of blame (King, 1978; Sharp and Green, 1975). It would be difficult to account in any other way, however, for the behaviour of Alan, a Year 4 member of Leonie's class, who had been regarded in earlier years as a placid, likeable, although not high-achieving, pupil. His parents were currently divorcing and Alan's behaviour had become noticeably more disruptive and aggressive. Ken was undergoing no such stress, but he had been noticed during every previous visit as attention seeking, frequently calling out, rarely settling to work with concentration and ready to disturb other children. Ken was an only child of affluent parents; his father was particularly anxious about his progress and frequently visited the school without appointments, asking to look at Ken's books. (In the following year, Ken was taken to a centre where he was diagnosed as dyslexic; he then entered a boarding school said to specialize in treating this.)

In addition, the school accommodated a shifting population of travellers' children from a nearby camp, some of whom settled happily while others were considered to cause immense problems. In Leonie's class, there were four such children, three of whom, although they were in Year 3 or Year 4, had never attended school before and were non-readers. David, who is mentioned above, was a non-reader who was receiving extra help and enjoying word-building computer games; although he had previously been excluded from a school in the area, he seemed to be happy and settled at Lawnside. Wayne, however, who had rarely spent more than a few months at any school, was the focus of serious concern, in spite of Leonie's obvious efforts to help and support him. The school had adopted a positive behaviour policy, ignoring unacceptable conduct, as far as possible, and praising good behaviour; Wayne took full advantage of this. Leonie discussed in an interview her strategies for helping pupils whose needs were different from those of their peers:

> Leonie: Some of them are lovely children in many ways, but they're nearly all very confident and loud, although sometimes they haven't even been to school before. David came last term and he literally hadn't even started to read.

> Interviewer: Is that why he spends so much time on the computer? I noticed that he's usually occupied with language games.

> Leonie: Yes, he doesn't know it's for that reason; he thinks he's just having fun. But I'm pleased; his reading is coming on so well. Wayne is another matter altogether. He worries me so much; he's so full of anger and aggression. As I told you, we're using a positive behaviour policy, stressing good conduct and ignoring bad as far as possible, but his behaviour is so extreme ... I'm worried about the messages other children receive; I feel that Alan and Ken, at least, are behaving badly more often since Wayne arrived. They see him refusing to do anything he doesn't feel like doing and being praised for quite ordinary behaviour. What are they supposed to think?

It is difficult to see how any teacher could have made more efforts to answer the needs of such a pupil as Wayne. He was provided with work designed to stimulate and interest without over-challenging him; his frequent outbursts were received calmly. If he did not wish to go to the school assembly, he was allowed to stay outside, which meant arranging for supervision. Leonie's priority was to follow the school's policy on behaviour, de-fusing difficult situations and diverting Wayne's attention to more productive areas, but she admitted sometimes feeling close to despair, and her worries were shared by Jane, a part-time colleague who taught the class during Leonie's non-contact time and her absences on courses. 'I don't know what I'm doing wrong,' Jane commented,

'I've tried every way I can think of to stimulate Wayne and Alan, to interest them and to form a good relationship, and they just don't want to know.' This sounds like the reverse of the attitude described by King and by Sharp and Green; Leonie's and Jane's instincts were to make great efforts to form happy class relationships and to blame themselves when these appeared to be unsuccessful.

Field notes made at the time describe what happened when the children were asked to paint illustrations of a Greek myth of their own choice. While Leonie was introducing the activity, Wayne repeatedly tapped a pencil on a wooden block, which Leonie quietly removed, ignoring the thumping on the table which followed. Soon afterwards, she sat with Wayne, hearing him read and warmly praising his efforts. When she moved off to another group, Wayne called out, 'Everybody here is crap and this is a crap school.' When Leonie was asked what nymphs were, she explained that they were 'like beautiful young women', and that there were seven of them in that story, to which Wayne shouted, 'And they all pissed in the same pot.' When Leonie ignored this and several similar episodes, Wayne went outside and knocked at the classroom's fire exit door for other children to let him in. Later, when the class split into groups for different science activities, Wayne would not settle but disrupted his group's activity on light and reflection by hitting other children and pushing them about. He then rushed outside, broke down two newly planted saplings and ran out onto the road, shouting that he was going home.

Long as this account is, it omits many similar incidents; when school had ended that day Leonie herself was clearly distressed. It was arranged, after discussion with Wayne's parents, that on the following day he would meet, and be assessed by, the head of the local Special Needs unit. This meeting, however, never took place; Wayne was taken home by his mother, who repeated that she and her husband could not 'do anything with him'. He did not appear at school the next day and his cousins, from the same site, said that the family had left, for a caravan site in a distant area. This, Leonie suspected, had often happened in the past; Wayne would stay at a school until there was an episode of severe disruption and would then be taken away. The effects on his education can be imagined; Leonie was extremely concerned about him, and, while admitting that his absence made life easier, hoped that the family would return so that Wayne could be helped.

It would be difficult to overestimate the effects on the quality of teaching and learning in a class of the presence of even a few such pupils. HMI (1985) stressed the importance of 'recognising the different causes of low motivation among pupils' and to teachers being, 'alert and sensitive to the varying needs of the individuals to change in family circumstances' (para 12). Leonie appeared to fulfil all of these conditions, but interaction is a two-way process, and Wayne's problems and needs were clearly related to factors outside the classroom, as well as to his probable unhappy awareness of the gap between his attainment level and that of most of his age group.

Criticism of Wayne or his parents would be pointless and presumptuous on the part of an observer who was unaware of their full circumstances; he was clearly disturbed and in need of help which might have been available if he had not left the area so abruptly. The point here is that the presence of disruptive pupils in a class intensifies the demands already made on teachers and reduces the attention and time available to other pupils, with obvious effects on the quality of their education. Wayne was an extreme case, but he demonstrates that no amount of planning, expertise and care will guarantee success in learning, although they are prerequisites for this — they are essential but not sufficient.

8.6 GROUPWORK AND THE ZONE OF PROXIMAL DEVELOPMENT

Leonie's vivid searchlight metaphor for the National Curriculum, above, summarizes some of what she saw as constraints on her teaching, but she also had to accommodate local advice:

> I went on the LEA science course and it looks as though we're going to have to change our approach pretty radically ... I've always used a lot of work cards, outlining the experiments and tasks and so on, but now we're going to ask the children to design their own experiments and investigations.

Leonie continued to explain that she found groupwork in science rather difficult to organize, but that this, too, was urged on teachers in the LEA course. The science lesson observed in Leonie's class demonstrated some of the problems she faced in a genuine effort to use the approach advocated by the advisers. One group worked with Leonie in the dark stockroom, experimenting with light beams, another tried to make work cards to instruct other children in how to make sundials; other activities included experiments in dropping objects of different weights and research from books on planets. Leonie felt that she needed to stay with the group in the dark stockroom, so the rest of the class had to work without her supervision. She later expressed her disappointment:

> Leonie: Some of the groups cooperated and worked out their activities very well, but I do think we're asking an awful lot of children of this age. I gave Richard's group of Y4 children a worksheet asking them to design a workcard for other children to use to make a sundial, and they just didn't manage it.

> Interviewer: I sensed that you were a bit disappointed; you didn't criticize their work, but you told them you thought it had been rather too hard, and that they could try something else another day.

> Leonie: I wasn't all that surprised, actually; both Richard and Malcolm are high-achievers, but Richard, particularly, always wants to be boss and do everything himself. He hasn't got the social skills to make him a good group leader, let alone a group member. Now Jenny, who's even further ahead in her overall work, is very quiet and unassuming; she fits in beautifully with her group, makes suggestions, but listens to the others; and her group did very well.

> Interviewer: What do you feel about the activity itself, making the worksheet? It needs a sort of two-layered approach, doesn't it — first they have to think about making a sundial and then about how to introduce the activity to other children. You felt that was asking rather too much of them?

> Leonie: I did, yes. Maybe I should have split it into two separate activities.

> Interviewer: Lee and his group were doing research from books, on the planets; were the others working on gravity?

> Leonie: Yes, I asked them to investigate whether it's true that a light object will take the same time to drop the same distance as a heavier object would, and to work out a fair test for that.

Interviewer: How do you think they got on?

Leonie: Oh, that seemed very successful. I wasn't at all happy about the afternoon in general, though; it did seem to get so chaotic. When I've done group activities like that in the past, I've usually chosen a time when I had plenty of other adult help available, someone with each group if possible. Today I ended up by feeling that I had to go into the stockroom to keep an eye on the group working on light, as they could have been put off by being in the dark, and I felt that I was letting the others manage on their own more than I liked.

Leonie's comments demonstrate the detailed knowledge of her pupils which is often seen as a strength of British primary education. Her expressed concern, however, raises questions not only about the practical difficulties experienced by teachers who adopt advice, sometimes against their better judgement, on class organization, but also about the quality of learning possible in such circumstances. In terms of this particular area, science, teachers' aims include encouraging children to think as scientists, to understand the concept of fair tests and to record and interpret results. These are not easy skills for children to acquire or for teachers to assess, but groupwork, which was encouraged by Leonie's science tutors, intensified her problems. Was it realistic to expect eight- and nine-year-olds to work in this way? In this case Leonie had planned and prepared in advance of the lesson varied and interesting activities and had conscientiously followed the advice provided on local courses. Observation and later interviews with children made it possible to attempt some evaluation of the quality of learning that had taken place.

Lee's group were involved in no practical activities; they were asked to research facts about planets, using a selection of books and dividing the work among themselves. Everyone in the group seemed to work with great concentration, and there was no disagreement at all about choice of planets or about sharing books. The children then copied out their work on large sheets of paper which were pinned to the wall as posters; they decided on the media used — paint, felt pens, crayons — and on the illustration and design of the posters. They thus had a fair amount of autonomy and control: apart from the initial general instruction to research planets, framing, to use Bernstein's term, was weak. The style of what was written suggested that the children had copied directly from the books, so at the end of the period — about forty minutes — they were questioned to examine their level of awareness and understanding of what they had written. Lee had chosen to read and write about Saturn; he wrote:

Speed another 400 million miles out ward to reach Saturn which orbits 888 million miles from the sun would appear as a tiny disc one ninetieth the sixe we see from the earth. Obviously, Saturn is even darker and colder than Jupiter, with an average daytime temperature of minus 223 de grees. After mars, going away from the sun, came the planets Jupiter, Saturn, Uranus, Neptune and Pluto. They are all to cold to support life forms. Both Soviets and Americans have sent probes to Mars. In 1965 Mariner

Questions to Lee

Interviewer: What's it like on Saturn?

Lee: Hot — I can't remember.

Interviewer: How far away is Saturn?

Lee: 400 million miles from here.

Interviewer: How far away is it from the sun when it is in orbit?

Lee: 120 thousand million miles.

Interviewer: What does 'orbit' mean?

Lee: I don't know.

Interviewer: What did you write about probes?

Lee: What are they?

Angus, who was not available for questioning, wrote simply:

Jupiter
Perspective on the planet
Jupiter 142,800 kms

John, regarded as a high-achiever, wrote:

Mars

The red planet. more like Earth than any other planet: two moons.
On 20 July, 1989, 20 years to the day since man first stepped on the moon, President Bush of America set a new goal; to land people on Mars by 2019.

Questions to John

Interviewer: What colour is Mars?

John: Red; the air is pinky because of the red rocks.

Interviewer: What does President Bush want to do?

John: He wants to send people there by 2019.

Interviewer: How far away is Mars?

John: 16,000 million miles. [John's poster stated: Mars is sometimes as close as 35,000 million miles.]

Interviewer: Is Mars bigger or smaller than Earth?

John: Bigger. [John's poster stated: Volume: 15 times Earth.]

Elsa wrote about Mercury:

Mercury

Is the closest of all, 350° C hotter then the highest temperatere in the wlod named after the swift-coated messenger of the gods in Roman myth.

Questions to Elsa

Interviewer: Is Mercury nearer to the sun than Earth is, or further away?

Elsa: Further away.

Interviewer: Is it hotter or colder there than on Earth?

Elsa: Hotter.

Interviewer: Why is it called Mercury?

Elsa: I don't know.

This recalls criticisms of topic work (Alexander *et al.*, 1992) to the effect that too much of it entails copying from text books with little attempt to evaluate what is being learnt. Leonie had stressed that the children should not simply copy from the books, but should read them and write in their 'own words', and she planned to discuss this work with the children later:

> I haven't really had a chance to look properly yet at what they've written, but they seemed to be hard at it. They can't very well do hands on activities about the size of planets and so on, but they do seem to find it very interesting.

Nevertheless, there seems to be sobering evidence here that obvious absorption in, and apparent enjoyment of, research from books does not always result in high quality learning, and the children's experience raises questions about the non-fiction books available for classroom and school libraries. Those used by this group were varied and well produced, copiously illustrated with attractive pictures, but the prose seemed unnecessarily stylized and difficult to interpret. Perhaps authors of non-fiction for this age group need to develop a straightforward, direct style, enabling children to extract solid information easily.

Jenny, a child seen as the highest achiever in her year, wrote very neatly:

> Are own sun
> We went outside and mearsured 26 metres and held the sun one end and the earth and moon the other end. Then we read our book and found that the earth was 93 million miles away from the sun. We also found out that the sun is always opposite to the moon.

The comment written on Jenny's work was, 'I'm not sure what you mean by this Jenny. Will you see me and explain please.'

These, and other written accounts, even those of generally high-attaining children like Jenny and Sally, suggest some confusion about the area discussed: the relative sizes of the sun, the earth and the moon. In spite of Leonie's careful advance instructions and workcards, the children seemed unable to relate their small-scale measuring and counting to the vast numbers involved in astronomical distances. Having held up cut-outs, measured and counted, the children looked up the relevant facts in a book. Had Leonie been able to observe, hear and question the group, there is little doubt that she would have 'scaffolded' the children's learning and guided them to reach useful conclusions, remembering her expressed preference for restricting varied investigative groupwork to times when 'plenty of other adult help is available'. But is it acceptable to require teachers to work in a system that relies on support from several adults when strict funding limits mean that such help would probably need to be voluntary and unpaid, and would be less easily available in those schools where children's needs may be greatest?

It may be that direct input from a teacher is needed for such abstract ideas as 'fair tests', or that the concepts are too difficult for children of this age group without adult support. Tharp and Gallimore (1988) discuss Vygotsky's 'Zone of Proximal Development' (ZPD), the area between a child's achieved developmental level and the potential level attainable through guidance or collaboration. The need for close attention and careful guidance from the teacher, and for the conditions which make this possible, are accentuated by Tharp and Gallimore's discussion of teaching as 'assisting performance':

> 'Assistance' offered at too high a level will disrupt child performance and is not effective teaching ... our definition of teaching emphasises that *teaching can be said to occur when assistance is offered at points in the ZPD at which performance requires assistance.* Careful assessment of the child's abilities ... is a constant requirement for the teacher. (p. 41)

It is difficult to see how Leonie, or any teacher, could have provided the carefully judged interventions needed by her pupils on this occasion; it certainly seems likely that the challenging activities of the science session were too ambitious for groups of children to tackle without support. Galton and Williamson (1992) cite the strong endorsement by Reid *et al.* of groupwork, 'a manageable and flexible base from which the teacher can work to provide the best learning experience for the class', but are sceptical. In practice, they argue, and cite research to support their view, teachers find such organization problematic. Alexander (1992) similarly suggests that local authority advisers underestimate the complexity of collaborative groupwork and advocate its use when it may not be appropriate. It was clear from Leonie's comments that she had serious misgivings about the appropriateness of these group activities in her science lessons but that she was following LEA advice; it may be thought that her own professional judgement was more reliable in this case.

8.7 PRESCRIPTIONS FOR TEACHING?

In the early years of the National Curriculum there were mixed views about its probable effects on primary education. Its supporters argued that it would add both breadth and depth to children's experience, focusing teachers' minds on the content of their teaching and providing benchmarks for evaluation. Fears were expressed, however, that the more expressive, creative side of the curriculum would be pushed to the margin, and that national assessment would encourage 'teaching to the test', making it difficult for teachers to respond to their pupils' individual needs. There is no evidence that Leonie's teaching has suffered in this way; she was alert to her pupils' needs and was constantly monitoring classroom interaction:

> Interviewer: How far were you consciously assessing during the cooperative science group work today?
>
> Leonie: Oh, all the time, virtually; you can't always write down what's being said, but you try to note and remember it, and to notice who is contributing and who needs drawing out.
>
> Interviewer: There was a lot of that going on during your activity based on newspaper articles, wasn't there? I noticed that you were trying to make sure that everyone contributed and no-one had a chance to dominate.
>
> Leonie: Oh yes, I think Diana and Ken would have taken over the whole period if I'd let them.

Pollard (1985) analysed macro- and micro-factors affecting coping strategies in classroom interaction, and reveals the complexity of the social situation in which teachers and pupils meet. Some OFSTED and government publications tend to ignore this complexity, and guidance is offered selectively, to teachers who are only one element in the quality of education received by pupils. It could hardly be expected that children would receive written advice and judgements from such sources, but there is a danger in formulaic prescriptions; teaching and learning are not part of a simple input – output model. This is to take the 'empty vessel' view of children's learning, seeing pupils as passive receivers of knowledge, poured into them by the teacher. As we have seen, education is a deeply interactive process in which pupils have an active role. Pupil understandings of curriculum tasks, behaviour and relationships with others and capacity to respond appropriately to all learning opportunities act as constraints on the teaching process. As events in the classroom described here indicate, there is no simple equation: careful planning + subject knowledge + differentiation + various other attributes, skills and qualities of the teacher = high quality learning for every pupil. These are essential requirements, and they were all part of Leonie's teaching, but she had to draw on additional reserves of patience, quick decision-making, humour and adaptability as she and her pupils jointly constructed the process and outcomes of classroom learning.

Chapter 9

Playing the System? Pupil Perspectives on Curriculum, Pedagogy and Assessment in Primary Schools

Andrew Pollard

9.1   INTRODUCTION

The analysis in this chapter updates and extends the account of pupil perspectives which was offered in the report of the first phase of the PACE project (Pollard *et al.*, 1994). Once again, the data are presented in terms of Bernstein's three 'message systems' (1975): curriculum, pedagogy and assessment.

One of the fascinating aspects of the first round of PACE findings was the fact that, despite the scale of changes in public policy and in the experiences of headteachers and teachers, classroom life for pupils seemed relatively unaffected. Indeed, in the midst of the turbulence of the struggle over educational values, power and understanding, there was remarkable continuity in pupil experience, as indicated by comparison of previous research with our observations of pupil behaviour and interviews with pupils. Several reasons for the relatively modest extent of experienced change in classrooms may be suggested. First, there is the central finding of the first PACE book that many Key Stage 1 teachers in the early 1990s tried to 'protect' pupils from effects of the curriculum and assessment reforms which they felt to be inappropriate or damaging to them. For instance, teachers monitored the growth of subject teaching and classroom direction for their effect on the teacher–pupil relationships to which they were committed. Similarly, they moderated the impact of new assessment requirements so that pupil stress could be minimized. Teachers, in other words, mediated change with the specific intention of protecting what they felt to be important qualities of their existing provision. Similarly, as Campbell and Neill (1993) have argued, this mediation also extended to ensure maintenance of many features of the old, established 'elementary school' curriculum which has been such a large influence on primary school teachers' routinized classroom practices. Such curricular conservatism was reinforced by the media and parental emphasis on 'the basics' and by the priority the core curriculum was given within new assessment and inspection procedures. 'The basics' thus retained a very high profile, and this undermined the stated intention of the Education Reform Act, 1988, that the curriculum should be 'broad and balanced'.

A second set of reasons for the maintenance of relative continuity in pupil experience is more structural, and relates to the nature of classrooms as settings for educational interaction between a teacher and many children. From this sociological perspective, the basic influences on pupil experience have not changed at all. In particular, classrooms remain closed and evaluative. Indeed, Jackson's (1968) description of classroom 'crowds, praise and power' are as important today as they were when he first coined them: 'crowds' constitute the audience for success, or for humiliation; the issue of 'praise' draws attention to the evaluative dimension of schooling; and a consideration of 'power' makes it clear that it is teachers who hold the initiative. Seen in this way, we can observe that pupils who experienced relative powerlessness before the Education Reform Act, 1988, still do.

The main focus of this chapter is on the evidence that, as the pupils in our sample have grown older through the early 1990s, they seem to become progressively instrumental and concerned to satisfy the classroom requirements of teachers. Of course, such arguments about pupil concerns are far from new. Indeed, Jules Henry (1955) in his article on 'docility, or giving teacher what she wants' offered an early analysis of the ways in which pupils seek to please teachers. This analysis had another famous manifestation in Becker *et al., Making the Grade* (1968) and has also been one focus of my own work on coping strategies (Pollard, 1985). In some ways then, the pupil perspectives which are reported in the paper constitute another version of an old story, but, as the longitudinal PACE data accumulate, we may begin to identify some new issues within the old pattern.

The data on which this chapter is based were gathered from 54 children in nine schools from across England, who were interviewed annually in their Year 1, Year 2, Year 3 and Year 4. The same basic questions were asked on each occasion so that it is possible to make direct comparisons of the children's views over time. Where target children were absent during the data-gathering period or had left the school, they were replaced by others drawn at random from each class. By the end of the fourth year of the study, the period reported here, 87 children had participated in the research. Each pupil interview was coded and analysed on the PACE pupil database. For the purpose of this paper the results have been aggregated for each round or for Years 1 and 2 and Years 3 and 4, thus providing easy comparison between pupil perspectives in Key Stage 1 and in the early years of Key Stage 2.

9.2   CURRICULUM

As in PACE 1, we gathered data on 'best liked' and 'least liked' curricular subjects or activities. Pupils nominated two subjects or activities in each category and we used these data to produce 'league tables' of pupils' curricular preferences for each year. These were based on the rank order of the net score when the percentage 'best liked' was set against the percentage 'least liked' for each subject or activity in each year. Table 9.1 sets out the results from this procedure for the first four years of the PACE project.

Table 9.1 *Comparative 'league table' of pupils' favoured curricular activities*

Rank	Year 1 net rank	Year 2 net rank	Year 3 net rank	Year 4 net rank
1	Physical Education	Physical Education	Maths	Maths
2	Painting	Maths	Singing	Drawing
3	Home corner play	Home corner play	Reading to teacher	Writing
4	Sand	Painting	Writing	Singing
5	Stories	Singing	Physical Education	Teacher Reading
6	Singing	Reading alone	Drawing	Physical Education
7	Construction	Construction	Teacher reading	Topic work
8	Reading alone	Reading lesson	Topic work	Reading to teacher
9	Reading lesson	Sand	Reading alone	History
10	Science	Science	Science	Reading alone
11	Writing	Stories	History	Music
12	Maths	Writing	Technology	Technology

Source: PACE 1 and 2 child interviews
Sample: 54 children in Years 1–4
Date: Autumn 1990 and 1991, summer 1993 and 1994

Some notable changes are apparent over the four years. In particular, in Years 3 and 4 writing rose dramatically to become amongst the most preferred activities, perhaps reflecting children's growing mastery of the basic skill and new confidence in expressing their ideas in written form compared with Years 1 and 2. Physical education became a little less popular in the transition from Key Stage 1 to 2. Maths consolidated the position at the top of the league table which had been ascribed to it in Year 2, after its very low rank position in Year 1. In both Years 3 and 4 maths had the highest net ranking for our sample. Science on the other hand, perhaps not recognized very discretely as a subject by the pupils, was not within the top 12 in Year 4.

In both PACE 1 and PACE 2 the children were asked to compare their best-liked and least-liked curricular activity nominations. Their comments provide some insights into the criteria which underlay their thinking. For instance, among the comments made by the children in the summer of Year 3, when most of them were 8 years old, were:

[PE/reading] You've got more stuff to do in PE and it's more exciting.

[Computers/singing] It's just like playing a game and you pretend you're the people on the computer. I hate singing in assembly. It's embarrassing.

[Maths/reading] 'Cos I can do maths really quickly and I'm good at it.

[Drawing/history] You can draw lots of things. You can choose and I'm good at it. My dad is. He draws cars and designs them.

[Maths/drawing] I'm better at maths.

[Painting/maths] Maths is much harder. You have to sit down and it's tiring. Painting you can move around.

[Maths/science] I find maths a lot easier.

[PE/writing] In PE you can do lots of moves and it's fun. [When I'm writing] I feel I'm going to get the words wrong and everyone may laugh.

[Maths/painting] I get maths all right. When you paint and pick up a colour it drips and splodges.

[Maths/topic work] Sums are better. They take dead long and I'm good at them.

[Maths/science] Because maths is a bit easy and science is hard and I like easy things and I don't like hard things and in science you can't use a calculator. Science is boring and maths is quite good.

[Maths/topic work] 'Cos I always do the best at maths and I do it fast.

[Maths/spelling] I prefer adding up 'cos it's my favourite thing and I use my hands. I don't bother to use the counters and I'm good at it.

[Writing/reading] 'Cos I like writing I don't like reading. I like discovering things 'cos I feel like doing it. Like doing things.

[PE/history] You can move in PE and I like it.

The pupils show a particularly strong awareness of just how hard or easy they felt the activitites to be in a particular curriculum area, and this was often linked to the issue of achieving success and recognition, rather than, at the extreme, humiliation. In addition, the children favoured activities which they intrinsically enjoyed and in which they were interested.

In Year 4 with data gathered when most of the children were 9 years old, a similar range of points was made and, as before, patterns in these responses were sought.

The *ease* of accomplishing a task or activity continued to be an important factor. For instance:

[Sewing/maths] You have to think *very* hard about maths, but with sewing you can just do it and relax.

[Maths/making models for technology] Maths is easy, I can do it. Models I can't do it.

In many such cases, there seemed to be a link to the degree of ambiguity and risk which was associated with achieving success in that subject area. For example:

[Maths/reading] Maths you can really work hard. You don't have to tell anybody and just get on with it. In reading you have to do it out loud and other children disturb you.

[Maths/science] I like solving problems. In science we just find out things and do experiments and you don't really know if you're right or not.

[Maths/history] I don't know. I just like sorting out the answers in maths.

For other children, however, the priority was seen more in terms of their intrinsic *interest* in the subject or in the activities which it made possible. In particular, the children valued opportunities for *autonomy* and personal expression:

[Writing stories/science] In science its hard but when we write stories, we can make up our own minds.

[Writing/science] You can make them stories, funny, exciting, adventurous. Science is hard — you have to find things out and it takes you a long time to figure things out.

[Painting/history] I like painting because we can mix colours and sometimes we can paint what we want. Sometimes she puts up a famous painting and we do a painting in the same style. In history she often asks us things and we don't know much about it.

[Writing stories/other writing] Writing stories is imaginative, like. When you write about other things, you have to think about that thing and you can't imagine anything.

[Writing stories/reading] I get ideas and I write it really fast and it's enjoyable. I don't like reading because sometimes the books are too hard.

Sometimes, they emphazised 'having fun':

[Technology/RE] Technology is fun and I like getting messy. RE; I'm not religious and it's boring anyway.

[Writing/science] Well, writing makes me better at it and I think it's fun. I don't really like doing experiments and answering questions. Science isn't the thing for me; I just haven't got it inside me.

[Painting/history] Painting is more fun and I really like the paint.

[Drawing/writing] In writing you're doing nothing: drawing's funnier.

However, relatively few children gave reasons for their choices which might be termed 'educational' or reasons which prioritized 'activity'. The latter was a particular surprise, for this had been significantly more important to the children when the sample was younger.

The criteria underpinning such pupil statements were coded and compared with those given in Years 1 and 2. The results are shown in Table 9.2.

Table 9.2   *Pupil criteria for preferred curricular activities (percentages of codings)*

	Years 1 and 2	Years 3 and 4
Success/ease	29	44
Interest	26	31
Fun	19	17
Activity	14	2
Educational	5	2
Other	7	4

Source: PACE 1 and 2 children interviews
Sample: 54 children in Years 1–4
Date: Autumn 1990 and 1991, summer 1993 and 1994

Table 9.2 shows how, in both Years 1 and 2 and in Years 3 and 4, almost a fifth of the children distinguished between their most and least liked curricular activities in ways which were coded as reflecting a criterion of 'fun'. Having said that, however, the progression from Key Stage 1 to the early years of Key Stage 2 seemed to have produced significant changes. As noted above, there was a big decrease in emphasis on activity itself, which was associated with the fall in popularity of physical education, and there was a 5 per cent increase in children favouring subjects or activities because of their intrinsic 'interest'. However, the most notable change, a 15 per cent rise, lay in the pupil emphasis on 'success' or 'ease'.

Various issues may be embedded in this. For instance, many of the children clearly favoured curricular activities which they experienced as being low in evaluative risk and task ambiguity, thus suggesting linkages with the work of Walter Doyle (e.g. Doyle, 1986; Doyle and Carter, 1984). Following this argument, one interpretation of Table 9.2 is that as the children became older they became even more concerned to succeed at their work than they had been in Key Stage 1. They monitored the difficulty of such challenges and had a growing awareness of the relative degrees of interest which were offered by different curricular activities. Of course, there were also variations within this broad description and, in particular, there was a tendency for having 'fun' to be mentioned by children attaining at relatively lower levels.

In the first major report of the PACE project (Pollard *et al.*, 1994) we offered a model of 'zones of influence' within classrooms which provides a representation of the power context. The two most important zones are those of the pupils and of the teachers, with a third zone being intermediate between the two. In the zone of pupils' major influence, concerns which articulate with child culture and individual experience are prominent and these are reflected in the pupil criterion of 'having fun' and 'activity'. In the zone in which teachers provide the major influence, pupils have to respond to the tasks with which they are presented and through which the curriculum is manifested. This is particularly reflected in the pupils' comments on the 'success' and 'ease' of the curriculum they experienced and, to a very small extent, in pupil views on long-term educational value. In the intermediate zone, pupils may concern themselves more with the intrinsic interest, fulfilment and autonomy which they feel they are able to obtain from their work.

Applying this model to the transition from Key Stage 1 to Key Stage 2 we have a very clear pattern. Almost half of the concerns of the pupils are now associated directly with the concerns of the teacher zone of influence. The expectation of 'activity', with which pupils evaluated the curriculum in Key Stage 1, has almost vanished and, in its place, we have pupils who are predominantly concerned that they should be able to achieve success in teacher directed tasks without too much difficulty. From the overall analysis of PACE 2 data, it appears that curriculum activities have become much more tightly framed in Key Stage 2 and that pupils recognize adjustments in the ways in which they are evaluated. Changes in pupil perceptions of curriculum articulate with new patterns of experience and to the power relations and expectations which existed within the social contexts of the Key Stage 2 classrooms.

9.3 PEDAGOGY

In both PACE 1 and PACE 2, one way in which we investigated pedagogy was by asking the target pupils, 'Do you choose what you do at school, or does your teacher choose for you most of the time?'. The results are shown in Table 9.3.

Table 9.3 *Children's perspective of who selects tasks at school (percentages)*

	Year 1	Year 2	Year 3	Year 4
Teacher	59	80	98	98
Children	13	2	2	0
Both	26	13	0	2
No data	2	5	0	0

Source: PACE 1 and 2 child interviews
Sample: 54 children in Years 1–4
Date: Autumn 1990 and 1991, summer 1993 and 1994

There is a strong pattern here, with almost all pupils at Year 3 and 4 feeling that their teachers decided upon activities and tasks. Of course, the children's perceptions at Year 1 and 2 may have been a little naïve, and certainly the relative autonomy which they experienced then was regulated within the routines and practices of the classroom organization. Nevertheless, the difference in pupil perception of control following the transition from Key Stage 1 to Key Stage 2 is notable. Whilst this may have simply reflected changes in methods of task assignment which teachers deemed appropriate as the children grew older, data from teacher interviews suggest that it also reflected a tightening in teacher direction of pupil activities over the period.

Did the pupils accept this tightening of control? Table 9.4 offers data on a second aspect of pupil views of pedagogy: perceptions of relationships with their teachers, which is very relevant to this question. The children were asked, 'How do you get on with your teacher?' and their responses were coded positive, neutral or negative.

Table 9.4 *Year 1, 2, 3 and 4 pupils' perceptions of their relationships with their teacher (percentages)*

	Year 1	Year 2	Year 3	Year 4
Positive	57	48	56	63
Neutral	35	46	39	35
Negative	2	4	5	2
Don't know	2	0	0	0
No data	4	2	0	0

Source: PACE 1 and 2 child interviews
Sample: 54 children in Years 1–4
Date: autumn 1990 and 1991, summer 1993 and 1994

The pattern here is fairly consistent across all four years for which data have been gathered, with the children tending to feel, if anything, increasingly positive. Only one or two children each year made comments which were coded as indicating negative perceptions of their teacher. For each year, almost two fifths expressed neutral views, but almost three fifths were positive about the ways in which they 'got on with' their teacher. Some of the things which the children answered as Year 3 and 4 pupils will illustrate their feelings.

Statements coded as 'positive' included:

Really well, she's a really nice teacher, very helpful.

All right, 'cos she's kind.

Excellent, really. On Parents' Evening he said 'You'll be glad to know your son has done nothing wrong and I wish I had another 32 like him'!

Very well. He's a good teacher and he's funny as well.

OK, he's always cracking jokes.

Statements coded as 'neutral' included a number which were conditional, such as:

All right, but noisy when people keep talking. And I don't like it because you never know anything.

Quite well. M' mates always talk to me, so if he sees you talking and you don't finish, he might send you to Mr R. He made my mate change places. I changed places a lot. I'm on my third table.

I get on quite well – last year and year before I got silly at the end of term and my two teachers got quite cross but now I seem to be much better.

In the middle, because sometimes I'm naughty and sometimes good.

Well OK really, but not brilliant. Sometimes I get my work right because Anthony does, and sometimes I get it wrong 'cos Anthony's told me wrong.

Not bad. Sometimes I disagree with her when she says something unfair.

Statements coded as 'negative' were:

Not very well — when I'm working she tells us to sit down.

Not so well; N told Miss that M wrote his name under the table and Miss asked us if we told him to do it.

Not at all. She's very strict.

The criteria which were deployed by the children are well established in the research literature (Pollard, 1985; Goodnow and Burns, 1988; Woods, 1990). They liked teachers to be kind and helpful, fair, interesting and fun. They were uneasy if their teacher acted in ways which they deemed to be unfair, inappropriate or boring.

In the PACE 1 project, a pattern of Year 1 and 2 girls tending to be more positive than boys was noted, and this was echoed by the children's statements at Year 3 and 4. For those years, the responses of 63 per cent of girls were coded as positive, as against 55 per cent of boys, whose responses were more often coded as neutral or negative. A pattern of variation in the child-perceived quality of teacher relationships by pupil attainment was also again found, as it had been by PACE 1 when the children were in Years 1 and 2. Higher attaining children tended to be more positive about their teachers than children who were experiencing more curricular difficulties at school.

Despite such variations, the overall message from these data is that pupils both recognized and accepted the greater control over their activities which the teachers in Key Stage 2 exercised. Indeed, as ethnographic data from Woods (1990) and Pollard and Filer (forthcoming) would suggest, one consequence of 'becoming a junior', with its contribution to the development of pupil identity through status passage (Van Gennep, 1960), is acceptance of the changing nature of school work. Children tend to recognize and accept that the lived experience of the juniors will be significantly different from that in the infants. They know that they cannot begin to grow up without accepting something of the terms of such passage.

9.4   ASSESSMENT

'Evaluation' is the third of Bernstein's message systems through which classroom practices can be characterized. In the school context of the 1990s, it takes the form of assessment of both formative and summative types and, at this mid-point in the overall PACE project, we were mainly concerned with pupil perspectives on the continuous, formative types of assessment to which they were subject in routine classroom work. We were particularly interested in the degree of positive feelings or, on the other hand, vulnerability and exposure, which the pupils perceived in those classroom episodes in which assessment or evaluation played a part.

Pupils in their Years 3 and 4 were asked, as they had been in their Years 1 and 2, 'Do you like it when your teacher asks to look at your book?'. As previously, their answers were coded using four codes: positive, negative, mixed and neutral.

Table 9.5 provides an overview of the results for all four school years from which data was gathered.

This table shows a decline from Year 1 to Year 4 in the eagerness with which pupils welcomed teachers asking to see their work. As 5/6-year-olds (Year 1), almost three-fifths of the children were pleased to show what they had done, but as 8/9-year-olds (Year 4) the figure had fallen by 14 per cent, with a matching increase in negative

Table 9.5 *Responses of pupils to the question 'Do you like it when your teacher asks to look at your book?'* (*percentages*)

	Year 1	Year 2	Tear 3	Tear 4
Positive	57	52	44	43
Mixed	15	20	18	17
Neutral	6	7	6	4
Negative	22	21	32	36

Source: PACE 1 and 2 child interviews
Sample: 54 children in Years 1–4
Date: Autumn 1990 and 1991, summer 1993 and 1994

comments. The transition from Key Stage 1 to Key Stage 2, and the consistency of the trend, was marked in these respects.

Among the statements coded *'positive'* and made by the children during their Year 3 and 4 were:

> Yes. I feel proud if she says it's good.

> Yes. Then I know what I've done wrong and what right and I can go away and correct it and it will be OK.

> Yes. Because normally they put comments and for me it's a good one. When I wrote the story of a frog learning to swim, Mrs G wrote a comment — 'You'll make a good swimming teacher.'

> Yes. Like with my poster, Miss said it was very good and I was all happy after.

> Yes. It feels like you've done something really good.

The more mixed responses included the following:

> Sometimes I don't like it if I haven't done very much. If I've done a lot, I like Mrs H to come over and say she's pleased with me; then I feel I've done something good.

> [Nods] Sometimes, when it's nice writing. I think is she going to say it's messy writing or not.

> In between, like this [makes rocking gesture with hand], I don't really know what she's going to say. Sometimes glad if I think the work's good; a bit worried if work's not all that good.

> Yes. If I think I haven't done much or if I've rushed because I didn't feel like it, I feel a bit worried, but if I think it looks nice I'm proud for her to see it.

> Yes. Sometimes I like it, sometimes I don't. I like her to look if it's neat, not if it's untidy.

> When I've only done a bit I feel worried. When I've done loads I'm all right.

The more negative comments by the children showed their concerns with 'getting things wrong' or being seen to get things wrong.

> I'm worried — I go like this [mimes praying]. You never know when she does a line if it's going to go like this or like this [mimes X and tick]. When she marks them right I'm so happy. A bit disappointed if I'm wrong.

> Not much. She might put you down to an easy book or cross them wrong.

> No. 'Cos I say 'Oh no! She's going to say, "Do that again Claire!"'

> No. I'm a bit scared so he'll say I've got to do it again. That's the problem.

No. I feel worried I might get them all wrong.

No. Nervous, scared — I think she may say, 'Go back and do that again!'

Sometimes I feel a bit worried. Because sometimes I get things wrong and teacher shouts at us.

I feel worried. 'Cos I don't hardly ever finish. But I did finish my spellings — two pages. I done the second page on me own.

No. Worried — in case she says, 'Good gracious me, that's terrible!'

Yes, but not when I'm in the middle of something 'cos I like to get on with it. I feel that I've finished it at last. Sometimes I have to say I don't like work or the others in my class call me a wimp.

No. I think I might have to stay in and work and not have a break.

No. My writing — I can't write properly. I just don't look at him when he's doing it, then I feel all right.

The overriding impression from reading these pupil comments is of their awareness of the risk which is involved in the key evaluative moment when the teacher inspects their work. They may 'get it wrong', be 'told off', have to 'do it again' or even be laughed at by their peers. Whilst there is considerable awareness of the importance of the appearance of the work and of the need to be correct, there is little sense that the pupils were alert to more educational criteria which their teacher might use. Rather, they hoped that their work would be 'all right', or, more probably, remained 'a bit worried'. Here, we have an indication of the perceived ambiguity of many classroom tasks and of pupil uncertainty about teacher responses.

The children were also asked, 'Why do some children do better at school work than others?', and their answers also illuminate something of their thinking about how to achieve classroom success. Table 9.6 summarizes the results.

Table 9.6 *Responses of pupils to the question 'Why do some children do better at school work than others?' (percentages)*

	Years 1 and 2	Years 3 and 4
Age	13	3
Effort	45	56
Ability	19	14
Skill	14	7
Dont't know	9	2
Other	0	8

Source: PACE 1 and 2 child interviews
Sample: 54 children in Years 1–4
Date: Autumn 1990 and 1991, summer 1993 and 1994

'Effort' was perceived as being the most important factor in school success in both Years 1 and 2 and in Years 3 and 4, but when the children were older it was particularly pronounced, recording an increase of 11 per cent and being cited by 56 per cent of children. 'Age' was no longer considered to be significant and the two explanations which could be regarded as encapsulating inherent capacities, 'ability' and 'skill', had also both decreased in perceived importance. For the Key Stage 2 children, what mattered was making sufficient 'effort' and application. For instance:

They just try harder.

Some people are dawdling about and not listening.

Maybe they have more patience and they concentrate, and some of the others rush and only do a little bit. The patient ones write two pages and they look things up in dictionaries.

Some people get on and don't talk as much; some people want to get on and others chat and chat and do, like, perhaps a couple of lines in half an hour.

It's because some are faster and they're good writers and they try harder.

They practise more at home.

Because they spend more time over it.

Because when we go to the [swimming] baths some people go learning, so they have more chance of getting a certificate. Because they're better workers and they can do faster writing, and they're on higher levels.

They're neater and they get the hang of it.

Some people concentrate more.

'Cos they don't scribble, they don't care about the people [messing around with them], they care about the work.

Well, because they work harder and they're clever because they don't talk.

'Cos some children mess around and some don't.

Some work harder and don't talk. I never talk until I've finished it all. Alex only did one line between 9 and 10.30

'Cos they just stick their fingers in their ears and get on. They bring ear plugs. If they get hit by a paper-clip they don't take any notice.

These results match Nicholls' studies of children in the United States at similar ages, where it was found that 'effort' was by far the most common attribution given by children for educational success (Nicholls, 1989). Nicholls suggested that the younger children were not able to differentiate effort and outcome and attributed an almost tautologous relationship between trying hard and succeeding. A previous study of British schoolchildren using open-ended responses has also shown the importance of effort in children's attributions of academic success and has shown an increase in this attribution with age in a similar way to our findings (Little, 1985). The Little study had a category of 'behaviour' which was also a reason commonly given by children for success. Behaviour is not differentiated from effort in our coding but some of the quotations above show how it figures in children's responses. The responses quoted above also show how, for some children, trying hard is also linked with notions of strategy, of having particular approaches to getting on with work. These ideas may link to the more general theme of children progressively learning pupil roles in the primary school.

When asked what happened when children 'did their work really well' about one quarter of the children in Year 3 and 4 simply expected to be praised by their teacher. However, almost 70 per cent reported that they would receive some sort of reward in the form of a 'star', 'team point', badge, certificate or other form of public recognition. Such symbolic rewards were more common than they had been at Key Stage 1, during which PACE 1 data showed approximately 9 per cent of teachers reinforcing exceptional pupil performances with choice of activities and a further 8 per cent occasionally providing material rewards such as sweets. The reward structure in the first two years of Key Stage 2 seemed to be more systematic and was often tied into whole-school structures for behavioural and academic reinforcement.

However, such external rewards were certainly not the prime concern for the pupils in the everyday run of classroom life. We asked them about the 'sorts of things' which would make them feel 'worried' about their work, and again, what would make them feel 'pleased' about it. The children's responses were coded to produce Table 9.7

Table 9.7 *Responses of pupils when asked 'What sort of things make you feel worried and pleased about your work?' (percentages)*

	Worried	Pleased
Teacher criticism/praise	7	38
Appearance	33	24
Correctness	32	17
Quantity	6	3
Quality	9	4
Completion	2	7
Other	5	3
Don't know	5	3
No answer	1	1

Source: PACE 2 child interviews
Sample: 54 children in Years 3 and 4
Date: Summer 1993 and 1994

From Table 9.7 it is clear that, when in Year 3 and 4, the pupils were primarily concerned that their work should be presented with a satisfactory appearance, a finding which reinforces the findings on assessment which were presented earlier. They also worried that their work should be 'correct' and were pleased if this was confirmed. However, correctness seemed to be rather more important to them than quality *per se*.

The evaluative context of the classroom was reflected in the emphasis the children gave to teacher praise. This was mentioned by 38 per cent of the children. As they put it:

When I've done writing I don't really know and it's all wrong and I show it to Mrs L and I don't want to do it again.

If the teacher tells other people off. I worry about what she's going to do to me.

'Cos I hadn't done much or it was messy.

The numbers were wrong or not neat and I think she won't tick it.

If I've done too much rubbing out and there's a hole in my page.

Not using a ruler, blunt pencil, and if you've been thinking about something else.

When it's not neat and I think I may have to do it again if it's scruffy.

If it didn't look neat and if I didn't care about my spellings.

If I think 'Oh no, that's not right.' If my spelling's wrong and it's too late, Mrs H is marking it.

If it wasn't neat or if I had lots of mistakes; if I'd been cheating and hadn't done very much. I think 'Oh God, she's going to tell me off.'

If I don't do neat writing Miss B gets angry.

9.5   CONCLUSION

The pupils studied tended to like curriculum subjects which either allowed them some autonomy or tended to produce tasks with low ambiguity — the best example being maths, where the scheme systems which are so dominant in Key Stage 2 permit children to 'be good' routinely. Children want success and ease, which can be seen as being in tension with risk and ambiguity. Teacher–pupil relationships remained good in the successive classrooms through which the children passed, but at the same time there was pupil awareness of tighter teacher control over the curriculum and tasks set. In terms of pupil awareness of evaluation, they were more aware of the high stakes and risk associated with teacher assessment but believed that this could be met by making more 'effort' of various sorts. In particular, they aimed to produce work with the right 'appearance' which was 'correct', — i.e. as the teacher expected or wanted. Pupils derived great pleasure from teacher approval.

Overall then, the PACE data on pupil perspectives seems to indicate that the sample of children adopted an increasingly refined 'pupil' role as they grew older and learned to 'play' the systems which existed in their successive classrooms.

Some of the consequences of such findings can be illustrated through a conversation with a Year 5 pupil. I asked David why he had found his topic work so hard to complete.

AP: Can you tell me about the topic work which was so difficult?

David: The topic was about Celebrations, and it was this picture, oh, it took me ages to figure out, and on the 50th time, I went up to Miss and it was OK. But then, I had to copy again because it was all horrible.
  And there was something else again in my topic book. I was thinking about what to put on these two pages I had left. And I couldn't think about anything. So finally, I went up to Miss and she shouted a lot, and then she went, 'Oh, just do pictures about it and put it on the pages.'

AP: She shouted at you did she?

David: Yea, she was in a ratty mood that time.

AP: Did you think that you ought to have known what to put?

David: Yea. But maybe I wasn't there when she explained.

AP: Why didn't you go up a bit sooner?

David: I kept on going up and going up and going up, and it was only the last time that she said that.

AP: So was she getting fed up with you?

David: Yea. But I didn't understand it at all. It was about 'celebrations'. We had all these books and we had to copy down all the stuff about celebrations. We had loads of sheets. It was hard and we had this big map and there's like Hinduism, Christianity ... oh, there's millions [sighs].

AP: But you did get it done after she shouted at you. Why was it that when you went to talk to her before it didn't work, but after she shouted at you, it did?

David: I don't usually understand it, but I always understand it when she shouts because she tells you the answer. Because she gets fed up of you coming up and coming up and coming up, so she shouts and she says ... 'just — do — pictures'.

AP: Why do you think she doesn't tell you the answer earlier?

David: She thinks we have to find it out.

AP: So do you like that, having to find it out?

David: Its all right sometimes, but on some bits when I don't know even what it is, ... its hard.

AP: Why is it that she doesn't tell you what to do straight away.

David: She wants you to find out for yourself because when you're older, she won't be there to help you.

AP: So why do you keep asking her and asking her until she tells you?

David: Well, because we're only little and we don't know what to do.

AP: Does it matter if you get it right? What would happen if you got it wrong?

David: She just says, 'start again'.

AP: So you want to avoid that?

David: One time I kept on trying, but I had to start again and start again until there was no pieces of topic paper left. I kept on trying ... but nothing seemed right.

This short excerpt illustrates several aspects of the analysis which has been developed in this chapter and elsewhere in the book. David's teacher, who was consciously resistant to what she saw as the 'constraining requirements of the National Curriculum', pursued her philosophy of self-directed pupil learning and had high expectations of what David could achieve. However, her motivational rationale for topic work foundered, for this pupil at least, in his uncertainty about 'what to put' and was further compromised by the fragmentation and quantity of the content she felt required to present — as David put it, 'oh, there's millions'. David understood many elements of the situation and even appreciated his teacher's educational intentions — 'when you're older, she won't be there to help you'. However, this didn't help him avoid task ambiguity and, in tackling this overriding concern, he had evolved what we might call an 'attrition' strategy. Thus he asked questions *repeatedly*, until the patience of the teacher cracked and, in her frustration, all ambiguity was removed — 'just — do — pictures'. The highest risk to David was the boredom which would result from 'starting again' and it is evident that the possibility of 'Miss getting ratty' was felt to be the lesser of the two evils, given what was fundamentally a warm reciprocal relationship between them.

It could be argued that this teacher started off by setting high expectations for David and her other pupils. But high teacher expectations are often perceived by pupils as increasing the ambiguity of tasks and risk of failure and public exposure. As Doyle and Carter (1984) found, pupils then tend to attempt to negotiate to reduce these difficulties. This is a form of coping strategy. In David's case above, the strategy he adopted was one of attrition and, in her own desperate attempt to cope with the multitude of pressures on her classroom time, his teacher ultimately capitulated and reduced her expectations of him.

'Raising teacher expectations' is often invoked as a means of increasing educational standards (see, for instance, The Annual Report of Her Majesty's Chief Inspector of Schools (OFSTED 1995)) but I would suggest that such rhetoric is contextually naïve.

Teachers' attempts to sustain high expectations often mean increasing the ambiguity and risk of the curricular tasks which pupils face. Such initiatives are thus likely to be contested by pupils using strategies to 'play the system' and to maximize ease and success. With relatively high class sizes, the result can be that high teacher expectations can produce a more fraught classroom atmosphere as the children are challenged and then respond. As I have argued elsewhere (Pollard 1985), both parties have to cope with their classroom experiences and may reach a mutual accommodation which avoids such tensions and renegotiations. Unfortunately, one outcome of the mesh of teacher–pupil strategies which often results is routinized teaching and pupil drift. However, this should be seen as a product of the practical circumstances of classroom life no less than as some sort of 'failing' on the part of teachers. As pupils cope by 'playing the system', the reduction of high expectations, and of the associated risk and ambiguity, is one of their goals.

Chapter 10

A Curriculum for All? Special Educational Needs and the National Curriculum

Paul Croll

10.1 Introduction

10.2 The National Curriculum in special schools

10.3 Special educational needs in mainstream primary schools: Teacher and headteacher perceptions

10.4 The classroom experience of children with learning difficulties

10.5 Conclusions

10.1 INTRODUCTION

One of the most contested areas in discussions on the impact of the National Curriculum on children's educational experience is that relating to the education of children with special educational needs. This is an area where the claims made for the educational advantages of the National Curriculum and the educational problems it brings differ most widely. The initial presentation of the National Curriculum by the Department for Education and the National Curriculum Council (NCC) strongly emphasized the notion of all children having an entitlement to the full curriculum and explicitly included children with special educational needs in this entitlement. The National Curriculum Council document on special educational needs in the National Curriculum was entitled, *A Curriculum for All* and opened with the statement that 'All pupils share the right to a broad and balanced curriculum, including the National Curriculum' (NCC, 1989). The NCC set up a Special Educational Needs Task Group to consider access to the National Curriculum for children with special educational needs. This produced circulars of curriculum guidance, and papers and resource materials were produced in particular curriculum areas such as science and modern foreign languages (NCC, 1991; 1993a). Although there are procedures within the National Curriculum for the modification or disapplication of its curricular requirements in the case of children with special educational needs, it was explicitly intended that these should be used 'rarely' (NCC, 1989, p. 9). The design of the PACE project enables us to consider some of these issues, drawing on teacher and headteacher perceptions and on direct observation in classrooms.

A number of commentators have argued that the National Curriculum has the potential for expanding the educational opportunities available to pupils with special educational needs. Writers such as Galloway (1990) have argued that the entitlement to a common curriculum will reduce the marginalization of such children and that the notion of curriculum entitlement will help prevent the exclusion from the mainstream curriculum which has often been a characteristic of the educational experience of children with special educational needs.

On the other hand, critics of the National Curriculum have claimed that its introduction will reverse the advances in the education of children with special educational needs which have begun to be made following the report of the Warnock Committee and the implementation of the 1981 Education Act (Heward and Lloyd-Smith, 1990). Criticisms have focused on the likelihood of increased pressure on teachers leading to less time being available for children with special educational needs, the appropriateness of some of the content of the National Curriculum for children with special educational needs, and on the impact of compulsory assessment procedures on children who are likely to attain poorly on such assessments. Concern about the impact of the National Curriculum on children with special educational needs has also been linked with concerns about the effects on such children of other educational changes introduced in the 1988 Education Act (Bowe *et al.*, 1992). These wider concerns centre on the devolution of budgets to schools and the publication of comparative tables of pupil achievement with the aim of introducing a more competitive climate between schools. It has been argued that the publication of 'league tables' will make children who are not likely to perform well academically unattractive to schools, while at the same time increased budgetary pressures will reduce the level of resources available to such children, especially those who are not the subject of statements.

Any attempt to consider the actual impact of the introduction of the National Curriculum on children with special educational needs is greatly complicated by the variety of these needs, both with regard to the nature of the difficulties which pupils have and the range of severity of a particular sort of difficulty. Children may experience learning difficulties, emotional and behavioural difficulties and a wide range of physical, sensory and health-related problems. There may also be a complex pattern of overlap between such problems (Tizard, 1974; Croll and Moses, 1985).

For the most part, children with the most demanding level of educational needs are the subject of a Statement of Special Educational Need. Most of these children are educated in special schools rather than in mainstream primary or secondary schools. In the early 1990s about one in forty children of school age had statements of special educational needs and about sixty per cent of these children were educated separately in special schools (DfE, 1994; Norwich, 1994). However, in addition to the small number of children with statements of special educational needs who are placed in mainstream schools, there is a much larger number of children whose problems are usually less severe but who, nevertheless, can be regarded as having special educational needs.

The Report of the Warnock Committee argued that special educational needs should be seen as a continuum rather than as a set of categories of handicap applying to a small number of children (DES, 1978). The Report suggested that up to one in five children might experience some form of special educational need. A large-scale survey of primary schools showed that the figure of approximately one in five matched teachers' experiences of the difficulties their pupils faced. In this survey, more than 18 per cent of primary-age pupils were described by their teachers as having special educational needs. The most common type of difficulty was associated with learning problems and especially reading problems, but significant proportions of pupils had behavioural and emotional difficulties, and about one in twenty had physical, sensory or health-related difficulties (Croll and Moses, 1985). This means that all teachers will experience children with special educational needs fairly frequently in their careers and that the experience for teachers of implementing the National Curriculum is certain to include the issue of special educational needs.

10.2 THE NATIONAL CURRICULUM IN SPECIAL SCHOOLS

It is perhaps surprising that in the early discussions of the likely effects of the National Curriculum on the education of children with special educational needs there was rather more support for the National Curriculum from special schools than there was from those concerned with special educational needs within the mainstream. While head-teachers and teachers in mainstream schools tended to emphasize the difficulties that the pressures of the National Curriculum, and especially the associated assessment procedures, would create in regard to children with special educational needs, staff, and especially the headteachers, of special schools often welcomed the inclusive approach of the National Curriculum and saw it as an opportunity for curriculum development in special education.

A large-scale survey of headteachers of special schools conducted in 1990 showed that over 80 per cent welcomed the introduction of the National Curriculum while fewer than one in ten expressed opposition to it. The pattern of response was broadly similar across all types of special school (Davies, 1990; Davies and Landman, 1991). Few of the headteachers felt that they currently met National Curriculum requirements, and a large majority agreed with the statement that the National Curriculum would, 'help in introducing changes that are needed' (Davies, 1990, p. 6). The content of the head-teachers' responses included very positive feelings about special education being included along with the rest of the education system, a recognition that the introduction of a broader curriculum in special schools was overdue and the view expressed by some heads that it would provide them with a lever for making changes which would otherwise be resisted by staff. The reservations expressed were typically to do with the range of staff expertise available to them to cover the whole of the curriculum, especially in the areas of science and foreign languages. The heads did not typically identify limitations inherent within their pupils as obstacles to following the National Curriculum, except in the area of foreign languages. Most heads expressed a reluctance to use the procedures for exemption or disapplication of the National Curriculum in the case of pupils with special educational needs (Davies, 1990; Davies and Landman, 1991).

Reports on consultation exercises carried out by the National Curriculum Council with teachers of children with special educational needs has confirmed the support among such teachers for the entitlement of all children to access to the National Curriculum (NCC, 1993b). The experience of working with the National Curriculum had not changed the initial enthusiasm for the notion of curriculum inclusion for all but it had led to the identification of many practical difficulties. Staff of special schools and special units were still opposed to the disapplication of the National Curriculum for pupils with special educational needs. However, this was because of the negative associations of the notion of disapplication: many teachers were looking for a more positive way of expressing the process of modifying the National Curriculum requirements for some children. There is a suggestion here of a rather cosmetic change in the way the process of modification or disapplication is expressed but which will, nevertheless, have the same practical outcomes. Teachers in special schools and special units also wanted to emphasize that the National Curriculum was only part of the curriculum needs of many children with special educational needs and that the personal, social and developmental aspects of the curriculum for such children should be given equal status with the National Curriculum.

The most recent evidence on the responses to the National Curriculum in special schools comes from a series of interviews with special school headteachers conducted in 1994 (Lewis and Halpin, forthcoming). Although this study was limited to twelve headteachers, and must therefore be treated cautiously, some interesting perspectives emerge. A number of headteachers matched the picture of special school heads that emerged from the large-scale survey conducted at an earlier stage of National Curriculum implementation and discussed above. These headteachers were enthusiasts for the National Curriculum and particularly the notion of the rights of children to equal access to the curriculum. A second group of heads were also supportive of the National Curriculum in principle but had deviated considerably from the letter of the requirements in order to make it workable for their pupils, for example, by arguing that much curriculum coverage was accomplished in cross-curricular themes. There are some echoes of this sort of perspective in the results of the NCC consultation exercise where teachers supported the National Curriculum but also had additional priorities which they wanted recognized. A third group of heads in the Lewis and Halpin study saw the National Curriculum as irrelevant to the needs of their pupils and had made little response beyond token curriculum modifications. This is a perspective which had not emerged from other evidence on special schools and the National Curriculum.

The Lewis and Halpin study is small-scale and cannot be generalized. However, it fits in with an emerging pattern within the special-school sector: an initial positive response to the National Curriculum on the grounds of the entitlement of all pupils and a recognition that the existing special school curriculum was too narrow, has been tempered by experience to include a recognition that there are important aspects of some children's educational needs which fall outside the National Curriculum. Data from the PACE project enable us to consider these issues with regard to mainstream schooling.

10.3 SPECIAL EDUCATIONAL NEEDS IN MAINSTREAM PRIMARY SCHOOLS: TEACHER AND HEADTEACHER PERCEPTIONS

The schools studied in the PACE project were all mainstream primary schools and the perspectives on the National Curriculum and pupils with special educational needs to arise in the study were concerned with the experience of such children in mainstream classes. Although a small minority of children in mainstream classes have difficulties which overlap in severity with those of children in special schools, for the most part teachers in the mainstream are thinking of children with considerably less severe problems when they describe special educational needs.

Although the PACE project was not primarily concerned with the issue of special educational needs and the National Curriculum, data relevant to this issue emerged from a variety of aspects of the study. The data to be presented in this section of the present chapter come from the interviews conducted with teachers and headteachers at different stages of the implementation of the National Curriculum and locate special educational needs in the broader context of responses to educational change.

In the first two rounds of interviews in 1990 and 1992 class teachers were asked how well they thought the curriculum content of the National Curriculum was matched to the needs of their pupils. At an earlier stage of the first interview they were also asked to describe the characteristics of the children they taught. Using the responses to the question about children's characteristics, teachers can be categorized into those who described their classes in terms of a preponderance of children having special educational needs and those who did not. Twenty of the 88 teachers interviewed said that they had many pupils with learning problems and/or had many children with emotional and behavioural difficulties. In Table 10.1 the responses to the question on the match of the National Curriculum to pupils' needs are presented separately for those teachers who did and those who did not characterize their pupils in terms of learning or emotional/behavioural difficulties or both.

Table 10.1 shows a substantial shift over time in teachers' perceptions of the match of the National Curriculum to their pupils' needs. In 1990, at an early stage in the process of implementation, well over half of the teachers interviewed (54.4 per cent) said that the National Curriculum matched their pupils' needs well, while less than one in five (17.0 per cent) felt that it was poorly matched. But by 1992, with several years experience of the National Curriculum, only a quarter of teachers (25.8 per cent) felt that it matched their children's needs well and a third (32.3 per cent) felt that it was not well matched. The numbers of teachers giving mixed or uncertain responses increased considerably from 28.4 per cent in 1990 to 41.9 per cent in 1992.

It is clear that, over time, teachers became less sure that the National Curriculum matched their pupils' needs, with the proportion saying that it did halving between 1990 and 1992 and the proportion saying it did not doubling. The comparison between teachers who described their classes in terms of learning or behavioural difficulties and other teachers, presented in Table 10.1, shows that, in both rounds of interviews, the teachers of the classes characterized by learning or behavioural difficulties were less positive about the match of the National Curriculum to their pupils needs than were other teachers. In 1990 rather under a half (45.0 per cent) of such teachers said that the National Curriculum was well matched to their pupils' needs while just over a third (35.0 per cent) said that it was not well matched. More of these teachers supported the match of the National Curriculum than disputed it, but the perception of these teachers was less favourable than was the perception of teachers who did not describe their classes in terms of learning and behavioural difficulties.

In 1992, the perception of match among teachers of classes with learning and behavioural difficulties was overwhelmingly negative. Only 15 per cent of these teachers now thought that the National Curriculum was well matched to their pupils' needs while exactly a half said that it was not well matched. It is clear that teachers of pupils who they perceive in terms of special educational needs are strikingly more likely than other teachers to see the content of the National Curriculum as inappropriate for their classes and that this perception of inappropriateness increased considerably over two years of experience of implementing the National Curriculum. The impact of the experience of the National Curriculum has tended to move all teachers in the direction of perceiving it as less appropriate than their initial reaction, but this reaction has been more decisive in the case of teachers who have classes they see in terms of special educational needs than it has among other teachers.

Table 10.1 *Special educational needs and the match of the National Curriculum to children's needs (percentages)*

	1990			1992		
	Classes with learning or behaviour difficulties	Other classes	All	Classes with learning or behaviour difficulties	Other classes	All
Well matched	45.0	57.4	54.5	15.0	28.8	25.8
Mixed	20.0	30.9	28.4	35.0	43.8	41.9
Not well matched	35.0	11.8	17.0	50.0	27.4	32.3

Source: PACE 1 teacher interviews
Sample: 88 Key Stage 1 teachers
Dates: Summer 1990 and summer 1992

At a later stage in the project interviews were conducted with teachers of KS1 pupils and with headteachers in 1994. Many, although not all, of the class teachers were the same people whose interview responses on the question of the match of the National Curriculum to their pupils' needs were discussed above. In the 1994 round of interviews the question of the National Curriculum and various sorts of special educational needs was addressed directly. Headteachers and class teachers were both asked directly what they thought had been the impact of the National Curriculum on particular groups of children, compared with its impact on children more generally. This question was asked about children with learning difficulties and also about children with emotional and behavioural difficulties.

In Table 10.2 the responses of headteachers and class teachers to the question about the impact of the National Curriculum on children with learning difficulties are presented. It is apparent that there is a considerable divergence of view across the sample as a whole but no substantial difference between teachers and heads. The most common response of both teachers and heads is that children with learning difficulties have been disadvantaged by the introduction of the National Curriculum: just under a half (48.5 per cent) of heads and a slightly smaller proportion (44.3 per cent) of teachers support this view. On the other hand, a fairly substantial minority of both groups, exactly a third of heads and just under a quarter (22.7 per cent) of teachers, think that the National Curriculum has brought particular benefits to children with learning difficulties.

Analysis of the further comments made in the interviews shows that people who thought there were advantages to children with learning difficulties stressed both the value of individualized assessments and the greater degree of structure which the

National Curriculum had introduced. The assessment arrangements for the National Curriculum and, especially, the teacher assessments were seen as helping the teacher to get to know children in a way that was particularly helpful for those who might have very individual needs. Associated with this, the clear targets for attainment within a more structured curriculum were seen as helping the teacher to identify children who were failing. Some comments suggested that it had been too easy in the past to accept unduly low goals for children who were experiencing difficulties and that the requirements of the National Curriculum would lead to more demanding expectations.

While teachers and heads who thought the National Curriculum would benefit children with learning difficulties placed an emphasis on the identification and diagnosis of these difficulties and the setting of appropriate aims, those who thought it would bring particular disadvantages for such children put more emphasis on pedagogy and on curriculum content. These comments stressed most of all the increased time pressure on teachers and the likely pressure to move towards more whole-class teaching and to focus on class average levels of achievement. These, it was argued, were making it harder to meet the needs of children with learning difficulties. Some people also commented on the broadening of the curriculum which had to be studied by all pupils, including those who, it was claimed, needed more time on basic skills before they could usefully address a broader curriculum:

> These are children who desperately need basic literacy. Anything that is a distraction from that isn't helping them

and from another teacher:

> A broader curriculum is OK in theory, but not for children who are struggling with basic skills.

Table 10.2   *The impact of the National Curriculum on children with learning difficulties (percentages)*

	Headteachers	Teachers
Particular benefit	33.3	22.7
No particular effect	12.5	17.0
Particular disadvantage	48.5	44.3
Don't know/No answer	8.3	15.9

Source: PACE 2 headteacher and teacher interviews
Sample: 48 headteachers, 88 teachers
Date: Spring 1994

The teachers and heads were also asked about the particular impact of the National Curriculum on children with emotional and behavioural difficulties. The response to this question are presented in Table 10.3. As with the question about children with learning difficulties, there is relatively little difference between the replies of teachers and headteachers and, as with the earlier question, there is considerable variation in the views expressed. In the case of learning difficulties the main difference to emerge from the data was between those who thought there were particular advantages and those who thought there were particular disadvantages. However, in the case of emotional and behavioural difficulties the main difference is between those who think there are particular advantages and those who were undecided or thought there would be no particular effect.

Very few of either heads or teachers (2.1 per cent and 6.8 per cent respectively) thought that there were particular benefits in the National Curriculum for children with emotional difficulties. In contrast, four in ten of both groups (39.6 per cent and 40.9 per cent) thought that there would be particular disadvantages. Well over half either could not answer or thought there would be no particular effect, a much higher proportion than in the case of learning difficulties. These figures seem to indicate that, while the National Curriculum is clearly seen as relevant to learning difficulties, although with considerable divergence of view of the nature of that relevance, it is not necessarily seen as relevant to emotional and behavioural difficulties. However, those teachers who do see it as relevant almost all see its influence as negative.

The content of teachers' comments on the National Curriculum and children with emotional and behavioural difficulties parallels the negative comments on its impact on children with learning difficulties. Many people emphasized the time pressure on teachers and the difficulty they faced in finding enough time for the social and pastoral aspects of their work and also fulfilling the requirements of the National Curriculum. Some teachers questioned the appropriateness of the curriculum content of the National Curriculum for children for whom they had more pressing concerns:

> I want to spend time helping these children make relationships and understand their behaviour. There are social priorities at this very early stage of schooling.

Table 10.3   *The impact of the National Curriculum on children with emotional and behavioural difficulties (percentages)*

	Headteachers	Teachers
Particular benefit	2.1	6.8
No particular effect	33.3	19.3
Particular disadvantage	39.6	40.9
Don't know/No answer	25.0	33.0

Source: PACE 2 headteacher and teacher interviews
Sample: 48 headteachers, 88 teachers
Date: Spring 1994

10.4 THE CLASSROOM EXPERIENCE OF CHILDREN WITH LEARNING DIFFICULTIES

The classroom observation conducted in nine of the classrooms involved in the PACE study makes it possible to describe some aspects of the classroom experience of children with special educational needs and to contrast it with the classroom experience of other pupils. In each class a week of classroom observation was carried out on four separate occasions, two at Key Stage 1 and two at Key Stage 2. Six children in each class were selected as the particular focus of the observation. These children were selected to give a cross-section of the class and not with regard to representing children with special educational needs. However, teachers were asked to describe children in their class to the researchers, and on the basis of these descriptions children can be described as having learning or other difficulties, as perceived by the teacher. For the present analysis, nine children who were most consistently characterized by their various teachers as having problems with learning have been categorized as low-achievers. These children come from seven of the nine classes which were the subject of intensive study. They were not necessarily the lowest-achieving nine children in the sample, but are children who were consistently perceived by their teachers as having special problems related to learning. The children identified as low-achievers constitute 16.7 per cent of the sample of 54 children observed. This is a very similar proportion to the 15.4 per cent of pupils described by their teachers as having learning difficulties in the large-scale survey by Croll and Moses of junior-age classes (Croll and Moses, 1985).

Earlier evidence about the classroom experiences of children with various sorts of special educational needs in mainstream primary classes also comes from the Croll and Moses study. This research reported that children with learning difficulties and also children with emotional and behavioural problems had broadly similar classroom experiences to other children in terms of teaching contexts and curriculum content. They were included in class lessons and experienced the same broad categories of curriculum content. However, children with special educational needs had significantly lower levels of task engagement and considerably higher levels of distraction from work than other children. They also received more individual teacher attention than other pupils, although this was necessarily still only for a very small part of their total classroom time.

Data from the PACE study comparing aspects of the clasroom activities of the nine 'low-achieving' children with that of other children in the sample are presented in Table 10.4. The observation data were obtained on four separate sessions of one week's observation, but for simplicity of presentation the data from the two Key Stage 1 observation sessions have been combined as have the two Key Stage 2 observation sessions.

Overall, pupils spend 58.2 per cent of their time in class directly task-engaged in the Key Stage 1 observation and 60.0 per cent in the Key Stage 2 observations. This figure excludes task-management, waiting and other approved activities and describes only direct involvement with curriculum tasks. The level of task-engagement is virtually identical to the figures reported in the ORACLE study of pupils in a much larger sample of primary classrooms (Galton *et al.*, 1980). At both Key Stage 1 and Key Stage 2 children in the low-achiever group spent substantially less time task-engaged than other pupils. Their figures for task-engagement were about ten per cent below other pupils on both occasions. Put another way, most children in these primary classrooms were spending about twenty per cent more time working on the curriculum than were the low-achieving pupils. The figures for distraction from task, also given in Table 10.4 show a considerably higher level of distraction among the low-achiever group. This result shows that the lower level of time on task for low-achieving children comes about, for the most part, because they are entirely off-task rather than because they are spending more time in task-management activities, waiting for the teacher or other approved activities.

This difference between the levels of task-engagement of the two groups is very similar to that found by Croll and Moses (1985) in an observational study of 34 primary school classrooms. It illustrates the difficulties teachers face with pupils who are both achieving poorly and spending less time than others on curriculum tasks. Although it might seem obvious that the lower-achieving children spend less time working than others, this is not necessarily the case. It could also be hypothesized that academically more successful children would complete their tasks quicker, leaving the lower-achievers to spend longer attempting to complete their work. This alternative hypothesis is clearly not supported by the data which show the task-management issues as well as those of appropriate match to children's attainments faced by teachers.

Table 10.4 also provides figures on various aspects of the pedagogical and curriculum contexts which structure pupils' classroom experiences. The teaching contexts are shown in terms of the experience the pupils have of interaction with the teacher either one-to-one, as part of a group or as part of the teacher's class audience. As other studies of classroom interaction have shown, although teachers typically spend a majority of their time interacting with pupils on a one-to-one basis, pupils typically experience teacher interaction as part of whole-class patterns of interaction. At Key Stage 1 a third (32.1 per cent) of the pupils' time in class is spent as part of the teachers' class audience. At Key Stage 2 this figure is about a quarter of class time (24.6 per cent). In contrast, the class time spent one-to-one with the teacher is 3.1 per cent at Key Stage 1 and 4.3 per cent at Key Stage 2 for the average child.

Previous research on children with special needs in mainstream schools suggests they receive higher-than-average levels of one-to-one teacher interaction (Croll and Moses, 1985, p. 128). Other research on the National Curriculum also suggests that teachers attempt to meet the needs of children with 'additional educational needs' through individual attention and group work (West *et al.*, 1995). As we have seen in the interviews conducted as part of the PACE study, teachers expressed a concern that the pressures of the National Curriculum will reduce the possibilities for giving children with special educational needs the additional time they need. The figures in Table 10.4 lend some tentative support to the claim that children with special educational needs may not be getting additional individual attention. At Key Stage 1 the children in the low-achiever group had slightly less one-to-one time with the teacher than did other children although they also had slightly more group work. At Key Stage 2 the children in the low-achiever group had slightly more one-to-one but slightly less group work.

The role of the 'basic subjects', generally taken to be English and mathematics under the National Curriculum, has been a matter of considerable debate. The National Curriculum was explicitly intended to broaden the curriculum, but was introduced with much accompanying rhetoric about improving standards in the basic subjects. As Campbell (1993) has shown, a large number of studies have demonstrated the heavy predominance of English and mathematics within the primary curriculum. A full implementation of the National Curriculum must necessarily reduce the time available for the 'basics'. In considering the implications of the National Curriculum for pupils with special educational needs, two different kinds of concern have been expressed about curriculum balance. As was described earlier in the chapter, some teachers are concerned that the pressure to broaden the curriculum will mean that children who are struggling with the basic skills in English and mathematics will spend less time than they need on these areas. On the other hand, it has also been argued that the pressure to reach attainment targets in English and mathematics will lead to a restricted rather than broader curriculum for children experiencing learning difficulties.

The figures for curriculum time on the 'basics' (English and mathematics), in Table 10.4 show that at both Key Stage 1 and Key Stage 2 children are spending, on average, just over half their time working in these curriculum areas. This is the kind of level which Campbell (1993) identifies as typically arising from studies of classrooms both before and after the introduction of the National Curriculum and is a rather higher proportion than that envisaged in the National Curriculum. This may be because the core curriculum, which consists of English and mathematics, as well as science, was introduced first and has consequently dominated teachers' curriculum planning. Table

10.4 also shows that both at Key Stage 1 and Key Stage 2, children in the low achiever category spent more time than other children on English and mathematics; 56.3 per cent compared with 50.3 per cent at Key Stage 1 and 62.2 per cent compared with 50.8 per cent at Key Stage 2. The numbers of children involved is small and the figures should be treated tentatively. However, they give some reason to think that the continued heavy emphasis on the basic subjects in the primary curriculum following the introduction of the National Curriculum has been experienced even more strongly by children regarded by their teachers as low achievers than by other children.

Table 10.4 *Low–achieving children in the primary classroom (percentages)*

	Key Stage 1		
	Low-achievers	Others	All
Task engaged	50.4	59.8	58.2
Distracted	26.9	19.1	20.4
Teacher: one-to-one	2.6	3.3	3.1
Teacher: group	8.8	6.8	7.1
Teacher: whole class	31.7	32.3	32.1
Time on basics	56.3	50.3	51.3
	Key Stage 2		
Task engaged	51.1	61.6	60.0
Distracted	25.1	17.7	18.9
Teacher: one-to-one	5.9	4.1	4.3
Teacher: group	2.5	2.7	2.7
Teacher: whole class	19.8	25.4	24.6
Time on basics	62.2	50.8	52.7

Source: PACE 1 and PACE 2 Systematic Observation
Sample: 18 Key Stage 1 classes and 18 Key Stage 2 classes
Dates: Autumn 1990, autumn 1991, summer 1993 and summer 1994

10.5   CONCLUSIONS

At the beginning of this chapter we identified the particularly acute contrasts between the claims made for the effect of the National Curriculum on the education of children with special educational needs. On the one hand, it was claimed that it would guarantee the curriculum entitlement of these children and would provide their teachers with clear targets and procedures for the diagnosis of their difficulties. On the other hand, concerns were expressed that the pressures it introduced on teachers would make it more difficult for them to meet children's special educational needs and that the content was inappropriate for children struggling with the basic skills or experiencing emotional and behavioural difficulties.

Studies of the responses of special schools to the National Curriculum have documented a degree of enthusiasm for the principle that the pupils of these schools have the same curriculum entitlement as other pupils and for a broadening of the special school curriculum. However, they have also shown a number of qualifications of this positive response following the experience of implementing the National Curriculum in these schools and a view expressed by many in special schools that the National Curriculum is only a part of their pupils' educational needs.

Teachers and headteachers in mainstream schools have expressed a variety of views about the consequences of the National Curriculum for pupils in mainstream primary schools with special educational needs. Positive responses include the views that more structured assessment and more demanding and structured aims will help teachers to meet special educational needs. However, the balance of responses is more negative and is dominated by concerns about pressures on time and the pressure to focus on the whole class and the class average, as well as a concern about the appropriateness of the curriculum content for children experiencing either learning difficulties or emotional problems. The observational data give tentative support to the arguments both that teachers are no longer able to give children with special educational needs more individual attention than other children and also that the emphasis on the basics of English and mathematics which has been maintained despite the notion of a 'broad and balanced' curriculum, is even more marked for these children.

In earlier chapters, and in a previous book (Pollard *et al.*, 1994), we have documented the difficulties created for teachers by the undefined and very open-ended nature of their perceptions of their professional role. This dilemma is probably particularly acute in the case of children with special needs, where the tensions created by competing demands on time and the importance of a pastoral as well as curricular commitment may be most evident. The discussion in this chapter is also relevant to our argument about the way that teachers operate as 'policy-makers in practice'. The pressures of meeting new demands in the context of a curriculum introduced sequentially has meant that, contrary to policy intentions to broaden the curriculum, the real curriculum in classrooms has concentrated on English and mathematics. This has been particularly the case for children with learning difficulties.

Chapter 11

Continuity and Change in English Primary Education

Patricia Broadfoot and Andrew Pollard

11.1 Introduction

11.2 The salient empirical findings of the book

11.3 Values, understanding, power and processes of mediation

11.4 Conclusion

11.1 INTRODUCTION

The Primary Assessment, Curriculum and Experience project was designed to address a wide range of issues concerning the feelings and behaviour of both teachers and pupils in the primary classrooms of the 1990s. Whilst the research team was particularly concerned to document the changes which followed the 1988 Education Reform Act, we also sought to illuminate more enduring features of classroom life in primary schools in England. The longitudinal design of the project, which has allowed us to follow the progress of a sample of 54 pupils in 9 geographically dispersed primary schools, is particularly significant in this respect since, by the end of the third phase of the project, it will enable us to chart the changing perspectives of both teachers and pupils over the six years of the project's life. Indeed, the decision by the Economic and Social Research Council to fund the third stage of the study will now enable the project team to chart the views and experiences of our pupil sample over the entire course of their primary schooling and to document the views of the teachers who worked with them during a period of unprecedented turbulence in educational policy in England. In addition to the detailed insights that we have been able to gain from our case study schools, we have also been able to draw on data on perspectives and experiences collected from teachers in our wider sample of 48 schools to whom we have returned regularly.

The findings from the first stage of the PACE project were published in *Changing English Primary Schools?* (Pollard *et al.*, 1994) as well as in a number of journal articles. This sequel has been specifically concerned with the results of PACE 2, which are necessarily closely linked with those of PACE 1. We have therefore invoked some of the analytical themes that characterized PACE 1 and developed them in the light of the insights that have emerged from PACE 2. At the same time we introduce the concept of 'mediation' as a new analytic theme to reflect both the developments that have taken place during PACE 2 and the new insights that a longer period of study have made possible.

11.2   THE SALIENT EMPIRICAL FINDINGS OF THE BOOK

Overall, our evidence suggests that in the early 1990s, once the initial adaption to the Education Reform Act, 1988, had been accomplished, headteachers continued to face particularly great pressures from external forces and new responsibilites. Meanwhile teachers continued to accommodate to continuing change, but some began to reassert a degree of professional control. In the midst of the externally generated turbulence, we found relative continuity in pupils' classroom experience.

The National Curriculum

In contrast with the earlier stage of the study, the National Curriculum became a more accepted part of primary schooling. The children studied had been taught under the National Curriculum for four years by the end of the PACE 2 project and an increasing number of mainly young teachers had had experience of teaching the National Curriculum exclusively. Despite the continued pressures they were under, teachers and heads felt that they had successfully implemented a major curriculum innovation. More than one in three teachers thought that children were getting a better educational experience following the introduction of the National Curriculum and fewer than one in twenty thought that children were getting a worse experience. However, many headteachers and classroom teachers felt that improvements were occuring despite, rather than because of, some aspects of government policy. Many saw themselves as 'mediating' new requirements deriving from a turbulent external environment, and we were able to document the relative continuities in pupils' classroom experience which have resulted.

Headteachers

Headteachers experienced a great deal of pressure, and they frequently reported overload and stress. This came about at least as much from developments such as Local Management of Schools, new provision for special educational needs, and new accountability and inspection requirements as from the implementation of the National Curriculum. While many headteachers thought that the new managerial aspects of their role took them away from the things that had brought them into teaching, some others welcomed the new challenges and autonomy. The values held by headteachers were important in their feelings about the job, and in 1994 over half of those interviewed felt there had been a reduction in their job satisfaction.

Teachers

Teachers continued to have a broad conception of their role and to emphasize the personal and developmental aspects of their work as well as their curriculum responsibilities. Teaching was experienced as increasingly pressured and constrained by external factors. Key Stage 2 teachers felt the curriculum for older primary school pupils was particularly overloaded, and they were concerned about the impact of new assessment requirements.

In comparison with data collected in the first stage of the PACE project, Key Stage 1 teachers in the second stage were more positive about the National Curriculum and more optimistic about the future of primary education. This partly reflects a process of normalization or routinization of innovation, but also reflects the fact that some of those least happy with the changes have chosen to leave the profession, while an increasing proportion of young teachers have only known the National Curriculum.

Teachers and the teaching profession have been cast in a variety of roles with regard to education policy: as partners in the traditional Schools Council model of curriculum change, as unthinking and passive implementers of policy and as active opponents of current policy developments. We developed a model of teachers as policy-makers in practice and documented the way that the realities of professional working situations can operate to mediate policy in a systematic way due to common features of professional ideologies and structural constraints. While some actions by the teaching profession represent collective action in response to policy (for example on testing), action may also be taken not collectively but in common, due to common features of working situations. The study has shown how, in areas like curriculum balance and assessment, the realities of teachers' working situations had a systematic effect on the implementation of change.

Pupils

The evidence on pupil perspectives as they move from Key Stage 1 to Key Stage 2 suggests that it was features of their classroom experiences *per se*, rather than any specific influence of the National Curriculum, which predominantly impacted on their experience of schooling. Our evidence shows pupils becoming progressively socialized into the pupil role, adopting a somewhat more instrumental approach to school as they move into Key Stage 2, valuing educational success and seeking 'easy' tasks which would ensure success. Pupil–teacher relationships remained good, although pupils were increasingly aware of teacher power and control and were very aware of the extent to which their activities were evaluated by teachers.

The education of children with special educational needs was a particular concern for many teachers who were worried about the time they would have for these children and the appropriateness of the National Curriculum for them. However, a minority of teachers thought that more explicit assessment and structured targets would help children with learning difficulties. The observational data give tentative support to the claim that teachers are now not able to give additional attention to children with special educational needs, and also suggest that the curriculum for such children is more restricted to the basic skills than is true for other pupils.

Curriculum

Although the National Curriculum was explicitly intended to broaden children's curriculum experience, evidence from PACE classroom studies showed clearly that over half of curriculum time is devoted to the basic skills of English and mathematics: a figure very similar to evidence from before the introduction of the National Curriculum. This may be a result of the way the National Curriculum was progressively implemented with an initial emphasis on the core subjects. Data from Stage Three of the PACE study will show whether a genuine broadening of the curriculum takes place at later stages of implemetation.

Pedagogy

Most teachers continued to state their commitment to using a mixture of teaching approaches, as appropriate to the subject and task. When compared with Key Stage 1, systematic observation data from Key Stage 2 showed a gradual decrease in the use of group work and whole class interaction. However, individual work and the proportion of sessions in which there was no main pedagogic context increased as the children became older. In Key Stage 2 teachers spent approximately 30 per cent of their time in whole class interaction, and just over 50 per cent of their time with individual pupils. We documented, through case studies, the complexity of the teacher role when confronted with the immediacy of practical classroom realities and dilemmas.

Assessment

Teachers continued to be sceptical of the value of National Curriculum assessment procedures and held a view of assessment as something which was inherent in, and an ongoing part of, the teaching process. However, there was a marked difference between Key Stage 1 teachers who had experience of SATs and Key Stage 2 teachers who, at the time of the study, did not have this experience. Key Stage 2 teachers were relatively unwilling to plan for or devote time to assessment, while many more Key Stage 1 teachers considered assessment activities as a planned and explicit part of their teaching. Many had begun to identify assessment practices as part of their professional self-image, rather than simply following National Curriculum prescriptions.

11.3   VALUES, UNDERSTANDING, POWER AND PROCESSES OF MEDIATION

Our conclusion to *Changing English Primary Schools?*, the first PACE book, was structured in terms of a number of 'dimensions of change' in relation to teachers' perspectives and practice: headteachers' changing views of their role and their ways of performing it, changes in curriculum content, teaching approach and assessment. These were represented in terms of a broad trend away from autonomy for schools, teachers and pupils towards more explicit goals and requirements and the categoric labelling of both curriculum subjects and pupil achievement. The responses to these changes provoked among both teachers and heads were interpreted in terms of the three related themes of power, values and understanding. We argued that teachers' practice is a reflection of their fundamental values concerning what education is and should be for — values that are rooted in the professional culture and in the training, subsequent experience and life-histories of individual teachers. These values, we suggested, are in turn reflected in particular ways of understanding how learning takes place and thus how teaching, and the practices associated with it, such as assessment and classroom management, should be conducted. A similar relationship between practice, and the values and related understandings underpinning it, was also found to characterize head-teacher behaviour.

Policy is ultimately about power: the power to decide what should be done and the power to implement these priorities in practice. In the minds of many politicians both in Britain and elsewhere, such implementation has not been seen as problematic provided that the necessary regulations and resources are in place. However, PACE 1 showed clearly that such simplistic, even coercive, notions of power are neither appropriate nor realizable in the context of education. Teachers' values cannot be commanded. They are not vulnerable to 'power–coercive' strategies for change (Chin and Benne, 1975). While they may be responsive to more 'normative–re-educative' approaches, change ultimately depends on teachers themselves being convinced of the need for it. Further testimony to the strength of this argument is provided by research on primary school teachers in France which parallels the PACE project. Whilst the values and understanding of French primary teachers are typically very different from those of their English counterparts (Broadfoot and Osborn, 1993), the ways in which they operate to inhibit coercive attempts to impose new policies are strikingly similar to those of English teachers (Broadfoot *et al.*, 1994).

In PACE 1 we identified five different responses that teachers in the study were making to the imposed changes: compliance, incorporation, mediation, retreatism and resistance. Whilst there were a few 'resistors', and a not inconsiderable number of 'retreatists' many of whom were looking for retirement as a way out, most of the teachers studied were adopting strategies of 'incorporation' — apppearing to accept the imposed changes but incorporating them into existing modes of working. The effect was that existing modes of working were adapted rather than changed more fundamentally, and the effect of change was considerably different from that which was intended by policy-makers. Such teachers were effectively resisting the imposition of attempts to change their understanding of desirable and appropriate practices and were using their classroom autonomy to avoid a more fundamental change of orientation. A rather different pattern of response was evident among the fifth and final group, the 'mediators' who had internalized the new requirements in such a way that they could take control of them and use them as a stimulus to develop new, professionally rewarding, insights and strategies.

In PACE 2 this concept of *mediation*, in the broadest sense, emerged as being particularly salient in explaining the rather different climate which characterized primary schools from 1992 to 1994. As the curriculum changes which had followed the Education Reform Act, 1988, became more understood and normalized, the sense of panic or even despair which many classroom teachers felt was replaced with a more positive outlook. Indeed, by 1994 only 5 per cent of Key Stage 1 teachers who we interviewed thought that children would be receiving a worse education than they would have before the Reform Act, and 71 per cent of them said that they would still choose to be a teacher if they had a chance to do so again. This compared with only 46 per cent making this choice in 1990.

Nevertheless, power struggles over education policy and practice during the early 1990s continued to reflect tensions of values and understandings. The policies of the Conservative Government of the period increasingly reflected their drive towards the 'marketization' of education (Bowe *et al.*, 1992) and this impacted on primary as well as secondary schools (Menter *et al*, forthcoming). Thus the rhetoric of 'parent choice' was articulated, schools were encouraged to 'opt out' of their local education authorities, standardised testing of pupils was imposed at age 11 and formal inspection of schools, with publication of reports, was introduced. As we commented in *Changing English Primary Schools?*, the emphasis on competition and consumerism which this market ideology reflects contrasts greatly with the values and commitments of most teachers in the state sector of education. For them, educational provision was seen as being more closely linked to community, opportunity and, in the case of primary school teachers, to the 'developmental tradition' which emphasizes individual growth (see Blyth, 1965 and Chapter 2 of *Changing English Primary Schools?*). The conception of 'child-centredness', which provided such a strong ideology for primary school teachers throughout the 1970s, was resilient and commitments to the well-being of children and to the quality of their experiences in school, and the relevance of these to learning, remained. Indeed, these commitments were complemented by awareness of the considerable personal fulfilment which pupils can bring to teachers as children's identities and potential are developed during the primary school years. The basic values and concerns of the Government and the profession thus continued to differ. Whilst the Government appraised the 'system' as a whole and sought mechanisms to 'lever up' standards through processes of competition and accountability, primary school teachers tended to be more concerned with the particularities of their school, the individuals in it and the formative processes through which pupil learning could be encouraged. A stark example of this difference in values and perception was the prioritization of parents as 'consumers' of education, with rights under the Parents' Charter of 1991, rather than as 'partners' with teachers in learning processes which would directly support the education of their children.

The case of the Dearing Review of the National Curriculum is of interest here. The National Curriculum had been introduced, subject by subject, from 1989. However, it became apparent that both it, and the assessment procedures associated with it, were overcomplex, too prescriptive and impractical to implement in schools. Indeed, we documented many of these difficulties in *Changing English Primary Schools?*. By the Summer of 1993 teacher opposition was considerable, and this was reinforced, particularly on assessment issues, by many parents and some industrialists as the power struggle between government and teachers over curriculum and assessment reached a climax. To defuse the situation, Sir Ron Dearing was then appointed to conduct a 'review', and the separate bodies for curriculum (the National Curriculum Council) and assessment (the School Examination and Assessment Council) were merged into the School Curriculum and Assessment Authority. In Dearing's subsequent report, coordinated by SCAA, the problems of overload, overprescription and unmanageability were accepted. 'Task Groups' of teachers were set up to 'slim down' the National Curriculum, considering it as a whole by Key Stage as well as by subject, and to enact a form of assessment using 'level descriptions' in which teacher-judgement would play a greater role. This episode can be seen as representing a victory for professional values and understandings of education as curriculum content and the forms of some assessments were amended. Indeed, in terms of our previous analysis in *Changing English Primary Schools?*, the changes can be interpreted as providing more autonomy for teachers, as an affirmation of their professionalism and as an acceptance that over-specification of knowledge to be learned is inappropriate where children need some flexibility to construct their own understandings. Alternatively, one might view the changes simply as a tactical retreat by a government which felt that it was prudent to de-fuse dissent, that it still controlled the structural framework of inspection and accountability, and that market forces would impose an ultimate discipline on schools. In any event, it is an episode which vividly illustrates the struggle for power, values and understanding which was such a fundamental feature of English primary school education in the early 1990s.

What then, reflecting these struggles, were the main features of continuity and change in primary schools since the start of the PACE 2 study in January 1993? As we indicated earlier, overall, our evidence suggests that there was relative continuity in pupils' classroom experience, whilst teachers struggled to accommodate to considerable change and headteachers faced particularly great pressure from external forces and new responsibilities. LEAs were also often called upon to implement national requirements and even faced threats to their continued existence.

One way of describing this conceptually is as a continuum flowing from turbulence in the external environment to relative stability in pupil experience. In essence, our argument is that this relative continuity in the midst of change was produced by successive layers of *mediation*, and that this reflected the influence of ideologies and values held by significant actors in the policy implementation processes.

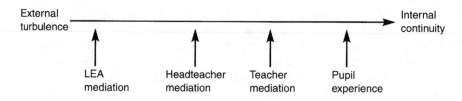

Figure 11.1   *From turbulence to continuity*

This basic analysis is represented in Figure 11.1. In what follows we review our findings in relation to this theme of mediation by headteachers, teachers and pupils.

Headteachers

Headteachers in the PACE sample saw themselves as being maximally exposed to new legal requirements, management responsibilites for curriculum, staff and finance, and new accountability procedures. However, although the inspection threat loomed in many of their thoughts, their commitment to pupils and the idea of staff collegiality meant that they actively sought to face external pressures and, in some sense, to protect staff from them. This, of course, reflects something of the ideological commitments to personal relationships which have been documented by Nias and her colleagues (Nias *et al.*, 1989). However, headteachers still made many new requirements of their teachers and other staff. There was evidence of agency and the use of residual autonomy as well as of strategic response to constraint.

Many heads spoke of their exhaustion and referred to their very considerably increased workload. There is no doubt that for all English primary heads their role significantly changed, following the Education Reform Act, from one in which they were essentially the head *teacher* to one in which they are typically much further removed from day-to-day contact with children. The scope of their role has increased to include broad managerial responsibility for every aspect of school life, with particular concern for financial management, trivial as well as important administration, and various aspects of accountability to parents, governors and inspectors. In 1994 no less than 86 per cent of heads said that there had been significant changes in the way the school was run. They pointed explicitly to the mediation which they were required to undertake — between teachers and governors, between teachers and parents, between teachers and the steady flow of instructions and requirements from government. Our 1994 data documents 64 per cent of heads who felt that they were constrained in what they could do as against 37 per cent who felt this way in 1990. Perhaps it was the combination of perceptions of their changing roles and of growing constraint that that led to 54 per cent of headteachers in 1994 recording a reduction in job satisfaction.

We believe that, between 1990 and 1994, there was an important shift in the point of maximum impact of the reforms. Initially, it was classroom teachers who were particularly pressurized by the imposition of new curricular requirements and professional responsibilities. They experienced tensions between existing practices and the prescriptions which flowed from politicians and the media, and this was combined with the pressures of excessive workloads through the 'overloaded' curriculum (Dearing, 1994). The result was a decline in self-confidence. However, by 1994 it was headteachers who manifested the greatest concern and stress, whilst in 1990 many had conveyed a more positive disposition. These contrasts suggest that, some years into the educational reform, it was headteachers who were the principal mediators of change and who were confronted by the more structural and fundamental legacy of the new policy requirements, particularly in respect of various forms of marketization (Menter *et al.*, forthcoming).

However, not all heads necessarily saw such changes as undesirable. Some did retain an optimistic view of the quality of primary schooling and the way it was likely to develop in future. Indeed, it is important to emphasize the range of different ways in which individual heads responded to these common trends. Whilst many deplored the loss of the satisfactions that had first brought them into teaching and, later, into school leadership, others were excited by the new management role and by the broader spread of responsibilities.

In this sense PACE 2 data on headteachers parallels the range of strategic responses to change which were documented for teachers in PACE 1. Depending on their personal values and aspirations, the stage in their professional career and other contextual factors such as the influence of colleagues, governors and parents, heads' responses spanned the full range from creative mediation to retreatism and even rebellion. Thus the themes of continuity and change may be traced both at the level of the role itself, in which the emphasis on change was very marked, and at the level of the individual performing that role. For many headteachers the loss of continuity and the challenge to established values was the cause of considerable regret, yet for others it brought new opportunities which were welcomed.

Teachers

PACE 2 studied two different cohorts of teachers: the teachers of Years 3 and 4 (which are the years our sample of pupils had reached) and Key Stage 1 teachers (who were revisited for a second interview following similar sampling in PACE 1). Although the responses of the two groups were in many ways similar, they also differed in certain respects, suggesting that the full impact of the reforms was felt later by Key Stage 2 teachers. In particular, Key Stage 2 teachers in 1994 felt less reassured by the Dearing Review of the National Curriculum and were less optimistic about the future. They felt the curriculum for older primary school pupils to be particularly overloaded and were concerned about new assessment requirements.

The qualitative data that the PACE team was able to collect over a period of years allowed us to penetrate these general, quantitative patterns. Using a life-history approach deriving from transcriptions of successive interviews with the same teachers, we have been able to identify the complex interaction of personal and institutional factors and external pressures and trends which influence the coping strategies of particular teachers. Whether teachers were able to mediate the demands of changing requirements in their working lives partly related to their personality, confidence, and aspirations but also, importantly, to how far they were able to reconcile the new ways of working with their fundamental professional values. In this respect, our data also revealed a tendency to 'burn out' for teachers who had been in the job a long time.

Although the 1994 picture of Key Stage 1 teachers was a much more positive one than for their junior school colleagues, and indeed in comparison with their own feelings in 1990, the longitudinal data again reveal significant differences in individual responses to change. Of particular interest was the variable capacity to mediate changes in ways that enabled professional satisfaction to be sustained or even enhanced. Thus for some, the very significant increase in perceived constraints (which was mentioned by 69 per cent of teachers) in fact led to an increase in professional satisfaction as a result of more clearly defined roles. Some assessment developments provide an example of this. Although from 1990 to 1992 assessment was the focus of both the greatest hostility and the most considerable change, by 1993 and 1994 there was a noticeable contrast between Key Stage 1 and Key Stage 2 teachers. Whilst the latter group remained unconvinced of the value of new assessment requirements, our data suggest that many Key Stage 1 teachers had internalized new, formative approaches to assessment which they found professionally enhancing.

The issue of confidence lies at the heart of our account of primary teachers' changing perspectives in recent years. Both in terms of what unites them as groups and in terms of what distinguishes them as individuals, the successful mediation of change required both that teachers felt sufficiently confident in their knowledge, skills and abilities to be able to adapt and that they were able to develop practices that accorded with their values and circumstances.

Pupils

The third group in our study, protected from external turbulence by headteacher and teacher mediation, consequently appeared to have experienced relatively little change in their classroom experiences. Indeed, such changes as there were in the curriculum and pedagogy experienced by pupils could be attributed as much to the pupils growing older as to government policy. Pupils' preferred orientation was one of pleasing the teacher, as has been found in many previous studies. There was evidence of a growing preoccupation with avoiding failure, which suggested the progressive adoption of an increasingly instrumental strategy of 'seeking to satisfy', rather than pursuing learning for its own sake. This may indicate that, despite the imposition of a clear structure of progression through the National Curriculum, the hierarchy of learning goals does not, at least as yet, have the same salience for English pupils as it does in other countries such as France, where the educational assumptions within the culture are more directly focused on learning outcomes. Research in France (Planel, 1994) has shown that pupils are actively aware of both short- and long-term learning goals that they feel they will need to master if they are to be successful, and that they regard the teacher as an important ally in this task. Whilst the children studied in the PACE project were influenced to some extent by the perceived interest of tasks themselves, there was little evidence of strategic motivation. Arguably this could be another manifestation of the effects of mediation — in this case, the still-dominant commitment of English teachers to the needs and interests of the individual child and hence the importance of an *individual* learning path, as against that of a *common* set of learning outcomes to be mastered as would be found among French teachers.

Our analysis of teachers' preferred assessment strategies led us to formulate the concept of 'diagnostic discourse'. This denotes the form of internal conversation that teachers conduct as they interpret the significance of pupil behaviour or learning outcomes and form judgements on an appropriate intervention. Our data document teachers' resistance to imposed standardized testing, which they continue to perceive as time-consuming yet unhelpful in supporting the learning process.

Detailed analysis of individual lessons which were conducted in case-study schools, raise serious questions concerning the practical possibility of implementing a pedagogy in which diagnostic data lead to the provision of learning experiences which match the *specific* learning needs of each pupil. It appears to be unlikely, given present class sizes, that even a highly skilled and committed teacher is able to provide adequately for the range of behavioural, cognitive and affective needs which pupils exhibit. Whether a strategy of whole-class teaching or group work is adopted, the match of task to need is unlikely to be perfect for any pupil and, for some, not even close. On the other hand, work which is predominantly offered on an individual basis may well be less stimulating and certainly will involve problems of supervision and organization.

Thus, like the impact of policy on teachers' practice, the impact of teaching on pupils should not be conceived in terms of a simple input–output mode. Its realization in practice is subject to the same mixture of pupils' personal values and motivations, their understanding of what is desirable and appropriate in terms of performance, and a list of contextual variables including interpersonal relationships.

The theme of power is also significant for understanding the changes which took place for pupils. Evidence both from interviews with pupils and from classroom observation indicates a steady decline in pupil autonomy as they moved from Year 1 to Year 4. This particularly related to their reduced power to choose learning activities and to the strengthening frame in classrooms, but it also affected pupils' capacity to introduce their own criteria of success and definitions of the situation. Whilst much of this decline must be attributed to the pupils getting older, it also lends support to teachers' reports of the growing constraints on their practice as a result of external directives. We will continue to trace such themes in the third phase of the PACE project as the pupils move through Years 5 and 6.

Teachers also have significant influence over the creation of individual pupil identities. However, whilst the literature on typifications would suggest that teachers are often responsible for 'labelling' pupils in a way that becomes reified and a basis for subsequent interaction, we found little evidence for this. Although our data on pupil careers reveals that the behaviour and attainment patterns of particular pupils were described in broadly similar terms by different teachers over the four years of study, variations were frequent enough to suggest that the teachers based their judgements on how they experienced the pupils, rather than on previously acquired pupil biographies, and that attainment levels were judged relatively independently of behaviour patterns. Moreover there seemed to be little evidence from our analysis that social class and gender were, in themselves, linked to teachers' typifications of pupils.

11.4   CONCLUSION

Classrooms are complex places. As Jackson (1968) suggested, they are characterized by crowds, praise and power, as well as delay, denial and interruption. They are places of compromised where a balance must be struck between the ideal and what is possible in a large group. They are also socially dynamic places in which the identities of teachers and pupils are constantly developing and changing as a result of social interaction and of the experience of trying to accomplish teaching and learning. Each participant in the process can be seen as monitoring their success — implicitly or explicitly — in achieving their chosen goals, and these goals are in turn a reflection of the values held by each individual in the light of their experience and understanding. If this representation is true of classrooms, it is also true of schools, which are equally embedded in a dynamic network of personal identity, values and understandings that are constantly developing in the light of internal and external interaction, pressure and constraint.

In the light of such realities, our analysis suggests that the impact of policy changes on education cannot be directly predictable or generalizable. Indeed, this may be inevitable in any struggle for power, values and understandings in a democratic society. In generating our analysis of these processes, we have used the concept of *mediation* to represent the series of transformations that take place in the process of translating policy directives into classroom practice. We have argued that headteachers and teachers are inevitably partners in the policy-making process, and it follows that pupils are as well. Whilst it may be tempting to conceptualize this process of transmission in engineering terms — perhaps as a series of articulated levers that relay load through the structure — such a metaphor ignores the creative interpretation by the actors involved at each successive stage of the process. Bernstein's analysis of the power to define, which is embodied in the discourse of primary, secondary and subsequent reconceptualizations of the original message, comes much closer to the picture which the PACE data describe.

In conclusion, we highlight four key points:

1. The struggle for power, values and understanding remain central themes in any analysis of recent developments in primary education. We have explored these in the light of evidence concerning both continuity and change in the early 1990s.
2. The progressive impact of externally derived policy changes can be seen as a complex synthesis of the successive mediations of the individual actors involved, as these are in turn influenced by broader changes in the social context.
3. In the early 1990s there was relative continuity in pupils' classroom experience. Whilst teachers continued to accommodate to change, headteachers faced sustained pressure from new responsibilities and external forces.
4. There were important variations between teachers in the ways in which they responded to change. This prompted us to try to identify, using more qualitative, longitudinal data, some of the reasons why some individuals developed in ways that they perceive to be positive, whilst others found new requirements progressively less acceptable.

Whilst the PACE project was originally conceived as a research response to major policy changes, we believe that its mixture of quantitative and qualitative methodologies and its longitudinal design has begun to yield more fundamental insights into the dynamics of teachers' work in English primary schools and the perspectives and experiences of their pupils. The third phase of the PACE project will allow analysis of the experience of primary education of the cohort of children in the sample from Years 1 to 6 and will provide a record of the changing experiences and perspectives of English primary school teachers from 1989 to 1996.

Appendix

The Design of the PACE Study

OVERVIEW

PACE is a large-scale and complex research project, and only an outline of the research design and data collection procedures are given here. Fuller details are given in Chapter 4 of Pollard *et al.* *(*1994). The PACE project will study pupils up to the end of their primary schooling but the outline below only describes the study up to Year 4 (1993/94), which is the last point at which the data discussed in this volume were collected.

Key features of the PACE project are: (a) its focus on a broad range of issues associated with the introduction of the National Curriculum, necessitating a wide range of data-collection procedures; (b) its focus on change, necessitating a longitudinal research design; and (c) its attempt to provide both a representative picture of primary education and to provide detailed descriptions of particular educational settings and processes, necessitating the embedding of case studies within a broader survey.

A range of methods

The outline below shows that a considerable variety of data collection procedures were used in the research in an attempt to capture the processes involved in multiple innovation. Personal interviews with headteachers, teachers and children were one of the most important sources of data. These included both open-ended questions and highly structured questions. The interviews with children incorporated special techniques involving visual stimuli and discussion of activities which the researcher had observed earlier. Self-completed questionnaires were used to collect demographic and career data and also attitudinal and similar data. The observations in classrooms included both systematic, quantitative procedures and qualitative approaches with open-ended or partially structured field notes. Other procedures included sociometry and tape recordings of teachers' interactions with children.

A longitudinal design

The principal longitudinal feature of the PACE design is its focus on the educational experiences of a cohort of children as they pass through primary education. The same group of children have been followed from their time in the Year 1 classroom through to Year 4 and will continue to be studied until the end of Year 6. For the most part, the teachers interviewed in the study were different at each round of data collection as the children moved into new classes. However, in Summer 1992, KS1 teachers were interviewed although the pupils being studied were then at KS2. This provides a picture of the changing perspectives of KS1 teachers over time. Headteachers were interviewed at all stages of the study. In the case of heads of all-through primary schools this makes possible a unique long-term analysis of headteachers' responses to educational change.

Classroom and assessment studies embedded in a survey

In order to give a representative picture of recent educational changes in the primary school a sample was obtained of 48 schools, six in each of eight Local Education Authorities sampled on a national basis. In each school the headteacher and two class teachers were interviewed and sent questionnaires at each round of data collection, except in the case of the assessment questionnaire, where only the head and teachers who had conducted national assessments were included. Within this sample, nine schools were selected for more intensive study, one from each of seven LEAs and two from the remaining LEA. Within each of these schools a single class of children was selected for intensive study and six children within the class were selected to be the focus of observation and interviews. One-week periods were spent in *classroom studies* concerned with curriculum and pedagogy. At times when SATs were being administered one-week periods were spent in *assessment studies* looking at the conduct of SATs and other assessment issues.

DETAILS OF SURVEY PROCEDURES

In surveys of teachers and headteachers in a sample of 48 schools from 8 LEAs, Data were collected by means of

1. A *questionnaire* covering demographic and career data, educational aims, notions of accountability and professional responsibility.
2. A *personal interview* covering perceptions of change following and in response to the National Curriculum, aspects of curriculum, pedagogy and assessment, relationships in school, views on education, perceptions of children and school strategies for change.
3. An *assessment questionnaire* completed following administration of national assessments and covering the management of SATs, responses of pupils and the value of SATs and teacher assessments.

Summer 1990: Questionnaire and personal interview data from 48 headteachers and 96 KS1 teachers in 48 schools.

Summer 1991: Assessment questionnaire data from 48 headteachers and 48 KS1 teachers administering SATs. (All heads and some teachers were the same as in the Summer 1990 round of data collection.)

Summer 1992: Questionnaire and personal interview data from 48 headteachers and 96 KS1 teachers in 48 schools. (All heads and some teachers were the same as in the Summer 1990 round of data collection.)

Summer 1992: Assessment questionnaire data from 48 headteachers and 48 KS1 teachers administering SATs. (All heads and some teachers were the same as in the Summer 1990 round of data collection.)

Autumn 1993: Questionnaire and personal interview data from 48 headteachers and 96 KS2 teachers in 48 schools. (In the case of all-through primary schools, the schools, and, therefore, the heads, except in a few cases where new heads were in place, were the same as in Summer 1990. In such schools the teachers were, with a few exceptions, different from those interviewed in the KS1 rounds of interviews. In the case of separate infant and junior schools, different schools were involved in this round of data collection.)

Spring 1994: Questionnaire and personal interview data from 48 headteachers and 96 KS1 teachers in 48 schools. (All schools, most heads and some teachers were the same as in the Summer 1990 round of data collection.)

DETAILS OF CLASSROOM STUDIES AND ASSESSMENT STUDIES

Case studies were conducted in 9 schools, one from each LEA in the case of 7 LEAs and two from the other LEA. Two kinds of case studies were conducted:

1. *Classroom studies* were conducted for one-week periods in the sample classrooms. The researcher carried out both qualitative observation and systematic observation, the latter focussed on six randomly selected children (3 girls and 3 boys). In addition, interviews were conducted with the class teacher and also with each of the six children. Sociometric and achievement data were also collected.
2. *Assessment studies* were carried out in classrooms where KS1 national assessments where being conducted. Pupils and teachers were observed using open-ended qualitative procedures during the administration of the SATs. Interviews were conducted with teachers and also with a selection of children who had been observed carrying out SATs.

Autumn 1990: Classroom Studies of a Year 1 class in each of 9 schools.

Summer 1991: Assessment Studies in a Year 2 classroom in each of 9 schools. (These were the same schools but different teachers and pupils from those in the Autumn 1990 Classroom Studies.)

Autumn 1991: Classroom Studies of a Year 2 class in each of 9 schools. (These were the same schools and the same pupils, except in a few cases where children had left, as in the Autumn 1990 Classroom Studies.)

Summer 1992: Assessment Studies in a Year 2 class in each of 9 schools. (These were the same schools and mainly the same pupils as in the

Autumn 1990 Classroom Studies and mainly involved the same teachers as the Summer 1991 Assessment Studies.)

Summer 1993: Classroom Studies of a Year 3 class in each of 9 schools. (These mainly involved the same pupils as the Autumn 1990 Classroom Studies. In the case of all-through primary schools they were in the same schools but in the case of separate infant and junior schools had changed schools.)

Summer 1994: Classroom Studies of a Year 4 class in each of 9 schools. (These were mainly the same pupils as were studied in the Summer 1993 Classroom Studies).

Bibliography

Abbott, D. with Broadfoot, P., Croll, P., Osborn, M. and Pollard, A. (1994) Some sink, some float: National Curriculum assessment and accountability, *British Educational Research Journal*, **29**(2), 155-74.

Acker, S. (1995) Carry on caring: the work of women teachers. *British Journal of Sociology of Education*, **16**(1) 21-36.

Acker, S. (1995) Gender and teachers' work, in M.Apple (ed.) *Review of Research in Education*, Washington DC: AERA.

Aitken, M., Bennett, N. and Hesketh, J. (1981) Teaching styles and pupil progress: a reanalysis. *British Journal of Educational Psychology*, **51**, 170-86.

Alexander, R. (1984) *Primary Teaching*. London: Holt, Rinehart and Winston.

Alexander, R. (1992) *Policy and Practice in Primary Education*. London: Routledge.

Alexander, R., Rose, J. and Woodhead, C. (1992) *Curriculum Organisation and Classroom Practice in Primary Schools*. London: DES.

Archibald, D. A. and Porter, A. C. (1994) Curriculum control and teachers' perceptions of autonomy and satisfaction. *Educational Evaluation and Policy Analysis*, **16**(1), 21-39.

Becker, H. S., Geer, B. and Hughes, E. C. (1968) *Making the Grade: The Academic Side of College Life*. New York: Wiley.

Bennett, N. (1976) *Teaching Styles and Pupil Progress*. London: Open Books.

Bennett, N., Desforges, C., Cockburn, A. and Wilkinson, B. (1984) *The Quality of Pupil Learning Experiences*. London: Lawrence Erlbaum Associates.

Bernstein, B. (1975) *Class, Codes and Control, Vol. III: Towards a Theory of Educational Transmission*. London: Routledge and Kegan Paul.

Black, P. J. (1994) Performance assessment and accountability: the experience in England and Wales. *Educational Evaluation and Policy Analysis*, **16**(2), 191-203.

Blyth, A. (1965) *English Primary Education*, Vol. II: *Background*. London: Routledge and Kegan Paul.

Bourdieu, P. and Passeron, J. (1970) *La Reproduction: éléments pour une théorie du système d'enseignement*. Paris: Les Editions de Minuit.

Bourdieu, P. and Passeron, J. (1977) *La Reproduction*. Paris: *Sage*.

Bowe, R. and Ball, S. with Gold, A. (1992) *Reforming Education and Changing Schools*. London: Routledge.

Boydell, D. (1978) *The Primary Teacher in Action*. Shepton Mallet: Open Books.

Briault, E. (1976) A distributed system of educational administration: an international viewpoint. *International Review of Education*, **12**(4), 429-39.

Broadfoot, P. (1979) *Assessment, Schools and Society*. London: Methuen.

Broadfoot, P. and Osborn, M. (1988) What professional responsibility means to teachers: national contexts and classroom contexts. *British Journal of Sociology of Education.* **9**(3), 265–87.

Broadfoot, P. and Osborn, M. (1993) *Perceptions of Teaching: Primary School Teachers in England and France.* London: Cassell.

Broadfoot, P., Osborn, M., Planel, C. and Pollard, A. (1994) Teachers' responses to policy changes in England and France. Paper given to the British Educational Research Association Annual Conference, University of Oxford.

Brophy, J. E. (1983) Research on the self-fulfilling prophecy and teacher expectations. *Journal of Educational Psychology.* **75**(5), 631–61.

Burgess, H., Southworth, G. and Webb, R. (1994) Whole school planning in the primary school. in A. Pollard *et al.* (eds.) *Look Before You Leap.* London: Tufnell Press.

Campbell, R. J. (1993) The broad and balanced curriculum in primary schools: some limitations on reform. *The Curriculum Journal* **4**(2), 215–39.

Campbell, R. J. and Neill, S. R. (1994) *Primary Teachers at Work.* London: Routledge.

Carrington, B. and Short, G. (1989) *'Race' and the Primary School: Theory into Practice.* Windsor: NFER-Nelson.

Chin, R. and Benne, K. (1975) General strategies for effecting change in human systems, in W. Bennis *et al.* (eds.) *The Planning of Change.* New York: Holt Rinehart and Winston.

Chitty, C. (ed.) (1991) *Changing the Future.* London: Tufnell Press.

Connell, R. W. (1985) *Teachers' Work.* Sydney: George Allen and Unwin.

Cortazzi, M. (1991) *Primary Teaching, How It Is: A Narrative Account.* London: David Fulton.

Coulson, A. (1976) The role of the primary head, in R. S. Peters (ed.) *The Role of the Head.* London: Routledge and Kegan Paul.

Craig, I. (1989) *Primary Headship in the 1990s.* Harlow: Longman.

Croll, P. (1981) Social class, pupil achievement and classroom interaction, in B. Simon and J. Willcocks (eds.) *Research and Practice in the Primary Classroom.* London: Routledge and Kegan Paul.

Croll, P. (1990) Norm and criterion referenced assessment: some reflections in the context of the National Curriculum, *The Redland Papers* **1**, 8–11.

Croll, P. and Moses, D. (1989) Policy and practice in special education: the implementation of the 1981 Education Act in England and Wales, in R. Brown and M. Chazan (eds.) *Learning Difficulties and Emotional Problems.* Calgary: Detselig.

Croll, P. and Moses, D. (1985) *One in Five: The Assessment and Incidence of Special Educational Needs.* London: Routledge and Kegan Paul.

Davies, J. D. (1990) *The National Curriculum in Special Schools*, mimeo. Bristol: University of the West of England.

Davies, J. D. and Landman, M. (1991) The National Curriculum in special schools for pupils with emotional and behavioural difficulties, *Maladjustment and Therapeutic Education,* **9**(3), 130–35.

de Gruchy, N. (1994) Let's take the credit for our boycott success. *Teaching Today,* **7**,4–5.

Dearing, R. (1994) *The National Curriculum and its Assessment: Final Report.* London: School Curriculum and Assessment Authority (SCAA).

Department for Education (1994) *Statistics of Education: Schools: 1993.* London: HMSO.

Department of Education and Science (1978) *The Education of Handicapped Children and Young People* (The Warnock Report). London: HMSO.

Department of Education and Science/ Welsh Office (1987) *The National Curriculum 5–16: A Consultation Document.* London: HMSO.

Department of Education and Science (1989) *National Curriculum: From Policy to Practice.* London: DES.

Doyle, W. (1986) Classroom organisation and management, in M. Wittrock (ed.) *Third Handbook of Research on Teaching.* New York: Macmillan.

Doyle, W. and Carter, K. (1984) Academic tasks in classrooms. *Curriculum Inquiry,* **14**(2), 129–49.

Dusek, J. B. and Joseph, G. (1983) The base of teacher expectancies: a meta-analysis. *Journal of Educational Psychology,* **75**(3), 327–46.

Evans, L., Packwood, A., Neill, R. and Campbell, R. J. (1994) *The Meaning of Infant Teachers' Work*. London: Routledge.

Flew, A. *et al.* (1981) *The Pied Pipers of Education*. London: Social Affairs Unit.

Fullan, M. (1991) *The New Meaning of Educational Change*. London, Cassell.

Galloway, D. (1990) Was the GERBIL a Marxist mole?, in P. Evans and V. Varma (eds.) *Special Education: Past, Present and Future*. Lewes: Falmer Press.

Galton, M. (1995) *Crisis in the Primary Classroom*, London: David Fulton.

Galton, M. and Simon, B. (eds.) (1980) *Progress and Performance in the Primary Classroom*. London: Routledge and Kegan Paul.

Galton, M. and Williamson, J. (1992) *Group Work in the Primary Classroom*. London: Routledge.

Galton, M., Simon, B. and Croll, P. (1980) *Inside the Primary Classroom*. London: Routledge and Kegan Paul.

Goodnow, J. and Burns, A. (1988) *Home and School: A Child's Eye View*. Sydney: Allen and Unwin

Hargreaves, A. (1994) *Changing Teachers, Changing Times: Teachers' Work and Culture in the Postmodern Age*. London: Cassell.

Hargreaves, D. (1988) Educational research and the implications of the 1988 Education Reform Act. Paper given at the BERA annual conference, University of East Anglia.

Hargreaves, D. (1975) *Interpersonal Relations and Education*. London: Routledge and Kegan Paul.

Hargreaves, D., Hester, S. H. and Mellor, F. J. (1975) *Deviance in Classrooms*. London: Routledge and Kegan Paul.

Hartley, D. (1985) *Understanding the Primary School*. London: Croom Helm.

Henry, J. (1955) Docility, or giving teacher what she wants. *Journal of Social Issues,* **2**, 33–41.

Her Majesty's Inspectorate (1994) *English from 5–16 London*: DES.

Her Majesty's Inspectorate (1985) *Education Observed 3*. London: DES.

Her Majesty's Inspectorate (1991) *The Implementation of the Curriculum Requirements of ERA*. London: HMSO.

Heward, C. and Lloyd-Smith, M. (1990) Assessing the impact of legislation on education policy, *Journal of Education Policy*, **5**(1), 21–36.

Hillcole Group (1993) *Falling Apart: The Coming Crisis of Conservative Education*. London: Tufnell Press.

Hoyle, E. (1974) Professionality, professionalism and control in teaching. *London Educational Review*, 3(2), 15–17.

Hoyle, E. (1980) Professionalisation and Deprofessionalisation in Education, in E. Hoyle and J. Megarry (eds.) *World Yearbook of Education 1980*. London: Kogan Page.

Hoyle, E. (1992) An education profession for tomorrow. Paper given to the annual conference of the British Educational Management and Administration Society, University of Bristol.

Huberman, A. M. (1993) *The Lives of Teachers*. London: Cassell.

Jackson, P. (1968) *Life in Classrooms*. New York: Holt Rinehart and Winston.

Jennings, A. (1985) Out of the Secret Garden, in M. Plaskow (ed.) *The Life and Death of the Schools Council*. Lewes: Falmer Press.

King, R. A. (1978) *All Things Bright and Beautiful? A Sociological Study of Infants' Classrooms*. Chichester: Wiley.

King, R. A. (1989) *The Best of Primary Education? A Sociological Study of Junior and Middle Schools*. Chichester: Wiley.

Kogan, M. (1975) *Educational Policy Making*. London: George Allen and Unwin.

Lawlor, S. (1993) *Inspecting the School Inspectors*. London: Centre for Policy Studies.

Lawn, M. (1988) Skill in schoolwork: work relations in the primary school, in J. Ozga (ed.) *Schoolwork: Approaches to the Labour Process of Teaching*. Milton Keynes: Open University Press.

Lewis, A. and Halpin, D. (forthcoming) The National Curriculum and special education: a report on the perceptions of twelve headteachers of special schools. *European Journal of Special Educational Needs,* **11**.

Lightfoot, S. L. (1983) The lives of teachers, in L. Shulman and G. Sykes (eds.) *Handbook of*

Teaching and Policy. New York: Longman.

Little, A. (1985) The child's understanding of the causes of academic success and failure. *British Journal of Educational Psychology*, **55**(1), 11–23.

Little, J. W. (1990) The persistence of privacy: autonomy and initiative in teachers' professional relations. *Teachers' College Record*, **91**(4), 509–36.

Lortie, D. C. (1969) The balance of control and autonomy in elementary school teaching, in A. Etzioni (ed.) *The Semi-professions and their Organisation*. New York: Free Press.

MacPherson, A. and Raab, C. (1988) *Governing Education*. Edinburgh: Edinburgh University Press.

Martin, E. (1993) Education of youths with disabilities in United States of America, in P. Mittler *et al*. (eds.) *World Year Book of Education 1993*. London: Kogan Page.

McCulloch, G. (1986) Policy, politics and education: the technical and vocational education initiative. *Journal of Education Policy*, **1**(1), 35–52.

Menter, I., Muschamp, Y., Nicholls, P. and Ozgar, J. with Pollard, A. (forthcoming) *Teachers' Work and Identity in Primary Schools: A Post-Fordist Analysis*. Buckingham: Open University Press.

Merton, R. K. and Nisbet, R. (eds.) (1976) *Contemporary Social Problems*, 4th ed. New York: Harcourt Brace Jovanovich.

Mortimore, P., Sammons, P., Stoll, L., Lewis, D. and Ecob, R. (1988) *School Matters: The Junior Years*. Wells: Open Books.

Munby, S. (1994) Marking out a Pyrrhic victory. *Times Education Supplement*, 15.7.94, 12.

NAHT (1994) Press release, 1.9.94.

National Curriculum Council (1989) *A Curriculum for All*. York: NCC.

National Curriculum Council (1991) *Science and Pupils with Special Educational Needs*. York: NCC.

National Curriculum Council (1993a) *Modern Foreign Languages and Special Educational Needs: A New Commitment*. York: NCC.

National Curriculum Council (1993b) *Special Needs and the National Curriculum: Opportunity and Challenge*. York: NCC.

National Curriculum Council (1993c) *Planning the Curriculum at KS2*. York: NCC.

Nias, J. (1989) *Primary Teachers Talking*. London: Routledge.

Nias, J., Southworth, G. and Yeomans, R. (1989) *Staff Relationships in the Primary School*. Lewes: Falmer Press.

Nicholls, J. (1989) *The Competitive Ethos and Democratic Education*. Cambridge MA: Harvard University Press.

Norwich, B. (1994) *Segregation and Inclusion*. Bristol: Centre for Studies on Inclusive Education.

OFSTED (1995) *Standards and Quality in Education, 1993/94*: The Annual Report of Her Majesty's Chief Inspector of Schools*. London: HMSO.

Osborn, M. and Black, E. (1994) *Developing the National Curriculum at Key Stage 2: The Changing Nature of Teachers' Work*. Birmingham: NASUWT.

Osborn, M. and Broadfoot, P., with Abbott, D., Croll, P. and Pollard, A. (1992) The impact of current changes in English primary schools on teacher professionalism. *Teachers' College Record* **94**(1) 138–52.

Osborn, M., Abbott, D., Broadfoot, P., Croll, P. and Pollard, A. (forthcoming) 'Teachers' professional perspectives: continuity and change, in R. Chawla-Duggan and C. Pole (eds.) *Education in the 1990s: Reshaping Primary Education*. Lewes: Falmer Press.

Pile, W. (1979) *The Department of Education and Science*. London: George Allen and Unwin.

Planel, C. (1994) Children's experience of primary school: A comparative study in England and France. Paper given at the British Educational Research Association Conference, University of Oxford.

Plaskow, M. (1985) A long view from the inside, in M. Plaskow (ed.) *The Life and Death of the Schools Council*. Lewes: Falmer Press.

Pollard, A. (1985) *The Social World of the Primary School*. London: Cassell.

Pollard, A. with Filer, A. (1995) *The Social World of Children's Learning*. London: Cassell.

Pollard, A. and Filer, A. (forthcoming) *The Social World of Children's Careers*. London: Cassell.

Pollard, A. and Tann, S. (1993) *Reflective Teaching in the Primary School,* 2nd ed. London: Cassell.

Pollard, A., Broadfoot, P., Croll, P., Osborn M. and Abbott, D. (1994) *Changing English Primary Schools? The Impact of the Education Reform Act at Key Stage One.* London: Cassell.

Raab, C. (1994) Theorising the governance of education. *British Journal of Educational Studies,* **42**(1) 6–22.

Rampton Report (1981) *West Indian Children in our Schools.* London: HMSO.

Rosenthal, R. and Jacobson, L. (1968) *Pygmalion in the Classroom: Teacher Expectation and Pupils' Intellectual Development.* New York: Holt, Rinehart and Winston.

Saunders, M. (1985) *Emerging Issues from TVEI Implementation.* Lancaster: University of Lancaster.

Sharp, R. and Green, A. (1975) *Education and Social Control.* London: Routledge and Kegan Paul.

Sikes, P., Measor, L. and Woods, P. (1985) *Teacher Careers: Crises and Continuities.* Lewes: Falmer Press.

Southworth, G. (1987) Primary school teachers and collegiality, in G. Southworth (ed.) *Readings in Primary School Management.* Lewes: Falmer Press.

Tharp, R. and Gallimore, R. (1988) *Rousing Minds to Life.* Cambridge: Cambridge University Press.

Tizard, B., Blatchford, P., Burke, J., Farquhar, C. and Plewis, I. (1988) *Young Children at School in the Inner City.* London: Lawrence Erlbaum.

Tizard, J. (1974) The epidemiology of handicapping conditions of educational concern, in M. Pringle and V. Varma (eds.) *Advances in Educational Psychology.* London: University of London Press.

Van Gennep, A. (1960) *The Rites of Passage.* London: Routledge and Kegan Paul.

Weatherley, R. and Lipsky, M. (1977) Street-level bureaucrats and institutional innovation. *Harvard Educational Review,* **47**(2), 171–97.

Webb, R. (1993) *Eating the Elephant Bit by Bit: The National Curriculum at Key Stage 2.* London: ALT.

West, A., Hailes, J. and Sammons, P. (1995) Classroom organisation and teaching approaches at Key Stage One. *Educational Studies,* **21**(1), 99–118.

Woods, P. (1977) Teaching for survival, in P. Woods and M. Hammersley (eds.) *School Experience.* New York: St Martins Press.

Woods, P. (1990) *The Happiest Days? How Pupils Cope with School.* London: Falmer Press.

Woods, P. (1995*) Creative Teachers in Primary Schools.* Buckingham: Open University Press.

Name Index

Subject Index